Reason in Law

Reason in Law
THIRD EDITION

Lief H. Carter **J.D., Ph.D.**
UNIVERSITY OF GEORGIA

HarperCollins*Publishers*

Library of Congress Cataloging-in-Publication Data

Carter, Lief H.
  Reason in law.

  Includes indexes.
  1. Judicial process—United States. 2. Law—
United States—Interpretation and construction.
3. Law—Philosophy. I. Title.
KF380.C325 1987   340′.11   87–23563
ISBN 0-673-39712-2

6 7 8 9 10 · PAT · 93 92

Printed in the United States of America

CREDITS

The author gratefully acknowledges permission to quote material from the
following sources.

  The Atlanta Constitution, October
7, 1977, p. 14–B. Reprinted by
permission of The Associated
Press.
  *The Atlanta Journal and Constitu-
tion,* November 30, 1986, p. 43–A.
Reprinted by permission of Reuters.

Judge Benjamin N. Cardozo, *The
Paradoxes of Legal Science* (New
York: Columbia University Press,
1928), pp. 70–71. Copyright ©
1928 Columbia University Press.
By permission.

(continued on p. 264)

For Nancy
Ratio legis est anima legis....

Preface

"Tu deviens responsable pour toujours de ce que tu as apprivoisé"
—Antoine de Saint Exupéry

Helpful users of the successful second edition requested a somewhat shorter edition for teaching purposes. I have therefore cut out the chapter on facts and law and have collapsed the two sets of questions after the illustrative cases into one. Even with the addition of an Appendix on judicial procedure and terminology for neophytes, and of Sanford Levinson's Ten Commandments interpretive problem at the end of the final chapter, the book is much tighter. The Appendix should be assigned in conjunction with chapter one and probably reassigned with chapter three.

In this new edition I have also added materials on the civil liberties aspects of the spread of AIDS. Both Judge Sorkow's ruling in the Baby M case and the applicability of the Boland Amendment to White House activities in the Iran Contra scandal present basic common law and statutory interpretation problems which this book addresses. These issues, plus the latest death penalty, right to bail, and other recent decisions also appear here.

The most important reason for a new edition is that I have grown unhappy with two positions I took in the earlier editions. First, I no longer waffle between defining legal reasoning as the psychology of choosing the outcome on one hand, and of justifying the outcome on the other. I now say clearly that legal reasoning is justification. How we choose is a mystery. I believe the art of justification feeds back into the choosing process. Just as a pianist's choice of fingering for a difficult passage or a painter's choice of color in a watercolor will reflect his or her experience with past choices, so legal reasoning values can enter the psychology of judicial choice. But we don't know how, and I doubt that, as students of law and politics, we need to know.

Second, I no longer find the *Carolene Products* footnote four solution to the constitutional law paradox adequate. I now believe that the nonexistence of any demonstrably correct method of constitutional interpretation is inevitable. Doctrinal open-endedness is part of the grand scheme which prevents the concentration of too much power in any single governmental institution. The Constitution is a motivation for, and a language that makes possible, talking about political values. Its goodness comes from the fact that we talk and how we talk, not from choosing only one view of what the Constitution means.

I like to think that recent scholarly trends have vindicated my assertion that good legal reasoning exists in the harmony among its main elements that the legal opinion creates. The tilt toward interpretation, and hence toward aesthetics, as an alternative to the demonstrable correctness of a conclusion has almost become a fad. In their book *Understanding Computers and Cognition* (1987), Fernando Flores and Terry Winograd state that presuming that knowledge is representational and rational dooms the current search for artificial intelligence to failure. They believe that knowledge is so completely intertwined with language and relationships, and is so thoroughly interpretive, that current computer designs may never achieve artificial intelligence. Fad or not, this book is committed to a comparable view of law.

Cheryl Mehaffey, Kevin Wilcox and Lori Safrit gave excellent research and production assistance in preparing this manuscript, as did Virginia Shine and Annette Hall. I am more grateful than ever for the help given by friends and strangers since I began writing the first edition eleven years ago. Some of their names appear in the prefaces of the second edition, but I cannot include an updated list here. It would be much too long! Besides, since I do not name them, I can avoid the conventional excusing of friends and strangers from responsibility for what I've written. St. Exupéry's fox tells the Little Prince that we become responsible forever for what we have tamed. A world that defines law as collaborative peace-making rather than adversarial truth-finding would necessarily accept that we are responsible, not for each other's choices, but for what we, together, become. This book, like all writing, is part of its author's continuous becoming.

Athens, Georgia
July 2, 1987

Contents

Reason in Law

I was much troubled in spirit, in my first years upon the bench, to find how trackless was the ocean on which I had embarked. I sought for certainty. I was oppressed and disheartened when I found that the quest for it was futile. I was trying to reach land, the solid land of fixed and settled rules, the paradise of a justice that would declare itself by tokens plainer and more commanding than its pale and glimmering reflections in my own vacillating mind and conscience.... As the years have gone by, and as I have reflected more and more upon the nature of the judicial process, I have become reconciled to the uncertainty, because I have grown to see it as inevitable. I have grown to see that the process in its highest reaches is not discovery, but creation; and that the doubts and misgivings, the hopes and fears, are part of the travail of mind, the pangs of death and the pangs of birth, in which principles that have served their day expire, and new principles are born.

What is it that I do when I decide a case? To what sources of information do I appeal for guidance? In what proportions do I permit them to contribute to the result? In what proportions ought they to contribute? If a precedent is applicable, when do I refuse to follow it? If no precedent is applicable, how do I reach the rule that will make a precedent for the future? If I am seeking logical consistency, the symmetry of the legal structure, how far shall I seek it? At what point shall the quest be halted by some discrepant custom, by some consideration of the social welfare, by my own or the common standards of justice and morals? Into that strange compound which is brewed daily in the caldron of the courts, all these ingredients enter in varying proportions. I am not concerned to inquire whether judges ought to be allowed to brew such a compound at all. I take judge-made law as one of the existing realities of life. There, before us, is the brew. Not a judge on the bench but had a hand in the making.

—*Judge Benjamin N. Cardozo,*
The Nature of the Judicial Process (1921)

Chapter I

WHAT LEGAL REASONING IS, AND WHY IT MATTERS

*Law, in all its divisions, is the strong
action of reason on wants,
necessities and imperfections.*
   —William Rawle (1832)

*I have grown to see that the [legal]
process in its highest reaches is not
discovery, but creation. . . .*
   —Benjamin N. Cardozo

OVERVIEW OF LEGAL REASONING

A fundamental political expectation in the United States holds that people who exercise power and authority over others must *justify* how and why they use their power as they do. We expect, both in private and in public life, that people whose decisions directly affect our lives will give reasons why they deserve to hold their power and show how their decisions serve common rather than purely selfish ends. We expect teachers to have and articulate grading standards. We expect elected politicians to respond to the needs of voters. In all such cases we reject the authoritarian notion that power justifies itself, that those with money or political office can therefore do whatever they please.

Courts in the United States hold and exercise political power. Judicial outcomes in lawsuits can literally kill and bankrupt people. Courts, as a coequal branch of government, also possess and use power to make law. This book describes how judges, and particularly appellate court judges, justify their exercise of this power. Whether appellate judges meet or fail to meet our fundamental expectation about the use of power depends almost entirely on the quality of their legal reasoning.

Appellate judges in most nontrivial cases write opinions explaining and thereby justifying the results they reach.[1] Legal reasoning is a shorthand expression for the many and at times competing and inconsistent standards judges, lawyers, and legal scholars use to evaluate judicial opinions. Just as elections hold legislators, governors, presidents, and many other politicians accountable, so their opinions hold appellate judges accountable.[2] Legal reasoning debates how judges may best meet their political obligation to justify their power.

Our culture encourages some misunderstanding about legal reasoning. Perhaps because, starting in the Renaissance, a stream of discoveries about the physical world has continuously bombarded Western civilization, we too often assume that legal reasoning is good when it discovers the law's "right answer," the correct legal solution to a problem. The idea that we live under a government of laws, not men, seems based on the assumption that correct legal results exist, like undiscovered planets or sub-subatomic particles, quite independent of man's knowledge.

---

[1] For an introduction to the legal procedures and terms by which cases reach the appellate level, see the Appendix, beginning at p. 255.

[2] All federal judges are appointed for life. Impeachment and removal from office are very rare. The majority of state judges are elected, but election challenges, especially at the appellate level, are also rare. The defeat of California Chief Justice Rose Bird and Associate Justices Cruz Reynoso and Joseph Grodin in November 1986 was an exception. See Henry J. Abraham, *The Judicial Process*, 5th ed. (New York: Oxford University Press, 1986), pp. 22–50.

Of course if law (and science) actually worked that way, a book on legal reasoning would be absurd. To see whether a judge settled a contract dispute correctly, we would study the law of contract. To determine the correctness of the U.S. Supreme Court's 1954 decision banning public school segregation by law, we would study the Constitution. In all cases trained lawyers and legal scholars would, like priests in olden days, have special access to correct answers that laypeople—most readers of this book—could not hope to match. The layperson would either defer to the conclusion of the expert or rebel.

Appellate judges do justify their power through the quality of the opinions they write. The quality of their opinions, however, depends on something other than proving that they got the law right. After all, when the law is clear enough that people on opposite sides of a case can agree on what it commands, people usually don't spend the many thousands of dollars that contesting a case in an appellate court requires. Legal reasoning, in other words, describes what judges do to justify the result when they *cannot* demonstrate or prove that they have reached the "right answer." As Benjamin Cardozo pointed out the better part of a century ago, appellate judges *create* law. The uncertainties and imperfections in law force judges to choose what the law ought to mean, not merely report on what it does mean.

To persuade us that the law ought to mean what the judge has created, the judicial opinion tries to persuade us to share the judge's beliefs about four kinds of things: (1) facts, events, and other observable conditions in the world (what I call "social background facts"); (2) social values and moral principles; (3) facts about the dispute established in the trial and preserved in the trial records; and (4) the lawyer's arguments about what the law has said in the past.

In this book's final chapter, I will argue that good legal reasoning exists when the opinion harmonizes or "fits together" these four elements—social background facts, moral assertions, the facts established at trial, and the rules at issue in the case itself. I hope the materials in this book will support and validate this abstract and fuzzy-sounding statement.

In a nutshell, legal reasoning describes how effectively an opinion's blend of case facts, prior law, social background facts, and moral values creates a legal outcome that makes some plausible sense of the moral and empirical world we know. From this definition, several immensely important corollaries follow. First, legal reasoning does *not* refer to what goes on in a judge's head. In 1929, U. S. District Judge Joseph Hutcheson confessed that the actual decision-making process revolved around the judicial "hunch."[3] Professor Warren Lehman in 1986 agreed: "What we call the capacity for judgment . . . is an intellectualized account of the capacity for decision-making and action, whose nature is not known to us."[4] Legal reasoning justifies the decision but does not explain how the judge arrived at it.

Second, two judges may reach different results in the same case yet each may reason equally well or badly. Like two excellent debaters, two opposing opinions may still persuade us that each judge has fit together a vision of a reality we can believe.

Third, legal reasoning is ultimately political, not legal. Laypeople who read judicial opinions can and should react to them and decide whether the opinion actually persuades them. No one opinion will persuade everyone, which is why the legal process becomes political. Reactions to judicial decisions about abortion or the rights of AIDS victims or the President's inherent war powers inevitably shape the development of law in the future. To return to my starting place, legal reasoning is for courts the mechanism by which the exercise of judicial power becomes politically acceptable or unacceptable.

Finally, the process by which judges seek to fit the four

---

[3]Joseph C. Hutcheson, Jr., "The Judgment Intuitive: The Function of the 'Hunch' in Judicial Decision," 14 *Cornell Law Quarterly* 274 (1929). Hutcheson defined "hunch" as "a strong intuitive impression that something is about to happen."

[4]Warren Lehman, *How We Make Decisions* (Madison: Institute for Legal Studies of the University of Wisconsin Law School, 1986), p. 12. For an analysis of the subconscious influences on a judge, see Richard Danzig, "Justice Frankfurter's Opinions in the Flag Salute Cases," 36 *Stanford Law Review* 675 (1984).

elements of legal reasoning together inevitably requires them to simplify and distort each element to some degree. Therefore, most opinions will fail to meet the requirements of pure legal logic. (The Supreme Court's rulings about establishment of religion—which allow churches and church schools many tax advantages yet prohibit the government from providing money to church schools for normal teaching aids—are notoriously incoherent by purely logical standards.) So too, opinions will simplify the moral and empirical issues in them. Simplification and alteration are a fact of life. We always must reshape raw materials if we want to fit them together smoothly.[5]

A DEFINITION OF LAW

Law is a process, not a collection of rules. What distinguishes the legal process from other ways of coping with life? Lawyers and judges attempt to prevent and solve other people's problems, but so do physicians, priests, professors, and plumbers. "Problem solving" therefore defines too much. Lawyers and judges work with certain kinds of problems, problems that can lead to conflicts, even physical fights, among people. It is the *kind* of problem with which judges and lawyers work that helps define law.

Contrary to the impression that television drama gives, with its emphasis on courtroom battles, most lawyers generally practice "preventive law." They help people discover ways to reduce their taxes or write valid wills and contracts. They study complex insurance policies and bank loan agreements. Such efforts reduce the probability of conflict. Most lawyers usually play a planning role. They help people create their own "private laws," laws governing their personal affairs and no more.

---

[5]This is equally true in the physical sciences. Geoffrey Joseph recently wrote, "What one finds [in the physical sciences] is a succession of theories, each of which resolutely ignores certain fundamental questions." "Interpretation in the Physical Sciences," 58 *Southern California Law Review* 9 (1985), p. 12.

But, of course, some conflicts start anyway. Why? Sometimes they start because a lawyer did the planning and preventing poorly or because the client did not follow a lawyer's good advice. Sometimes lawyers cannot find in rules of law a safe plan with which to prevent a conflict. Many conflicts, however, such as the auto collision, the dispute with a neighbor over a property line, or the angry firing of an employee, begin without lawyers. Then people may call them in after the fact, not for an ounce of prevention but for the pounding of a cure.

If a battle erupts spontaneously, lawyers may find a solution in the rules of law, though once people get angry at each other they may refuse the solution lawyers offer. If a struggle arises, however, and if the lawyers don't find a solution or negotiate a compromise, then either one side gives up or the opponents go to court; they call in the judges to give their solution.

You may now think you have a solid definition of law: Law is the process of preventing or resolving conflicts between people. Lawyers and judges do this; professors, plumbers, and physicians, at least routinely, do not. But parents prevent or resolve conflicts among their children daily. And parents, perhaps exasperated from coping with family fights, may turn to a family counselor to deal with their own conflicts. Many ministers too no doubt define their goals as reducing conflict. Lawyers, then, aren't the only people who try to resolve conflicts.

Law, like the priesthood and professional counseling, involves an immense variety of problems. Law requires the ability to see specifics and to avoid premature generalizing and jumping to conclusions. So do good counseling, good "ministration," and good parenting. But what distinguishes the conflict solving of lawyers and judges from the conflict solving of parents, counselors, or ministers? Consider these three not-so-hypothetical cases. What makes them distinctively *legal* problems?

- A Massachusetts supermarket chain's order of a carload of cantaloupe from Arizona arrives two weeks

late and partially rotten. The supermarket chain refuses to take delivery of the melons and refuses to pay
for them. Did the seller in the contract of sale guarantee their safe arrival? Did the delay cause the decay, or
had some spore infected the melons before shipment?
Did the railroad act negligently in causing the delay,
thus making it liable for the loss? Should the supermarket chain try to recover the profit it didn't make
because it had no melons to sell, and if so, from whom?
Do any regulations made by the Department of Agriculture or the Interstate Commerce Commission speak
to the problem?[6]

- A young man, entranced by the thought of flying,
  steals a Cessna from an airstrip in Rhode Island and
  manages to survive a landing in a Connecticut corn
  patch. He is prosecuted under the National Motor Vehicle Theft Act, which prohibits transportation "in interstate or foreign commerce [of] a motor vehicle,
  knowing the same to have been stolen. . . ." The statute
  defines motor vehicle to "include an automobile, automobile truck, automobile wagon, motorcycle, or any
  other self-propelled vehicle not designed for running
  on rails." Does the pilot's brief flight amount to transportation of the plane "in interstate . . . commerce?" Is
  an airplane a "vehicle" within the meaning of the act?[7]

- A United States president seeks to protect the confidentiality of his private conversations in office from
  prosecutors who suspect the conversations will reveal

---

[6]Real life provides us with a much more complicated version of this case
of the rotten cantaloupe. See *L. Gillarde Co. v. Joseph Martinelli and Co., Inc.*, 168
F .2d 276 (1st Cir. 1948) and 169 F .2d 60 (1948, rehearing). The case has
introduced a generation of students at Harvard Law School, myself among
them, to the complexities of the legal process in Henry M. Hart, Jr., and Albert
M. Sacks, *The Legal Process* (Cambridge: Harvard Law School, 1958), pp. 10–75.

[7]Cf. *McBoyle v. United States*, 283 U.S. 25 (1931). The letter abbreviations
following the names of cases identify the series of books that contains the
judicial opinion deciding the case. The first number indicates the volume in
the series that contains the opinion, and the second number is the starting
page of the opinion. The Appendix discusses *McBoyle* further.

evidence of a criminal conspiracy. In what circumstances does the Constitution allow a president to withhold such information?[8]

These are legal problems, not counseling or psychological or parental problems, because we define their nature and limits—but not necessarily their solution—in terms of rules that the state, the government, has made. The laws of contract and of negligence help define the problem or the quarrel between the melon seller and the melon buyer. So, as it turns out, do Department of Agriculture shipping regulations for farm produce. Criminal statutes passed by legislatures define, among many concepts, how the government may deal with thieves. The Constitution sets limits on presidential power. Governments have made these rules; they are laws. The process of resolving human conflicts through law begins when one person or several persons decide to take advantage of the fact that the government has made rules to prevent or resolve such conflicts. When people convert a problem into a legal conflict by taking it to court, the court's resolution of the problem has the force of the government behind it. Even in a noncriminal case, if the loser or losers don't pay up, the judge may order jail terms.

The legal process, then, is the process lawyers and judges use when they try to prevent or resolve problems—human conflicts—using rules made by the state as their starting point. To study reason in this process is to study how lawyers and judges justify the choices they inevitably make among alternative legal solutions. For example, legal reasoning studies how they justify saying an airplane is or is not a "vehicle" in the context of the National Motor Vehicle Theft Act. Throughout this book we shall study the legal process by asking the central questions lawyers and judges ask themselves as they do their work: What does the law mean as applied to the problem before me? What different and sometimes contradictory solutions to the problem does the law permit?

Now stop and compare this definition of law and legal reasoning with your own intuitive conception of law, with the

[8]*United States v. Nixon*, 418 U.S. 683 (1974).

definition of the legal process you may have developed from television, movies, and other daily experiences. Do the two overlap? Probably not very much. The average layperson usually thinks of law as trials, and criminal trials at that. But trials, by our definition, are one of the less legal, or "law-filled," parts of the legal process because much of the conflict-settling work of lawyers and judges involves deciding not what law means but what happened. In a sense this part of conflict solving is really not law at all but a microscopic kind of historical research: Did the deceased pull a knife on the defendant before the defendant shot him or didn't he? Did that witness really see the defendant run the red light just before the defendant hit the police car? We are confident enough that these historical problems do not require legal reasoning that we often turn the job of solving them over to groups of amateur historians better known as juries.

Laws do tell these historians what facts to seek. Pulling the knife *could* excuse the shooting through the law of self-defense, though if the deceased were a child of three it would almost surely not. Running the red light *could* establish legal negligence, though it presumably would not if the defendant were driving his car in a funeral procession at the time.

We cannot totally separate law and facts, but the heart of the reasoning part of law, and the subject of this book, lies not in analyzing what happened but in analyzing what facts the rules allow us to seek and what to do with these facts once we "know" them. Turning to the eager flyer, the historical problem we must solve is whether or not that particular defendant at some specified point in the past actually flew someone else's airplane to another state without permission. The legal reasoning problem, on the other hand, requires deciding whether or not we ought to call the plane a "vehicle" in this statute's context.

THREE WAYS TO CLASSIFY LAW

Sources of Law: Where Laws Originate

The range of legal problems and conflicts is practically infinite, but lawyers and judges will, one way or another, resolve the issues by referring to and reasoning about rules of law.

Despite the endless variety of legal problems, lawyers and judges usually resort to four categories of law: *statutes, common law, constitutional law,* and *administrative regulations.* The easiest category to understand is what we often call "laws"—the *statutes* passed by legislatures. Laypeople tend to think of statutes as the rules that define types of behavior that society wishes to condemn: crimes. However, legislatures enact statutes governing (and sometimes creating!) many problems without enacting criminal statutes—no-fault insurance, income tax rates, social security benefit levels, for example. For our purposes this statutory category also includes the local ordinances passed by the elected bodies of cities and counties.

But there is a problem here. Despite their freedom, legislatures do not enact statutes to cover everything. And when lawyers and judges face a problem without a statute, they normally turn to that older set of rules called *common law.*

Judges, not legislators, make common law rules, but not by calling together a judicial convention to argue, log-roll, draft, and finally vote on (or bury) proposed laws. Common law rules have emerged through a process introduced in England before the discovery of the New World. The process began essentially because the Crown in England chose to assert national authority by sending judges throughout the country to act, to decide cases, in the name of the Crown. The king did not in fact write rules to govern all judges' decisions. It was because the judges *acted* in the name of the central government, certainly a shaky government by our standards, that their decisions became law common to all the king's domain. Many of the rules for decision making originated in local custom or the minds of the judges themselves.

The process by which these decisions became "law" took a surprisingly long time. In the beginning, the reasons for judicial decisions were murky, and judges applied them inconsistently. But observers of the courts wrote descriptions of the cases, often just the facts and the result, and judges began to look to these descriptions for past examples to guide current judicial action. The formal practice whereby judges write opinions explaining their choices, which other judges in turn treat as legal authority called "precedents," is only a few hundred years old, but it is a powerful and stabilizing force in legal reasoning today. Precedents will receive much attention in this book because the facts and values embedded in the examples of precedents are fundamental tools of legal reasoning.

In Chapters III and IV, we examine reason in statutory and common sources of law, and Chapter V explores the third source of law: *constitutional law*. The Constitution of the United States and the 50 state constitutions set out the structure and powers of government. They also place legal limits on the way those who govern can use their power. While statutes (and common law where statutory law is silent) can govern anybody, constitutions govern the government.[9] The U.S. Constitution even governs presidents, although most constitutional cases involve an alleged conflict between the national or state constitutions and a decision made and enforced by lesser public administrators who claim to act under statutory authority.

Administrative regulations, of the Internal Revenue Service, or the San Francisco Zoning Board, or any of the thousands of national, state, and local administrative agencies, make up the fourth source of law. Executives and nonelected administrators can make rules only when a constitution or a statute gives them the authority to do so. Problems in administrative law can fascinate and perplex as much as any. Because the length of this book and your time have limits, we shall examine reasoning about administrative regulations only briefly. You should not, however, let this deliberate neglect mislead you into thinking the subject is unimportant. Administrative regulations are shaping law and our lives more and more.[10] The scope of this book is confined to historically more developed sources of law: *statues, common law,* and *constitutional law.*

---

[9]If I, as a private citizen, don't like a speech of yours and forcibly remove you from your soapbox, I will probably violate a principle of common or statutory law. And I would violate a normative principle favoring free exchange of ideas. This principle is what makes the heckling of public speakers by antagonists in the audience so despicable. I will not violate the First Amendment of the Constitution. If I did this to you while working as a government official, such as an FBI agent, however, that would be another matter.

[10]See my *Administrative Law and Politics* (Boston: Little, Brown, 1983).

Before concluding this discussion of the sources of law, I want to emphasize this central truth: Judges write opinions explaining their legal choices. They do so not only when they apply older, judge-made common law rules but also when they choose among alternative possible meanings of statutes, constitutional provisions, and administrative regulations. All these opinions create precedents, guides to help judges in similar future cases make similar kinds of decisions. *Judicial opinions, therefore, give meaning to all types of legal rules.* A judge who chooses to interpret a statute in a certain way creates a precedent that judges in future similar cases may incorporate into their own decisions. This is why we say that judges make law.

Functions of Law: The Problems That Laws Solve

The second way of classifying laws examines the various social objectives that different laws try to achieve. It examines the problems that laws try to solve.

Scholars classify these so-called functions of laws in varying ways. In one common method, examples of the kinds of problems laws attempt to prevent or resolve are simply listed. Some laws (but only a small fraction of the total) deter crimes by threatening punishments. These same criminal laws also diminish the occurrence of vigilante justice; they allow people outraged by crimes to vent their anger safely on the criminal through the punishments decided by the courts. Other laws, like those regulating the operation of radio and television broadcasters, do not prevent good people from doing bad things or punish bad people in hopes of making them good. Instead, these laws coordinate people with different but equally "good" wants, in this case the competing interests of broadcasters and listeners. Note that the problem here arises from a limited resource, the airwaves, which society must use wisely for its collective advantage.

Some laws promote government itself and keep it financially solvent by raising tax revenues. Other laws protect citizens from government. They preserve our freedoms not only to participate in politics but also to transact and enforce private economic agreements. Many laws, like building and sanitation codes, seek to protect our individual health. Others, like laws that prohibit racial discrimination, identify broad objectives for society as a whole.

Superficially, these classifications do seem important and useful. It *is* important to know the legal process helps people trust that government will try to make important immediate expectations about life come true. When this minimum trust collapses, societies quickly slip toward anarchy. Law *does* help people cope with many kinds of problems, and it will take more than a few simple formulas to understand law and legal reasoning. But, on closer inspection, how helpful is this classification of legal functions? Since policy makers in government generally (but not inevitably) express their policy choices as rules of law, the list of problems that laws address can become no more than a laundry list of public policies.

More to the point, a judge who knows that law X protects individual health or that law Y seeks to raise revenues does not, by that knowledge, move any closer to deciding the case before the court.[11] Indeed, in the typical case, the judge must evaluate a variety of legal rules with many functions—some directly opposing one another—all of which potentially apply to the case.

Thus the first two ways of classifying laws are not entirely satisfactory. In this book therefore we focus less on the sources and functions of law than on the choices judges must make when they decide legal cases and on the manner in which they can make such choices wisely. How can we begin to classify the kinds of choices judges make?

Dynamics of Law: The Choices That Laws Create

In most cases, judges must reconcile the competing pulls of constitutional values, the actual wording of legal provisions,

---

[11]Throughout this book the masculine gender, when I use it generically, refers to women and men equally. For an effective corresponding generic use of the feminine gender, see Charles L. Knapp, *Problems in Contract Law* (Boston: Little, Brown, 1976).

prior judicial opinions, and their own views of the facts and values—the social realities—of the cases before them. Judges must make difficult choices such as these:

- Does the case before me call for continued adherence to the historical meaning of legal words? Must I do what the framers of statutory or constitutional language hoped their language would accomplish? When do social, political, and technological changes permit or require a different or revised interpretation?
- Does this case call for judicial deference to the literal meaning of the words themselves? In what circumstances do I decide more wisely by ignoring the actual dictionary definitions of the words in a statute or constitution?
- Does this case obligate me to follow a judicial precedent the wisdom of which I doubt? When am I free to ignore a relevant precedent?

Throughout the following chapters we shall see that the judge's choice of change or stability, judicial discretion or legislative judgment, and literal or flexible interpretation of words and precedents depends on the nature of the relationship a legal choice addresses. We shall see that it becomes crucial for judges to know to what extent people (1) probably relied on past statements of law; (2) had a justifiable reason to rely on past law; (3) can benefit from judge-made changes in law; and (4) can or cannot use the courts in the future to implement a planned effort to solve problems. Judges must know all of these things, or at least guess at them as intelligently as possible, to reason persuasively in law.

WHY JUDGES WILL ALWAYS CREATE LAW

The necessity for discretionary choice in law will never end because our experience of the observable empirical world continuously changes. A glance at the news provides examples in which changing knowledge of the world forces a reconsideration of legal issues:

- A budget analyst for Broward County, Florida, was fired shortly after his employer learned he had AIDS. A federal statute defines a handicapped person as someone whose impairment substantially limits the activities of the afflicted person and protects such persons against discrimination. Did the employer discriminate by firing him? The employer claimed that other workers might get the disease through routine contact, but at the time (1986), no scientific research supported that belief.[12]

- A pregnant Georgia woman, Donna Piazzi, takes a drug overdose. She is brain-dead by the time she reaches the hospital. A respirator and intravenous feeding might keep her alive long enough to deliver a healthy baby, but the chances are slim. Robert Piazzi, Donna's husband, asks the hospital to disconnect the respirator and IV feed. However, a David Hadden claims to have fathered the fetus and insists that the hospital keep his future child alive. Neither Robert nor David can in fact pay the costs of keeping Donna and the fetus alive. Who should make the decision in this case, Robert, David, or the hospital?[13]

There exists a second reason why judges will continuously create law. The moral values that claim to govern a case collide. Thus, the Constitution contains language protecting the freedom of the press. It also contains language ensuring the fairness of criminal trials. But an unrestrained press can do much to prejudice the fairness of a trial.

In this instance, perhaps judges can do justice by reaching a fair compromise between these interests. A more difficult problem arises not when two interests collide but when two ideas of justice itself collide. Consider the occasional collision of general and particular justice. Is it just for the engineer to pull the train away from the station always exactly on time,

---

[12]See "Court Will Decide if AIDS's Victims Enjoy Rights of the Handicapped," *Wall Street Journal,* November 5, 1986, p. 39.

[13]See "Feud over brain-dead woman, fetus raises quagmire of legal issues," *Atlanta Constitution,* July 25, 1986, p. 16–A.

even though a G.I. racing down the platform to get home to his family for Christmas will miss it? Is it not true in the long run, to paraphrase the late Professor Zechariah Chafee, that fewer people will miss trains if everyone knows that trains always leave on the dot, that more people will miss trains if they assume that they can dally and still find the train at the station? While it is often possible to engineer compromises among competing interests, it is often impossible to compromise between different visions of justice itself. Unless he is corrupt or lazy, a judge will *strive* to do justice, but whether he succeeds often remains debatable.

The ways of making legal choices I describe and advocate here do not make judges or anyone else completely "objective," because legal decisions require choices from among competing values. The problem of general versus particular justice is a good illustration. A value, a preference, or a moral "feeling" is not a concept we can prove to be right or wrong. Those who adopt values that conflict with yours will call you biased, and you may feel the same way about them. A discussion of legal reasoning can stress that some values are better than others, but arguments on both sides will remain. If the argument gets heated, each side will accuse the other of being biased. In the final chapter, we will examine more fully the nature of bias and impartiality in law. If "biases" and "values" are identical psychological feelings or beliefs about right and wrong, then legal reasoning cannot eliminate them, but we will see that judges can act impartially nevertheless.

SUMMARY

In the study of law, as well as in its execution, getting the question right is always half the struggle and often all of it. Hence I summarize each chapter with a list of questions. If a question stymies you, some rereading may be in order.

- What is legal reasoning?
- What are the four elements of legal reasoning?
- What is law?
- How do common law, statutes, administrative law, and constitutional law differ?

- How and why do appellate judges "make" all four kinds of law?
- What problems do laws try to solve?
- What choices do laws and cases create for judges?
- Why do judges inevitably create law?

ILLUSTRATIVE CASE

At each chapter's end I give you a chance to apply some of the skills you have just learned to an actual instance of legal reasoning in a judicial opinion. At the end of the opinion I will pose questions that will help you extract the proper lessons from the opinion itself. Here is the first case.

Prochnow v. Prochnow
Supreme Court of Wisconsin
274 Wisconsin 491 (1957)

A husband appeals from that part of a decree of divorce which adjudged him to be the father of his wife's child and ordered him to pay support money. The actual paternity is the only fact which is in dispute.

Joyce, plaintiff, and Robert, defendant, were married September 2, 1950, and have no children other than the one whose paternity is now in question. In February, 1953, Robert began his military service. When he came home on furloughs which he took frequently in 1953 he found his wife notably lacking in appreciation of his presence. Although he was home on furlough for eight days in October and ten in December, after August, 1953, the parties had no sexual intercourse except for one time, to be mentioned later. In Robert's absence Joyce had dates with a man known as Andy, with whom she danced in a tavern and went to a movie, behaving in a manner which the one witness who testified on the subject thought unduly affectionate. This witness also testified that Joyce told her that Robert was dull but that she and Andy had fun. She also said that a few days before Friday, March 12, 1954, Joyce told her she had to see her husband who was then stationed in Texas but must be back to her work in Milwaukee by Monday.

On March 12, 1954, Joyce flew to San Antonio and met Robert there. They spent the night of the 13th in a hotel where they had sex relations. The next day, before returning to Milwaukee, she told him that she did not love him and was going to divorce him. Her complaint, alleging cruel and inhuman treatment as her cause of action, was served on him April 8, 1954. On September 16, 1954, she amended the complaint to include an allegation that she was pregnant by Robert and demanded support money.

The child was born November 21, 1954. Robert's letters to Joyce are in evidence in which he refers to the child as his own. He returned to civilian life February 13, 1955, and on February 18, 1955, answered the amended complaint, among other things denying that he is the father of the child born to Joyce; and he counterclaimed for divorce alleging cruel and inhuman conduct on the part of the wife.

Before trial two blood grouping tests were made of Mr. and Mrs. Prochnow and of the child. The first was not made by court order but was ratified by the court and accepted in evidence as though so made. This test was conducted in Milwaukee on March 21, 1955. The second was had in Waukesha September 29, 1955, under court order. The experts by whom or under whose supervision the tests were conducted testified that each test eliminated Robert as a possible parent of the child. An obstetrician, called by Robert, testified that it was possible for the parties' conduct on March 13, 1954, to produce the full-term child which Mrs. Prochnow bore the next November 21st. Mrs. Prochnow testified that between December, 1953, and May, 1954, both inclusive, she had no sexual intercourse with any man but her husband. . . .

BROWN, Justice. The trial judge found the fact to be that Robert is the father of Joyce's child. The question is not whether, on this evidence, we would have so found: what we must determine is whether that finding constituted reversible error.

Section 328.39 (1) (a), Stats., commands:

> Whenever it is established in an action or proceeding that a child was born to a woman while she was the lawful wife of a specified man, any party asserting the illegitimacy of the child in such action or proceeding shall have the burden of proving beyond all reasonable doubt that the husband was not the father of the child. . . .

Ignoring for the moment the evidence of the blood tests and the effect claimed for them, the record shows intercourse between married people at a time appropriate to the conception of this baby. The husband's letters after the child's birth acknowledge it is his own. The wife denies intercourse with any other man during the entire period when she could have conceived this child. Unless we accept the illegitimacy of the baby as a fact while still to be proved, there is no evidence that then, or ever, did she have intercourse with anyone else. The wife's conduct with Andy on the few occasions when the witness saw them together can justly be called indiscreet for a married woman whose husband is absent, but falls far short of indicating adultery. Indeed, appellant did not assert that Andy is the real father but left that to the imagination of the court whose imagination, as it turned out, was not sufficiently lively to draw the inference. Cynics, *among whom on this occasion we must reluctantly number ourselves* [emphasis supplied], might reasonably conclude that Joyce, finding herself pregnant in February or early March, made a hasty excursion to her husband's bed and an equally abrupt withdrawal when her mission was accomplished. The subsequent birth of a full-term child a month sooner than it would usually be expected if caused by this copulation does nothing to dispel uncharitable doubts. But we must acknowledge that a trial judge, less inclined to suspect the worst, might with reason recall that at least as early as the preceding August Joyce had lost her taste for her husband's embraces. Divorce offered her freedom from them, but magnanimously she might determine to try once more to save the marriage: hence her trip to Texas. But when the night spent in Robert's arms proved no more agreeable than such nights used to be she made up her mind that they could live together no more, frankly told him so and took her departure. The medical testimony concerning the early arrival of the infant does no more than to recognize eight months of gestation as unusual. It admits the possibility that Robert begat the child that night in that San Antonio hotel. Thus, the mother swears the child is Robert's and she knew, in the Biblical sense, no other man. Robert, perforce, acknowledges that it may be his. Everything else depends on such reasonable inferences as one chooses to draw from the other admitted facts and circumstances. And such inferences are for the trier of the fact. Particularly, in view of Sec. 328.39 (1) (a), Stats., supra, we cannot agree with appellant that even with the blood tests left out of consideration, the record here proves beyond a reasonable doubt that Joyce's husband was not the father of her child.

Accordingly we turn to the tests. The expert witnesses agree that the tests excluded Mr. Prochnow from all possibility of this fatherhood. Appellant argues that this testimony is conclusive; that with the tests in evidence Joyce's testimony that she had no union except with her husband is insufficient to support a finding that her husband is the father. . . . But the Wisconsin statute authorizing blood tests in paternity cases pointedly refrains from directing courts to accept them as final even when they exclude the man sought to be held as father. In its material parts it reads:

> Sec. 325.23 *Blood tests in civil actions.* Whenever it shall be relevant in a civil action to determine the parentage or identity of any child, . . . the court . . . may direct any party to the action and the person involved in the controversy to submit to one or more blood tests, to be made by duly qualified physicians. Whenever such test is ordered and made the results thereof shall be receivable in evidence, but only in cases where definite exclusion is established. . . .

This statute does no more than to admit the test and its results in evidence, there to be given weight and credibility in competition with other evidence as the trier of the fact considers it deserves. No doubt in this enactment the legislature recognized that whatever infallibility is accorded to science, scientists and laboratory technicians by whom the tests must be conducted, interpreted and reported retain the human fallibilities of other witnesses. It has been contended before this that a report on the analysis of blood is a physical fact which controls a finding of fact in opposition to lay testimony on the subject, and the contention was rejected. . . . When the trial judge admitted the Prochnow tests in evidence and weighed them against the testimony of Mrs. Prochnow he went as far in giving effect to them as our statute required him to do. Our opinions say too often that trial courts and juries are the judges of the credibility of witnesses and the weight to be given testimony which conflicts with the testimony of others for us to say that in this case the trial court does not have that function. . . .

. . . The conclusion seems inescapable that the trial court's finding must stand when the blood-test statute does not make the result of the test conclusive but only directs its receipt in evidence there to be weighed, as other evidence is, by the court or jury. We hold, then, that the credibility of witnesses and the weight of all the evidence in this action was for the trial court and error can not be predicated upon the court's acceptance of Joyce's testimony as more convincing than that of the expert witnesses.

Judgment affirmed.

WINGERT, Justice (dissenting). With all respect for the views of the majority, Mr. Chief Justice FAIRCHILD, Mr. Justice CURRIE, and the writer must dissent. In our opinion the appellant, Robert Prochnow, sustained the burden placed upon him by Sec. 328.39 (1) (a), Stats., of proving beyond all reasonable doubt that he was not the father of the child born to the plaintiff.

To meet that burden, appellant produced two classes of evidence, (1) testimony of facts and circumstances, other than blood tests, which create grave doubt that appellant is the father, and (2) the evidence of blood tests and their significance, hereinafter discussed. In our opinion the blood test evidence should have been treated as conclusive in the circumstances of this case.

Among the numerous scientific achievements of recent decades is the development of a method by which it can be definitely established in many cases, with complete accuracy, that one of two persons cannot possibly be the parent of the other. The nature and significance of this discovery are summarized by the National Conference of Commissioners on Uniform State Laws, a highly responsible body, in the prefatory note to the Uniform Act on Blood Tests to Determine Paternity, as follows:

> In paternity proceedings, divorce actions and other types of cases in which the legitimacy of a child is in issue, the modern developments of science have made it possible to determine with certainty in a large number of cases that one charged with being the father of a child could not be. Scientific methods may determine that one is not the father of the child by the analysis of blood samples taken from the mother, the child, and the alleged father in many cases, but it cannot be shown that a man is the father of the child. If the negative fact is established it is evident that there is a great miscarriage of justice to permit juries to hold on the basis of oral testimony, passion or sympathy, that the person charged is the father and is responsible for the support of the child and other incidents of paternity.... There is no need for a dispute among the experts, and true experts will not disagree. Every test will show the same results....
> [T]his is one of the few cases in which judgment of court may be absolutely right by use of science. In this kind of a situation it seems intolerable for a court to permit an

opposite result to be reached when the judgment may scientifically be one of complete accuracy. For a court to permit the establishment of paternity in cases where it is scientifically impossible to arrive at that result would seem to be a great travesty on justice. (Uniform Laws Annotated, 9 Miscellaneous Acts, 1955 Pocket Part, p. 13.)

In the present case the evidence showed without dispute that the pertinent type of tests were made of the blood of the husband, the wife and the child on two separate occasions by different qualified pathologists, at separate laboratories, and that such tests yielded identical results, as follows:

	3/17/55	9/29/55
	Blood types	
Robert Prochnow (Husband)	AB	AB
Joyce Prochnow (Wife)	O	O
David Prochnow (Child)	O	O

There is no evidence whatever that the persons who made these tests were not fully qualified experts in the field of blood testing, nor that the tests were not made properly, nor that the results were not correctly reported to the court. . . .

Two qualified experts in the field also testified that it is a physical impossibility for a man with type AB blood to be the father of a child with type O blood, and that therefore appellant is not and could not be that father of the child David. Both testified that there are no exceptions to the rule. One stated "There is no difference of opinion regarding these factors amongst the authorities doing this particular work. None whatsoever." The evidence thus summarized was not discredited in any way and stands undisputed in the record. Indeed, there was no attempt to discredit it except by the wife's own self-serving statement that she had not had sexual relations with any other man during the period when the child might have been conceived. . . .

QUESTIONS

1. This case requires the court to interpret several statutes. Which are they? The case also involves a procedural rule that

differentiates the work of appellate courts from that of trial courts. What is that rule?

2. What factual assertions about this dispute did the trial court accept as proved? What factual assertions did it reject?
3. What social background facts are at issue here? What choice did the appellate court have to make about social background facts in order to decide this case?
4. Did not the majority's decision to reject the conclusive proof of the blood tests rest on some value choices? Does the court articulate these choices? If not, what might they have been? Does this decision necessarily depend on a fundamentalist religious conviction that God can always alter nature if He wishes? Or might the court have believed that, in the interest of giving David any father at all, it was best to assign paternity to Robert despite science?
5. Why was the law ambiguous in this case?
6. Do you find the majority or the dissenting opinion does a better job of legal reasoning? Why? (Chapter VI will help you refine your answer to this question.)
7. How does this opinion change the law? That is, if the dissent had prevailed in this case, how would the reading of the rules of law at issue in this case change?
8. Suppose the majority in *Prochnow* believed that public opinion strongly favors children growing up with fathers rather than as illegitimate bastards. Is public opinion an appropriate basis on which to justify legal decisions? In this connection consider the case of Bernard Goetz. Goetz, a white male who had been previously mugged in New York City, shot and severely wounded four black males after they approached him on a subway and requested $5.00. The law of self-defense requires both a showing of an imminent threat of bodily harm and that reasonable means of retreating from or defusing the situation were not available. Two of the victims were shot in the back. Goetz did not retreat to the other, more populated end of the subway car, nor did he brandish his weapon before firing. Goetz then escaped from the scene and went into hiding for several days. A New York grand jury, which included blacks and Hispanics, refused at first to indict Goetz for attempted murder. Public support for Goetz was massive. Columnist Jimmy Breslin received an "avalanche of hate mail," much of it explicitly racist, after he criticized Goetz's actions.[14] Goetz was later indicted when fur-

---

[14]"A Goetz Backlash," *Newsweek*, 11 March 1985, p. 50.

ther evidence indicated he premeditated the shooting. Since we live in a representative democracy, is it appropriate for the legal system to reflect such strong public sentiment? What weight, if any, should judges give to public opinion? Why? In June, 1987, a New York trial jury acquitted Goetz of all charges except carrying an illegal weapon.

Chapter II

CHANGE AND STABILITY IN LEGAL REASONING

The person who first said, "Ask a simple question, you get a simple answer," probably didn't ask a lawyer.
—*Charles L. Knapp*

The first chapter began to narrow this book's scope of inquiry. We do not in this book put ourselves in the shoes of legislators, nor do we examine how elections or lobbying efforts or presidential leadership produce new law. We ask here whether *judges* have persuaded us that they have made their legal and hence political choices justly. A legal conflict has started. Lawyers have failed either to prevent it or to resolve it short of going to court. They have brought a case to a judge, who must in turn choose a sensible solution to the conflict from the competing arguments the lawyers make. Reason in law takes over when rules of law themselves fail to solve legal conflicts once the facts of the dispute between the parties are known. Rules fail to solve legal problems because judges and lawyers often cannot tell precisely what the words of the rule mean in their case.

The first section of this chapter explains why law is so often ambiguous. The second section asserts that this uncertainty and ambiguity benefits us more than it harms us, at least as a general rule. The third section examines the other side of the uncertainty coin, the general philosophical conditions in which judges should maintain legal clarity and stability at the expense of other values. The concluding section reviews some general and inevitable characteristics of law that make it forever changing, never perfected.

UNPREDICTABILITY IN LAW

Reasoning from Words

Cases often go to courts (and particularly appellate courts) because the law does not determine the outcome. Both sides believe they have a chance to win. The legal process is in these cases *unpredictable*. Legal rules are made with words, and we can begin to understand why law is unpredictable by examining the ambiguity of words, the "disorderly conduct of words," as Professor Chafee put it.[1] Sometimes our language fails to give us precise definitions. There is, for example, no way to define the concept of "table" so as to exclude some items we call "benches" and the reverse.[2] More often, words and state-

---

[1]Zechariah Chafee, "The Disorderly Conduct of Words," 41 *Columbia Law Review* 381 (1941).

[2]My thanks to Professor Martin Landau, University of California, Berkeley, for this example. If you don't believe it, try creating this definitional distinction paying attention to coffee tables and tool benches. Furthermore suppose a state enacts a statute exempting from its sales tax all "food and food stuffs." What is "food"? Is chewing gum food? Is coffee? Is beer? And is human blood for transfusions a "product" or a "service"? The distinction matters because in most states it is harder for an injured party to collect damages when injured by a "service" than when injured by a "product." The issue has arisen in cases involving blood for transfusions contaminated by the AIDS virus.

ments that seem clear enough in the abstract may, nevertheless, have different meanings to each of us because we have all had different experiences with the objects or events in the world that the word has come to represent. The experiences of each of us are unique in many respects, so no one word or set of words necessarily means the same thing to all of us. How many parents must reject some names for a new child because, while the mother associates a given name with a friend or hero from the past, the father once knew a villain of the same name?

Words, furthermore, are malleable: people can shape them to suit their own interests. To illustrate, in 1962 Congress, to encourage new business investment, allowed business people up to a 10 percent tax credit for investing in new personal property for their business. Investments like new machinery would qualify, but new buildings and permanent building fixtures would not. In 1982 the Justice Department sued the accounting firm of Ernst and Whinney for using words to disguise real property as personal property. What the accountants called "movable partitions," "equipment accesses," and "decorative fixtures" were in reality doors, manholes, and windows—all real property unqualified for the tax deduction. A "freezer" was in reality an entire refrigerated warehouse, "cedar decoration" was a wood-paneled wall, and "movable partitions—privacy" described toilet stalls.[3]

The disorderly conduct of words affects legal reasoning most immediately when a judge faces the task of interpreting a statute for the first time, when no judicial precedent inter-

---

[3]Jim Drinkhall, "Turnabout has IRS Accusing Taxpayers of Gobbledygook," *Wall Street Journal,* November 12, 1982, p. 1. Consider also in this regard John Train's compilation of "antilogies," words that can be used in opposite senses depending on contexts. Thus the infinitive "to dust" can refer to removing dust or to laying down dust, as in crop dusting. "To continue" can mean to proceed or to delay a proceeding. "To sanction" both authorizes and condemns. "To buckle" can fasten together or fall apart. The noun "cause" can in some contexts mean goal or consequence, as in the statement, "The final cause of law is the welfare of society." See "Antilogies," *Harvard Magazine,* November–December 1985, p. 18, and "More Antilogies," *Harvard Magazine,* March–April 1986, p. 17. See also Arthur Leff, "The Leff Dictionary of Law: A Fragment," 94 *Yale Law Journal* 1855 (1985).

preting the statute helps the judge to find its meaning. Therefore, we shall refine the problem of disorderly words in Chapter III, which examines judicial choices in statutory
interpretation.

Reasoning from Examples of Precedents

The previous paragraph suggests that precedents help narrow
the range of legal choices judges face when they resolve a case.
Indeed, precedents do just that, but they never provide complete certainty. Reasoning by example also perpetuates a degree of unpredictability in law. To see why, we proceed
through six analytical stages.

Stage One: Reasoning by Example in General

Reasoning by example, in its simplest form, means accepting
one choice and rejecting another because the past provides an
example that the accepted choice somehow "worked." Robert,
for example, wants to climb a tree but wonders if its branches
will hold. He chooses to attempt the climb because his older
sister has just climbed the tree without mishap. Robert reasons
by example. His reasoning hardly guarantees success: His
older sister may still be skinnier and lighter. Robert may regret
a choice based on a bad example, but he still reasons that way.
If he falls and survives, he will possess a much better example
from which to reason in the future.

   The most important characteristic of reasoning by example in any area of life is that no rules tell the decider *how* to
select the facts that are similar or different. Let us therefore
see how this indeterminacy occurs in legal reasoning.

Stage Two: Examples in Law

In law, decisions in prior cases provide the examples for legal
reasoning. For starters, a precedent contains the analysis and
the conclusion reached in an earlier case in which the facts
and the legal question(s) resemble the current conflict a judge

has to resolve. Even when a statute or a constitutional rule is involved, a judge will look at what other judges have said about the meaning of that rule when they applied it to similar facts and answered similar legal questions. Not only might a judge resolve Chapter I's case of the rotten cantaloupe in terms of common law precedents of contract, but a judge hearing the cases of the airplane thief or of Richard Nixon's "Watergate" defense of executive privilege would look beyond the National Motor Vehicle Act and the Constitution to see how judges have interpreted these rules or rules like them in earlier precedents.

To understand more fully how precedents create examples we must return to the distinction between law and history. How does a judge know whether facts of a prior case really do resemble those in the case now before him?

Trials themselves do *not*, as a rule, produce precedents. As we have seen, trials seek primarily to find the immediate facts of the dispute, to discover who is lying, whose memory has failed, and who can reliably speak to the truth of the matter. When a jury hears the case, the judge acts as an umpire, making sure the lawyers present the evidence properly to the jury so that it decides the "right" question. Often judges do the jury's job altogether. The law does not allow jury trials in some kinds of cases. When the law does allow jury trials, the parties may elect to go before a judge anyway, perhaps because they feel the issues are too complex for laypeople or perhaps because "bench trials" take less time.

Of course, a trial judge must decide the issues of law that the lawyers raise. The conscientious trial judge will explain to the parties orally for the record why and how he resolves the key legal issues in their case. In some instances he will give them a written opinion explaining his legal choices, and some of these find their way into the reported opinions. But since at trial the judge pays most attention to the historical part of the case, deciding what happened, he usually keeps his explanations at the relatively informal oral level. As a result other judges will not find these opinions reported anywhere; they cannot discover them even if they try. Hence few trial judges create precedents even though they resolve legal issues.

Thus the masses of legal precedents that fill the shelves of law libraries mostly emerge from the appellate process. You should not, however, lose sight of the fact that lawyers use many of the same legal reasoning techniques when they base their recommendations to their clients on appellate precedents to avoid trials as well as when they manipulate precedents to their advantage in litigation.

Stage Three: The Three-Step Process of Reasoning by Example

Legal reasoning often involves reasoning from the examples of precedents. Powerful legal traditions impel judges to solve problems by using solutions to similar problems reached by judges in the past. Thus a judge seeks to resolve conflicts by discovering a statement about the law in a prior case—his example—and then applying this statement or conclusion to the case before him. Lawyers who seek to anticipate problems and prevent conflicts follow much the same procedure. Professor Levi calls this a three-step process in which the judge sees a factual similarity between the current case and one or more prior cases, announces the rule of law on which the earlier case or cases rested, and applies the rule to the case before him.[4]

Stage Four: How Reasoning by Example Perpetuates Unpredictability in Law

To understand this stage we must return to the first step in the three-step description of the legal reasoning process, the step in which the judge decides which precedent governs. The judge must *choose* the facts in the case before him that resemble or differ from the facts in the case, or line of cases, in which prior judicial decisions first announced the rule. The judge no doubt accepts his obligation, made powerful by legal tradi-

[4]Edward Levi, *An Introduction to Legal Reasoning* (Chicago: University of Chicago Press, 1949), p. 2. Please do not confuse the six analytical stages I use in this chapter with the three-step reasoning process inherent in our legal system itself.

tion, to "follow precedent," but he is under no obligation to follow any particular precedent. He completes step one *by deciding for himself* which of the many precedents are similar to the facts of the case before him and *by deciding for himself* what they mean.

No judicial opinion in a prior case can require that a judge sift the facts of his present case one way or another. He is always free to do this himself. A judge writing his opinion can influence a future user of the precedent he creates by refusing to report or consider some potentially important facts revealed in the trial transcript. But once he reports them, precedent users can use the facts in their own way. They can call a fact critical that a prior judge reported but deemed irrelevant; they can make a legal molehill out of what a prior judge called a mountain. Thus the present judge, the precedent user, retains the freedom to choose the example from which the legal conclusion follows.

I call this judicial freedom to choose the governing precedent by selectively sifting the facts *fact freedom*. Our inability to predict with total accuracy how a judge will use his fact freedom is the major source of uncertainty in law. Thus we cannot say that "the law" applies known or given rules to diverse factual situations because we don't know the applicable rules until after the judge uses his fact freedom to choose the precedent.

Stage Five: An Illustration of Unpredictability in Law

Consider the following example from the rather notorious history of enforcing the Mann Act. The Mann Act, passed by Congress in 1910, provides in part that "Any person who shall knowingly transport or cause to be transported ... in interstate or foreign commerce ... any woman or girl for the purpose of prostitution or debauchery, or for any other immoral purpose ... shall be deemed guilty of a felony." Think about these words for a minute. Do they say that if I take my wife to Tennessee for the purpose of drinking illegal moonshine whiskey with her I shall be deemed guilty of a felony? What if

I take her to Tennessee to rob a bank? Certainly robbing a bank is an "immoral purpose." Is it "interstate commerce"? But we are jumping prematurely to Chapter III. For the moment, you should see only that the Congress has chosen some rather ambiguous words and then move to the main problem: choosing the "right" example to decide the following case.

Mr. and Mrs. Mortensen, owners and operators of a house of prostitution in Grand Island, Nebraska, decided to take some of the employees for a well-earned vacation at Yellowstone and Salt Lake City. The girls did lay off their occupation completely during the entire duration of the trip. Upon their return they resumed their calling. Over a year later federal agents arrested the Mortensens and, on the basis of the vacation trip, charged them with violation of the Mann Act. The jury convicted the Mortensens. Their lawyer appealed to an appellate court judge.

Unpredictability in law arises when the judge cannot automatically say that a given precedent is or isn't factually similar. To simplify matters here, let us now assume that he examines only one precedent, the decision of the U. S. Supreme Court in *Caminetti v. United States,* announced in 1917.[5] He must choose whether this example does or does not determine the result in *Mortensen.* Assume that in *Caminetti* a man from Wichita met but did not linger with a woman during a brief visit to Oklahoma City. After his return home, he sent this "mistress" a train ticket, which she used to travel to Wichita. There she did spend several nights with her friend, but not as a commercial prostitute. Assume that on these facts the Supreme Court in *Caminetti* upheld the conviction under the Mann Act. Does this case determine the Mortensen's fate? Does this precedent bind the court in *Mortensen?* To answer these questions the judge must decide whether this case is factually similar to *Mortensen.* Is it?

In one sense, of course it is. In each case the defendants transported women across state lines, after which sex out of

---

[5]*Caminetti v. United States,* 242 U. S. 470 (1917). *Caminetti's* facts and holding cover noncommercial as well as commercial sexual immorality.

wedlock occurred. In another sense it isn't. Without her ticket and transportation the Oklahoma woman could not have slept with the defendant. But if the Mortensens had not sponsored the vacation, the women would have continued their work. The Mortensens' transportation *reduced* the frequency of prostitution. The rancher maintained or increased "illicit sex." Should this difference matter? The judge is free to select one interpretation of the facts or the other in order to answer this question. Either decision will create a new legal precedent. It is precisely this freedom to decide either way that increases unpredictability in law.

Stage Six: Reasoning by Example Facilitates Legal Change

Why does judicial fact freedom make law change constantly? Legal rules change every time they are applied because no two cases ever have exactly the same facts. Although judges treat cases as if they were legally the same whenever they apply the rule of one case to another, deciding the new case in terms of the rule adds to the list of cases a new and unique factual situation. To rule in the Mortensens' favor, as the Supreme Court did in 1944, gave judges new ways of looking at the Mann Act.[6] With those facts, judges after 1944 could, if they wished, read the Mann Act more narrowly than *Caminetti* did. *Mortensen* thus potentially changed the meaning of the Mann Act, thereby changing the law.

But as the situation turned out, the change did not endure. In 1946 the Court upheld the conviction, under the Mann Act, of certain Mormons, members of a branch known as Fundamentalists, who took "secondary" wives across state lines. No prostitution at all was involved here, but the evidence did suggest that some of the women did not travel voluntarily. Fact freedom worked its way again[7] The Court ex-

[6]*Mortensen v. United States,* 322 U. S. 369 (1944).
[7]*Cleveland v. United States,* 329 U. S. 14 (1946).

tended *Caminetti* and by implication isolated *Mortensen.* The content of the Mann Act, then, has changed with each new decision and each new set of facts.

Is law always as confusing and unclear as these examples make it seem? In one sense certainly not. To the practicing lawyer, most legal questions the client asks possess clear and predictable answers. But in such cases—and here we return to the definition in Chapter I of legal conflicts—the problems probably do not get to court at all. Uncertainty helps convert a human problem into a legal conflict. We focus on uncertainty in law because that is where reason in law takes over.

In another sense, however, law never entirely frees itself from uncertainty. Lawyers always cope with uncertainties about what happened, uncertainties that arise in the historical part of law. If they go to trial on the facts, even if they think the law is clear, the introduction of new evidence or the unexpected testimony of a witness may raise new and uncertain legal issues the lawyers didn't consider before the trial. Lawyers know they can never fully predict the outcome of a client's case, even though much of the law is clear to them most of the time.

IS UNPREDICTABILITY IN LAW DESIRABLE?

Is it desirable that legal rules do not always produce clear and unambiguous answers to legal conflicts? Should the legal system strive to reach the point where legal rules solve problems in the way, for example, that the formula for finding square roots of numbers provides automatic answers to all square root problems?

Despite the human animal's natural discomfort in the presence of uncertainty, some unpredictability in law is desirable. Indeed, if a rule had to provide an automatic and completely predictable outcome before courts could resolve conflicts, society would become intolerably repressive, if not altogether impossible. There are two reasons why.[8]

[8]Levi, *An Introduction to Legal Reasoning,* pp. 1–6.

First, since no two cases ever raise entirely identical facts, society must have some way of treating different cases *as if they were the same* in a way litigants accept as fair. Of course, judicial impartiality is an important element of fairness, and we shall return to the problem of impartiality in the final chapter. But you should also think about this fact: If the legal system resolved all conflicts automatically, people would have little incentive to *participate* in the process that resolves their disputes. If the loser knew in advance he would surely lose, he would not waste time and money on litigation. He would not have the opportunity to try to persuade the judge that his case, always factually unique, *ought* to be treated by a different rule. Citizens who lose will perceive a system that allows them to "make their best case" as fairer than a system that tells them they lose while they sit helplessly.

Only in unpredictable circumstances will each side have an incentive to present its best case. Because the law is ambiguous, each side thinks it might win.[9] This produces an even more important consequence for society as a whole, not just for the losers. The needs of society change over time. The words of common law, statutes, and constitutions must take on new meanings. The participation that ambiguity encourages constantly bombards judges with new ideas. The ambiguity inherent in reasoning by example gives the attorney the opportunity to persuade the judge that the law *ought* to say one thing rather than another. Lawyers thus keep pushing judges to make their interpretation of "the law" fit newer shared beliefs about right and wrong.

I am not encouraging legislators and judges to create or applaud legal uncertainty. Rather, I am arguing that uncertainty in law is unavoidable. This uncertainty is, however, more a blessing than a curse. The participation that uncertainty in law encourages gives the legal process and society itself a vital capacity to change its formal rules with the less formal changes in human needs and values.

---

[9]The process also has the desirable effect of encouraging negotiation and compromise. Each side has an incentive to settle because each side knows it could also lose.

THE OTHER SIDE OF THE COIN:
STARE DECISIS AS A STABILIZING
AND CLARIFYING ELEMENT IN LAW

I hope that this discussion of unpredictability in law has not left the impression that law is never clear at all. If rules of law amounted to nonsense—lacked any meaning—government by law could not function. If society is to work, most law must be clear much of the time. We must be able to make wills and contracts, to insure ourselves against disasters, and to plan hundreds of other decisions with the confidence that courts will back our decisions if the people we trust with our freedom and our property fail us.

There is indeed a force pushing toward stability within reasoning by example itself: Once judges determine that a given precedent is factually similar enough to determine the outcome in the case before them, then in normal circumstances they follow the precedent. We call this the doctrine of *stare decisis,* "we let the prior decision stand."

Stare decisis operates in two dimensions. Students and lawyers tend to confuse the two, so let me explain them both, even though only the second really concerns us in this book. Stare decisis in the first, or "vertical," dimension acts as a marching order in the chain of judicial command. Courts in both the state and federal systems are organized in a hierarchy within their jurisdictions. Thus the supreme courts of Georgia and of the United States both sit at the top of an "organization chart" of courts. The rulings of the highest court in any jurisdiction legally control all the courts beneath it. Stare decisis stabilizes law vertically because no court should ignore a higher authoritative decision on a legal point. As long as the U. S. Supreme Court holds that airplanes are not "vehicles" within the NMVTA, all courts beneath it must legally honor that clear rule of law in any future airplane theft case that may arise under the Act.

There is, however, a more interesting "horizontal" dimension to stare decisis. What if a supreme court makes a decision but then, either a few years or many decades later, de-

velops nagging doubts about the wisdom of its precedent?
When should a court follow its own precedent in the face of
such doubts? As you begin to wrestle with the intricacies of
horizontal stare decisis, please note that the concept applies
only after a judge has reason to doubt the policy or wisdom
of the precedent. Judges do not need to resort to the doctrine
to justify following the example of a case whose analysis and
outcome are as convincing as the alternatives. Note also that
stare decisis does not substitute for reasoning by example.
Judges can seek guidance from the doctrine only *after* they
have used their fact freedom to conclude that a case from the
past legally governs or controls the case at bar. Professor
Thomas S. Currier has stated well the values that justify the
principle of stare decisis on this horizontal dimension:

1. *Stability.* It is clearly socially desirable that social relations
   should have a reasonable degree of continuity and
   cohesion, held together by a framework of reasonably
   stable institutional arrangements. Continuity and cohesion in the judicial application of rules [are] important
   to the stability of these institutional arrangements, and
   society places great value on the stability of some of
   them. Social institutions in which stability is recognized
   as particularly important include the operation of government, the family, ownership of land, commercial arrangements, and judicially created relations....

2. *Protection of Reliance.* [T]he value here is the protection of
   persons who have ordered their affairs in reliance upon
   contemporaneously announced law. It is obviously desirable that official declarations of the principles and attitudes upon which official administration of the law will
   be based should be capable of being taken as determi-
   nate and reliable indications of the course that such
   administration will in fact take in the future.... This
   value might be regarded as a personalized variation on
   the value of stability; but it is broader in that it is recognized even where no social institution is involved, and
   stability as such is unimportant.

3. *Efficiency in the Administration of Justice.* If every case coming before the courts had to be decided as an original
   proposition, without reference to precedent, the judicial

work-load would obviously be intolerable. Judges must be able to ease this burden by seeking guidance from what other judges have done in similar cases.

4. *Equality.* By this is meant the equal treatment of persons similarly situated. It is a fundamental ethical require-ment that like cases should receive like treatment, that there should be no discrimination between one litigant and another except by reference to some relevant differ-entiating factor. This appears to be the same value that requires rationality in judicial decision-making, which in turn necessitates that the law applied by a court be con-sistently stated from case to case. The same value is rec-ognized in the idea that what should govern judicial de-cisions are rules, or at least standards. The value of equality, in any event, appears to be at the heart of our received notions of justice.

5. *The Image of Justice.* By this phrase I do not mean that any judicial decision ought to be made on the basis of its likely impact upon the court's public relations, in the Madison Avenue sense, but merely that it is important not only that the court provide equal treatment to per-sons similarly situated, but that, insofar as possible, the court should appear to do so. Adherence to precedent generally tends not only to assure equality in the admin-istration of justice, but also to project to the public the impression that courts do administer justice equally.[10]

The next chapters will describe more precisely the cir-cumstances in which Currier's reasons for horizontal stare decisis do and do not compel a judge to follow rather than depart from a precedent. Here you should simply note that, in fact, most law is clear enough to prevent litigation most of the time. Lawyers can advise us on how to make valid wills and binding contracts. We do know that if someone steals our car and takes it to another state, federal officials, under the authority of the National Motor Vehicle Theft Act, can try to track down the car and the criminal. Without a system of prec-

[10]Thomas S. Currier, "Time and Change in Judge-Made Law: Prospective Overruling," 51 *Virginia Law Review* 201 (1965), pp. 235–238. See also George Fletcher, "Paradoxes in Legal Thought," 85 *Columbia Law Review* 1236 (1985).

edents it would be harder for us to predict judicial decisions and therefore more difficult for us to plan to avoid legal conflicts.

There is a paradox here. Because courts do exist to apply law to solve legal problems, and because we trust them in fact to do so, courts, particularly the appellate courts that concern us here, don't actually have to do this in the majority of disputes. In anticipation, private citizens who know what the law means in their case will, if for no other reason than to save money, usually resolve their problem without asking a court to review the law. They don't need to ask the meaning of the law; they know its meaning.

Perhaps in our legal system both clarity and unpredictability, and stability and change can benefit us, depending on the type of problem the law tries to address in a given case. You should reflect further on this possibility as you read the next and final section of this chapter.

LAW IN SOCIETY: AN OVERVIEW

This book tries to suggest new ways of thinking about legal reasoning to laypeople, lawyers, and judges. So far it has adopted the tactic of emphasizing (but not yet proving) many negative aspects of law: Law is not what it seems. Law is often unclear. Legal choices are not wise or fair or just in any absolute sense. Yet this book does state a constructive philosophy of legal reasoning. Lawyers and judges should isolate themselves less than they sometimes do from social realities. The premises of legal reasoning ought to rest on the best possible understanding of how people actually feel and act in their daily affairs. The goals of legal reasoning must serve real human needs rather than an abstract legal symmetry. Hence this overview.

To start, assume that modern governments should strive above all to create and then improve upon conditions that foster societal "health." Law should foster a social environment in which particular individuals and the citizenry collectively can develop their capacities and satisfy their needs.

In the narrow and immediate sense this means that societies must find ways to divide up their limited resources—food, clear air and water, shelter, and so forth—in a manner that most citizens can either tolerate or, more ideally, find fair.[11]

In the broader long-term sense this means that societies must work to increase the available resources relative to the size of the population. At least societies should do so when the current level of availability leaves some citizens in conditions in which they cannot satisfy basic needs.

People often fail to appreciate, however, that, although some tangible resources or wants have limits (so that the more Peter gets the less Paul has), other wants, equally desirable, have no such limits. Hart and Sacks make this point powerfully:

> There *can* be enough freedom of thought and speech for
> everybody and enough freedom of worship, if society
> wishes to recognize and protect these freedoms. So of
> friendship, peace of mind, self-respect, and the sense of
> participation in the life of the community. So of health. So
> of every kind of pleasurable activity which depends upon
> the development and exercise of personal talent. So, for
> most practical purposes, of the enjoyment of the personal
> talents of others. Given a minimum of material goods, the
> supplies of these and other intangible satisfactions depend
> mainly upon people having the wit to avoid placing limits
> upon them by their own folly.[12]

---

[11]Philip Selznick believes that our unruly and individualistic "frontier" culture is now facing for the first time the challenge of using limited resources efficiently. This change therefore inevitably produces shifts in legal doctrine that encourage cooperation. *Leadership in Administration* (Berkeley: University of California Press, 1983 ed), p. viii.

[12]Henry M. Hart, Jr. and Albert M. Sacks, *The Legal Process* (Cambridge: Harvard Law School, 1958), p. 112. More recently the Harvard Law School has led the movement to identify and apply the techniques of negotiating mutually satisfactory solutions to conflicts rather than litigating them. See the short but potentially revolutionary book by Roger Fisher and William Ury, *Getting to Yes* (New York: Penguin, 1983). See also Robert Axelrod, *The Evolution of Cooperation* (New York: Basic Books, 1984).

The legal process is not the only arm of government striving to achieve these basic social objectives. Our commitment to public education, for example, rests on the same philosophical ground. But the legal process, more than any part of government, affects the ability of people to work toward (or at least not against) these goals because all governmental activity—crime control and racial integration—and much private activity—business dealings—operate in a legal framework. We must judge the quality of judicial choices by asking whether they help achieve these goals. Judges who make such choices must do the same.

If we had to select one quality that societies and their legal systems should encourage to achieve these goals, would we not choose the quality of human cooperation? If so, we should judge legal choices by whether they foster some hope of encouraging or maintaining cooperation.

Cooperation doesn't necessarily mean total or perpetual agreement. Businesspeople compete, husbands and wives quarrel, and labor and management have bitter disputes about the conditions of work. Rather, it means that the people in conflict cannot resolve the disagreement without cooperating at a deeper level with each other by jointly agreeing to argue within the limits of disagreement that rules provide.

To illustrate, consider an extreme example of conflict. Here is a situation in which we *want* people to come to blows and hurt each other: the boxing match. You can probably think of many rules—weight classifications, weigh-in procedures, glove-weight rules, and methods for scoring rounds in the absence of a knockout—with which the fighters must cooperate. If they don't, the match loses its significance. Like sports rules, rules of law provide the cooperative framework within which disagreement works toward maintaining society's main goals. Now reflect upon the five values that support the principle of stare decisis. Does not each value appeal to us precisely to the extent that we think it fosters the kind of cooperation on which social harmony and progress depend?

By electing to encourage cooperation in society through the formal methods of law, as any complex human group must, we must nevertheless accept three imperfections inherent in legal systems.

1. The first imperfection economists call the problem of "opportunity costs." People who resort to law for problem solving often give up their chance to go somewhere else or to someone else for the solution. Turning to the rules of the state often draws battle lines and requires an investment of time and money so that, once started, people tend to get locked into the process. Solving a problem through law often prevents solving a problem through love or compromise. A legal solution of a conflict may be better than a shootout, but love and compromise are better still.

Additionally, resorting to law rather than some other method means not only abiding by the state's rules but also depending upon the state's machinery for making its rules work. The problem isn't that the strangers who run the machinery don't care about deciding justly. Usually they do care, but they care simultaneously about keeping the machinery running, and this sets limits on how they decide cases. Their time is limited. Sensitive and delicate though the machinery may be, a case must be whittled, pounded, smoothed, and fictionalized to some degree to fit the machine.

Much of what appears to the casual observer as injustice in law arises from the methods lawyers and judges unavoidably adopt to keep the legal machinery moving. More important, the legal system remains distant and formal in order to maintain the appearance of impartiality. Judicial systems will not remain effective for long if losers regularly accuse the system of crumbling into an unfair power struggle in which the judge simply sides with the winner against the loser.[13] In order to retain the appearance of impartiality, judges must often make decisions by blinding themselves to some facts of the conflict and the feelings of

[13]See Martin Shapiro, *Courts: A Comparative and Political Analysis* (Chicago: University of Chicago Press, 1981).

the parties. They must often act before they have fully settled the problem in their own minds. When we choose to go to law, we choose to pay all these opportunity costs.

2. The second imperfection raises the problem of generality. If legal rules, including both statutes and the principles judges announce in their opinions, are to direct cooperation, they must direct how people should behave in the future. Since we do not know the future, and since conditions change and unique events occur in ways we cannot always predict, rules must direct behavior in general terms. But if laws are general they cannot speak with precision, certainly not to each and every human conflict. We want law to define cooperative behaviors, but the generality we need in law also means that sometimes it will fail to resolve the always unique specific case.

3. The final imperfection deals with the problem of legal authority. Just as the boxers must believe that they *ought* to abide by boxing's rules to make the match more meaningful, so citizens should feel an obligation to law. We make law powerful in the coercive sense by backing it up ultimately with the power of armed policemen.[14] However, subjecting citizens to police force does not automatically develop a moral commitment to the rightness of law; in fact, I suspect it tends to produce the opposite psychological reaction, one of bitterness and resentment. But if the threat of force does not elicit a sense of obligation, what does?

The third imperfection arises because, I suspect, people develop a sense of obligation to law partly because they be-

---

[14]Armed policemen do more than enforce the criminal laws. Any time a court rules that one person has become legally liable to another, for example, for breaking a contract in business or negligently breaking a leg in an auto accident, armed policemen, usually called deputy sheriffs or marshals, may seize the debtor or his property to enforce the judicial judgment.

lieve law is certain, free of ambiguity, and evenly applied without, as the saying goes, bias or favor. As a result, judges regularly try to hide the uncertain and changeable side of law from us, even though uncertainty and change are desirable. Judges often pretend that legal reasoning *does* resemble the process of solving an arithmetic problem, that they have "found" the right law rather than created it or chosen it, in order to bolster the authority of law. I do not think we shall completely escape the drive of judges to make the law appear more certain and hence impartial than it is. Nevertheless, judicial wisdom lies in knowing when to acknowledge the presence of uncertainty and the necessity for choice that enables law to change for the better. This book's final chapter proposes a philosophy of impartiality that permits judges to admit that they make creative choices in an uncertain world.

SUMMARY

- Although in Chapter III we expose more thoroughly the "disorderly conduct of words," why, generally, do the words of legal rules so often fail to resolve legal problems?
- What is reasoning by example? Why do American judges resolve legal conflicts by doing so? Where do the judges' examples come from?
- Which of the steps in the three-step process of reasoning is the most crucial? Why?
- How does reasoning by example perpetuate uncertainty in law? Why is such uncertainty desirable?
- What are the stabilizing elements in law? Under what circumstances does the doctrine of stare decisis provide useful guidance to a judge?
- What are "opportunity costs" and why are they imperfections inherent in the legal process? Similarly, why is generality both a blessing and an imperfection?

ILLUSTRATIVE CASES

In the federal judicial system it is common for the intermediate appellate courts to hear cases in panels of three judges, with the outcome determined by majority vote. Here are two opinions written by Learned Hand sitting on two separate panels. The first is a precedent for the second. Notice that they were decided just a month apart. You should read the second case initially to see how Judge Hand uses his fact freedom to distinguish *Repouille* from *Francioso,* then to see how Judge Frank uses fact freedom a different way, and finally to explore the possibility that both judges in *Repouille* have used their fact freedom foolishly.

United States v. Francioso
164 F.2d 163 (Nov. 5, 1947)

L. HAND, Circuit Judge.

This is an appeal from an order admitting the appellee, Francioso, to citizenship. At the hearing the "naturalization examiner" objected to his admission upon the ground that he had married his niece and had been living incestuously with her during the five years before he filed his petition. Upon the following facts the judge held that Francioso had been "a person of good moral character" and naturalized him. Francioso was born in Italy in 1905, immigrated into the United States in 1923, and declared his intention of becoming a citizen in 1924. His wife was born in Italy in 1906, immigrated in 1911, and has remained here since then. They were married in Connecticut on February 13, 1925, and have four children, born in 1926, 1927, 1930, and 1933. Francioso was the uncle of his wife, and knew when he married her that the marriage was unlawful in Connecticut and that the magistrate would have not married them, had they not suppressed their relationship. They have always lived together in apparent concord, and at some time which the record leaves indefinite, a priest of the Catholic Church—of which both spouses are communicants—"solemnized" the marriage with the consent of his bishop.

In United States ex rel. Iorio v. Day, in speaking of crimes involving "moral turpitude" we held that the standard was, not what we personally might set, but "the commonly accepted mores": i.e., the generally accepted moral conventions current at the time, so far as we could ascertain them. The majority opinion in the United States ex rel. Berlandi v. Reimer perhaps looked a little askance at that decision; but it did not overrule it, and we think that the same test applies to the statutory standard of "good moral character" in the naturalization statute. Would the moral feelings, now prevalent generally in this country, be outraged because Francioso continued to live with his wife and four children between 1938 and 1943? Anything he had done before that time does not count; for the statute does not search further back into the past.

In 1938 Francioso's children were five, eight, eleven and twelve years old, and his wife was 31; he was morally and legally responsible for their nurture and at least morally responsible for hers. Cato himself would not have demanded that he should turn all five adrift. True, he might have left the home and supported them out of his earnings; but to do so would deprive his children of the protection, guidance and solace of a father. We can think of no course open to him which would not have been regarded as more immoral than that which he followed, unless it be that he should live at home, but as a celibate. There may be purists who would insist that this alone was consistent with "good moral conduct"; but we do not believe that the conscience of the ordinary man demands that degree of ascesis; and we have for warrant the fact that the Church—least of all complaisant with sexual lapses—saw fit to sanction the continuance of this union. Indeed, such a marriagé would have been lawful in New York until 1893, as it was at common-law. To be sure its legality does not determine its morality; but it helps to do so, for the fact that disapproval of such marriages was so long in taking the form of law, shows that it is condemned in no such sense as marriages forbidden by "God's law." It stands between those and the marriage of first cousins which is ordinarily, though not universally, regarded as permissible.

It is especially relevant, we think, that the relationship of these spouses did not involve those factors which particularly make such marriages abhorrent. It was not as though they had earlier had those close and continuous family contacts which are usual between uncle and niece. Francioso had lived in Italy until he was eighteen years of age; his wife immigrated when she was a child of four; they could have had no acquaintance until he came here in August, 1923, only eighteen months before they married. It is to the highest degree improbable that in that short time there should have arisen between them the familial intimacy common between uncle and niece, which is properly thought to be inimical to marriage. . . .

Order affirmed.

Repouille v. United States
165 F.2d 152 (Dec. 5, 1947)

L. HAND, Circuit Judge.

The District Attorney, on behalf of the Immigration and Naturalization Service, has appealed from an order, naturalizing the appellee, Repouille. The ground of the objection in the district court and here is that he did not show himself to have been a person of "good moral character" for the five years which preceded the filing of his petition. The facts are as follows. The petition was filed on September 22, 1944, and on October 12, 1939, he had deliberately put to death his son, a boy of thirteen, by means of chloroform. His reason for this tragic deed was that the child had "suffered from birth from a brain injury which destined him to be an idiot and a physical monstrosity malformed in all four limbs. The child was blind, mute, and deformed. He had to be fed; the movements of his bladder and bowels were involuntary, and his entire life was spent in a small crib." Repouille had four other children at the time towards whom he has always been a dutiful and responsible parent; it may be assumed that his act was to help him in their nurture, which was being compromised by the burden imposed upon him in the care of the fifth. The family was altogether dependent upon his industry for its support. He was indicted for manslaughter in the first degree; but the jury brought in a verdict of manslaughter in the second degree with a recommendation of the "utmost clemency"; and the judge sentenced him to not less than five years nor more than ten, execution to be stayed, and the defendant to be placed on probation, from which he was discharged in December, 1945. Concededly, except for this act he conducted himself as a person of "good moral character" during the five years before he filed his petition. Indeed, if he had waited before filing his petition from September 22, to October 14, 1944, he would have had a clear record for the necessary period, and would have been admitted without question.

Very recently we had to pass upon the phrase "good moral character" in the Nationality Act; and we said that it set as a test, not those standards which we might ourselves approve, but whether "the moral feelings, now prevalent generally in this country" would "be outraged" by the conduct in question: that is, whether it conformed to "the generally accepted moral conven-

tions current at the time.''[a] In the absence of some national in-
quisition, like a Gallup poll, that is indeed a difficult test to apply; often questions will arise to which the answer is not
ascertainable, and where the petitioner must fail only because
he has the affirmative. Indeed, in the case at bar itself the answer
is not wholly certain; for we all know that there are great numbers of people of the most unimpeachable virtue, who think it
morally justifiable to put an end to a life so inexorably destined
to be a burden on others, and—so far as any possible interest of
its own is concerned—condemned to a brutish existence, lower
indeed than all but the lowest forms of sentient life. Nor is it inevitably an answer to say that it must be immoral to do this, until
the law provides security against the abuses which would inevitably follow, unless the practice were regulated. Many people—
probably most people—do not make it a final ethical test of conduct that it shall not violate law; few of us exact of ourselves or
of others the unflinching obedience of a Socrates. There being no
lawful means of accomplishing an end, which they believe to be
righteous in itself, there have always been conscientious persons
who feel no scruple in acting in defiance of a law which is repugnant to their personal convictions, and who even regard as mar-
tyrs those who suffer by doing so. In our own history it is only
necessary to recall the Abolitionists. It is reasonably clear that the
jury which tried Repouille did not feel any moral repulsion at
his crime. Although it was inescapably murder in the first degree,
not only did they bring in a verdict that was flatly in the face of
the facts and utterly absurd—for manslaughter in the second degree presupposes that the killing has not been deliberate—but
they coupled even that with a recommendation which showed that
in the substance they wished to exculpate the offender. Moreover,
it is also plain, from the sentence which he imposed, that the
judge could not have seriously disagreed with their recommendation.

One might be tempted to seize upon all this as a reliable
measure of current morals; and no doubt it should have its place
in the scale; but we should hesitate to accept it as decisive, when,
for example, we compare it with the fate of a similar offender in
Massachusetts, who, although he was not executed, was impris-
oned for life. Left at large as we are, without means of verifying

[a]*United States v. Francioso,* 164 F.2d 163, (2d Cir., 1947). [Footnote in original.]

our conclusion, and without authority to substitute our individual beliefs, the outcome must needs be tentative; and not much is gained by discussion. We can say no more than that, quite independently of what may be the current moral feeling as to legally administered euthanasia, we feel reasonably secure in holding that only a minority of virtuous persons would deem the practise morally justifiable, while it remains in private hands, even when the provocation is as overwhelming as it was in this instance.

However, we wish to make it plain that a new petition would not be open to this objection; and that the pitiable event, now long passed, will not prevent Repouille from taking his place among us as a citizen. The assertion in his brief that he did not "intend" the petition to be filed until 1945, unhappily is irrelevant; the statute makes crucial the actual date of filing.

Order reversed; petition dismissed without prejudice to the filing of a second petition.

FRANK, Circuit Judge (dissenting).

This decision may be of small practical import to this petitioner for citizenship, since perhaps, on filing a new petition, he will promptly become a citizen. But the method used by my colleagues in disposing of this case may, as a precedent, have a very serious significance for many another future petitioner whose "good moral character" may be questioned (for any one of a variety of reasons which may be unrelated to a "mercy killing") in circumstances where the necessity of filing a new petition may cause a long and injurious delay. Accordingly, I think it desirable to dissent.

The district judge found that Repouille was a person of "good moral character." Presumably, in so finding, the judge attempted to employ that statutory standard in accordance with our decisions, i.e., as measured by conduct in conformity with "the generally accepted moral conventions at the time." My colleagues, although their sources of information concerning the pertinent mores are not shown to be superior to those of the district judge, reject his finding. And they do so, too, while conceding that their own conclusion is uncertain, and (as they put it) "tentative." I incline to think that the correct statutory test (the test Congress

intended) is the attitude of our ethical leaders. That attitude
would not be too difficul to learn; indeed, my colleagues indicate
that they think such leaders would agree with the district judge.
But the precedents in this circuit constrain us to be guided by
contemporary public opinion about which, cloistered as judges
are, we have but vague notions. (One recalls Gibbon's remark
that usually a person who talks of "the opinion of the world at
large" is really referring to "the few people with whom I happened to converse.")

Seeking to apply a standard of this type, courts usually do
not rely on evidence but utilize what is often called the doctrine
of "judicial notice," which, in matters of this sort, properly permits informal inquiries by the judges. However, for such a purpose (as in the discharge of many other judicial duties), the courts
are inadequately staffed, so that sometimes "judicial notice" actually means judicial ignorance.

But the courts are not helpless; such judicial impotence has
its limits. Especially when an issue importantly affecting a man's
life is involved, it seems to me that we need not, and ought not,
resort to our mere unchecked surmises, remaining wholly (to
quote my colleagues' words) "without means of verifying our conclusions." Because court judgments are the most solemn kind of
governmental acts—backed up as they are, if necessary, by the
armed force of the government—they should, I think, have a more
solid foundation. I see no good reason why a man's rights should
be jeopardized by judges' needless lack of knowledge.

I think, therefore, that, in any case such as this, where we
lack the means of determining present-day public reactions, we
should remand to the district judge with these directions: The
judge should give the petitioner and the government the opportunity to bring to the judge's attention reliable information on
the subject, which he may supplement in any appropriate way.
All the data so obtained should be put of record. On the basis
thereof, the judge should reconsider his decision and arrive at a
conclusion. Then, if there is another appeal, we can avoid sheer
guessing, which alone is now available to us, and can reach something like an informed judgment.[b]

[b]Of course, we cannot thus expect to attain certainty, for certainty on such
a subject as public opinion is unattainable. [Footnote in original.]

QUESTIONS

1. What legal questions does Judge Hand ask about Mr. Francioso's behavior? How does he answer them?
2. What facts about the *Repouille* case make *Francioso* factually similar enough to serve as a precedent?
3. The problem in both cases is how a court should determine whether an applicant for naturalization has the required good moral character. In *Francioso* Judge Hand uses a method that permits him to conclude that Francioso should become a citizen. How does he do so?
4. Does Judge Hand use the same method in *Repouille?* If so, what facts distinguish the two cases so that, even though Francioso won, Mr. Repouille lost?
5. What method would Judge Frank use? How, if at all, does it differ from Hand's method? Which of these two do you prefer? Why?
6. Do you agree with the following analysis of *Repouille* by Professor Michael Moore?

My intuition here is a simple one: you get better results if you ask judges to seek them explicitly rather than if you tell them to do something else. An example of this is Learned Hand's decision in *Repouille v. United States.* Hand had to interpret the naturalization statute, which allowed citizenship to those of "good moral character." Repouille aplied for citizenship, despite having killed one of his children, a retarded, crippled, helpless child that drained family resources from Repouille's other children. Hand denied Repouille citizenship, relying on what he took to be the conventional moral judgment that euthanasia, no matter how tragic the circumstances, manifested bad moral character.

My simple intuition is that Hand would have done better if he had judged the moral question himself, let his emotions grapple with the choice Repouille had faced. One hears this in every regretful line of Hand's opinion, dryly reciting the conventional judgment that all mercy killings are bad. Had Hand taken the responsibility for deciding whether **this** mercy killing of Repouille really constituted a morally bad act, he could not have allowed himself the comfort of a wooden recitation of a conventional moral norm. Forcing Hand to decide whether the act was really bad would have forced him, in Edmond Cahn's words, to have been "in session with himself, prepared to answer for the consequences." With sensitive moral beings, you get better judgment with such personal involvement than you do when a judge can claim the dispassionate air of the sociologist of other people's morals.[15]

7. Stanley Fish, the literary theorist, has strongly criticized the belief that rules of law dictate "correct" answers to legal conflicts. Which points made in the first two chapters does Fish's analogy to basketball illustrate?

Suppose you were a basketball coach and taught someone how to shoot baskets and how to dribble the ball, but had imparted these skills without reference to the playing of an actual basketball game. Now you decide to insert your student into a game, and you equip him with some rules. You say to him, for instance, "Take only good shots." "What," he asks reasonably enough, "is a good shot?" "Well," you reply, "a good shot is an 'open shot,' a shot taken when you are close to the basket (so that the chances of success are good) and when your view is not obstructed by the harassing efforts of opposing players." Everything goes well until the last few seconds of the game; your team is behind by a single point; the novice player gets the ball in heavy traffic and holds it as the final buzzer rings. You run up to him and say, "Why didn't you shoot?" and he answers, "It wasn't a good shot." Clearly, the rule must be amended, and accordingly you tell him that if time is running out, and your team is behind, and you have the ball, you should take the shot even if it isn't a good one, because it will then *be* a good one in the sense of being the best shot in the circumstances. (Notice how both the meaning of the rule and the entities it covers are changing shape as this "education" proceeds.) Now suppose there is another game, and the same situation develops. This time the player takes the shot, which under the circumstances is a very difficult one; he misses, and once again the final buzzer rings. You run up to him and say "Didn't you see that John (a teammate) had gone 'back door' and was perfectly positioned under the basket for an easy shot?" and he answers "But you said.... " Now obviously it would be possible once again to amend the rule, and just as

[15]"A Natural Law Theory of Interpretation," 58 *Southern California Law Review* 277 (1985), pp. 392–393.

obviously there would be no real end to the sequence and number of emendations that would be necessary. Of course, there will eventually come a time when the novice player (like the novice judge) will no longer have to ask questions; but it will not be because the rules have finally been made sufficiently explicit to cover all cases, but because explicitness will have been rendered unnecessary by a kind of knowledge that informs rules rather than follows from them.[16]

8. Try to imagine another example of the ambiguous meaning of words similar to the table/bench definitional problem. Alternatively, consider the meaning of two words you shall see fairly frequently in this book, "mean(s)" and "meaning." You ought to be able to think of at least six distinguishable meanings of these words. See Reed Dickerson, *The Interpretation and Application of Statutes* (Boston: Little, Brown, 1975), Chapter 4.

9. Recall the *Cleveland* case described in this chapter. In that case several Mormons transported their multiple wives across state lines, only to suffer prosecution under the Mann Act. Assume that the case of the vacationing prostitutes, *Mortensen,* represents the most recent prior judicial interpretation of the Mann Act. In that case, as you know, the court ruled that the act did not cover this instance of interstate transportation, even though the girls were prostitutes and even though without the trip home the girls could not have resumed their trade with the Mortensens. Reread the statutory language of the Mann Act, quoted above, and then prepare arguments both for the Mormons and for the prosecution. How are reasoning by example, stare decisis, and fact freedom reflected in these arguments? Try this problem: Apply the facts of the Mann Act precedents to argue that transporting a girl across state lines solely for the purpose of taking nude photographs of her for a magazine does or does not violate the Mann Act.[17]

---

[16]Stanley Fish, *"Fish v. Fiss,"* 36 Stanford Law Review 1325 (1984), pp. 1329–1330.

[17]See *United States v. Mathison,* 239 F.2d 358 (7th Cir., 1956).

Chapter III

STATUTORY INTERPRETATION

Whoever hath an absolute authority
to interpret any written or spoken
laws, it is he who is truly the
lawgiver, to all intents and
purposes, and not the person who
first spoke or wrote them.
   —Benjamin Hoadly

It is of course dangerous that judges
be philosophers—almost as
dangerous as if they were not.
   —Paul Freund

In some respects, legal reasoning resembles the hunt for game. This and the next two chapters examine three hunting grounds where judges seek their quarry: the resolution of the legal conflict before them on statutory, common law, and constitutional grounds.[1]

---

[1]Practicing lawyers hunt in the same places. They do so to help people plan their affairs, ideally without litigation. They also reason like judges when they prepare their positions on the legal issues in litigation itself. To avoid the constant repetition of the phrase "judges and lawyers" in the text, you should assume that comments about how judges reason usually refer to the lawyer's search for persuasive legal arguments as well.

As you cover this material, keep these points in the back of your mind:

1. Partitioning the hunting ground so neatly creates a very artificial simplification. Judges rarely settle an entire controversy by solving one isolated legal point. Many legal controversies, especially in their initial stages, *potentially* raise statutory *and* common law *and* constitutional legal points, to say nothing of the administrative law hunting ground this book omits.

2. Good lawyers and trial judges recognize that the psychological dynamics of a situation—such as the desire of a quarreling couple to compromise if each can somehow "save face" in the process—can contribute more than law can to settling controversies. We ignore that important dynamic in law here.

3. Never lose sight of the judge's objective. It always involves solving a problem, a concrete case, not merely evaluating legal questions in the abstract. The hunt for legal quarry is not a hunt for "a legal rule" in isolation but for a legal interpretation sufficient to resolve the case. Judges do not hunt always for "the one right solution," but to appear just they often pretend to do so.

4. Unlike the recreational hunter, judges cannot return from the hunt empty handed. They must decide by using the best available legal reasons, even if they are weak or unsatisfying. Like the primitive man hunting for survival, the judge may set out for an elk and feel fortunate to return with a turkey or a squirrel.

5. Finally, do not forget the message of the first two chapters: Despite the hunting metaphor's initial appeal, legal reasoning is *not* fundamentally a hunt at all. One of this century's finest teachers of legal reasoning, Karl Llewellyn, was fond of the similar metaphor of "quarrying" for some stone of legal truth. But hunting and mining can be seriously misleading metaphors because they suggest that the "truth" (the animal in the field or the nugget in the ground) is always there somewhere and needs only to be hunted down

or dug up. But the truth isn't really "there" waiting; the reasoning judge creates the truth. Maybe judges resemble artists more than hunters.[2]

WHAT ARE STATUTES AND WHAT SHOULD JUDGES DO WITH THEM?

"Statutes"—a dusty and unromantic word. One thinks of endless rows of thick books in inadequately illuminated library stacks. The librarians have the mildew under control, but its odor remains faintly on the air.

To understand better the significance of statutory law, we must abandon our reaction to statutes as dull and musty words; we must see them as vital forces in society. Statutes are the skeleton of the body politic. They form the framework that gives political power its leverage. People in government, when fortified by statutory authority, can take our property, our freedom, and our lives. Political campaigns and elections, indeed much in public life that does excite us, matter because they directly influence the making of laws that can dramatically affect the quality of our lives.

In the United States, the special legal meaning of statutes rests on two fundamental principles of government. First, although all officials, including judges, can and do make law, legislatures possess primary authority for doing so.[3] When leg-

---

[2]See my *Contemporary Constitutional Lawmaking: The Supreme Court and the Art of Politics* (Elmsford, N.Y.: Pergamon Press, 1985). Jerome Frank compared legal reasoning to musical interpretation in his "Words and Music: Some Remarks on Statutory Interpretation," 47 *Columbia Law Review* 1259 (1947). That metaphor doesn't work, either. See Reed Dickerson, *The Interpretation and Application of Statutes* (Boston: Little, Brown, 1975), pp. 24–26, for the explanation.

[3]This familiar principle of legislative supremacy has one important exception: Courts in the United States possess the authority to reject statutory supremacy when they conclude that the enforcement of a statute would violate a legal norm expressed in or implied by the constitutions of the states or the nation. Where judges find a violation, their expression of constitutional values becomes supreme, and this political dynamic is part of the familiar set of checks and balances that American government contains.

islatures make policy to address a public problem, in theory that policy controls or supersedes the policies of presidents, administrators, or judges. Second, legislatures can communicate their chosen policies in a legally binding way only by voting favorably on a written proposal. Without the vote by the legislature, no matter how forcefully legislators advocate a policy decision, they create no law. Committee reports, floor speeches, and so forth, may help us make sense of the law, but only the duly enacted statute has the force of law.

Statutes officially say, in effect: "Society has a problem. This is how society shall cope with it." Some statutory policies are incredibly general. Early antitrust statutes said that society has a problem preserving effective business competition, and it shall hereafter be illegal to restrain competition. In 1890 a nearly unanimous Congress passed with very little debate the Sherman Antitrust Act. Its first two sections state: (1) "Every contract, combination in the form of a trust or otherwise, or conspiracy, in restraint of trade or commerce among the several States, or with foreign nations, is hereby declared to be illegal"; and (2) "Every person who shall monopolize, or attempt to monopolize ... any part of the trade or commerce among the several States, or with foreign nations, shall be deemed guilty of a misdemeanor. ... " Such general language leaves to judges much freedom to shape and refine law. Other statutes create extremely detailed rules. Current tax laws say that government shall raise revenues, but it takes literally thousands of pages of rules and regulations to specify how government shall do it.

In the common law chapter to come, we shall see that courts can make and have made laws to handle many problems that legislatures now address by statute. This fact does not in any way conflict with the policy-making priority we now grant to legislatures. Furthermore, many modern social problems are so complex and their effects so synergistic that legislation, which is forward-looking and susceptible to an infinite variety of pragmatic compromises, is the preferred policy-making method.

A statute that states how society shall cope with business monopoly or revenue raising or any of thousands of other

problems really attempts to instruct judges to settle legal conflicts in one way rather than another. How should judges decide in concrete cases what statutes mean? When judges resolve specific cases in terms of statutes, they should seek first
the guidance of earlier case precedents dealing with the same
interpretive problem. But what if the problem has never
arisen before? Then a judge must address directly such questions as these: "What problem does this statute try to solve? Is
the case before me an example of such a problem? If so, how
does this statute tell me to solve it?" The judge who approaches statutory interpretation in the first instance this way
acknowledges legislative supremacy. He recognizes that it is
not *his* idea of the problem that resolves the case before him.
Rather, he knows that he must deal with the problem in the
way the statute communicates that problem and its solutions
to him.

Since he sees that statutes are a special kind of communication, the judge who approaches statutes wisely also knows
that he cannot treat the words as a series of Webster's definitions strung together. He understands the difficulties of clear
communication. He intuitively appreciates the saying, "The
greatest difficulty with communication is the illusion that it
has been achieved." He knows that words gain meaning not
from dictionaries, but from their context. He knows that a sign
on an outdoor escalator reading "Dogs Must Be Carried" does
not mean that everyone riding the escalator must carry a dog.[4]
He knows that the words of statutes become meaningful only
when they are applied to the solution of public problems.

WHAT JUDGES ACTUALLY DO WITH STATUTES

We have just outlined how judges should interpret statutes.
The rest of the chapter fills in the details. We must begin, however, by seeing that how judges actually interpret statutes
often bears little or no resemblance to our description.

[4]My thanks to Professor Allan Hutchinson for this illustration.

First Actuality: Sticking to the Literal Meaning of Words

In 1912 Lord Atkinson, speaking for the British House of Lords in its appellate judicial role, said:

> If the language of a statute be plain, admitting of only one meaning, the Legislature must be taken to have meant and intended what it has plainly expressed, and whatever it has in clear terms enacted must be enforced though it should lead to absurd or mischievous results.[5]

Lord Atkinson, no doubt, respected legislative powers and responsibilities—in this case, those of the House of Commons. The problem he perceived, we can safely guess, is this: If courts can go beyond the words at all, they can go anywhere they want, setting their own limits and destroying legislative supremacy in the process.

Legislative supremacy is important, but how would the good Lord react to this hypothetical statute: "A uniformed police officer may require any person driving a motor vehicle in a public place to provide a specimen of breath for a breath test if the officer has reasonable cause to suspect him of having alcohol in his body." Presumably Lord Atkinson would not exempt women from this law just because the last sentence reads "him" rather than "him or her." The earlier use of the word "person," even to a literalist, can cover both sexes. But how would he handle the following argument by an equally literalistic defendant? "The statute plainly says the officer may require the specimen from a person driving. I may have been slightly inebriated when the officer pulled me over, but when the officer required the specimen I was *not* 'driving a motor vehicle.' I wasn't even in my car. I was doing my imitation of a pig in the middle of the pavement when the officer requested the specimen."[6] This result is absurd, but Lord Atkinson seems willing to accept absurd results. Should he be?

---

[5]*Vacher and Sons, Ltd., v. London Society of Compositors,* A.C. 107 (1912), 121.

[6]See Sir Rupert Cross, *Statutory Interpretation* (London: Butterworths, 1976), p. 59. Or imagine a city ordinance requiring all liquor stores "to cease doing business at 10:00 P.M." Does the ordinance permit them to reopen at 10:01 P.M.?

American judges have also been seduced by the appeal of adhering to the words. A Virginia statute stated: "No cemetery shall be hereafter established within the corporate limits of any city or town; nor shall any cemetery be established within two hundred and fifty yards of any residence without the consent of the owner. . . . " In 1942, after the legislature passed this statute, the town of Petersburg, Virginia, bought an acre of land within its corporate limits on which to relocate bodies exhumed during a road-widening project. The acre adjoined and would be incorporated into a long-established cemetery. A city resident well within the proscribed distance of the added acre brought suit to prevent the expansion and cited the statute. He lost. Justice Gregory wrote for the appellate court:

> If the language of a statute is plain and unambiguous, and its meaning perfectly clear and definite, effect must be given to it regardless of what courts think of its wisdom or policy. . . .
>
> The word, "established," is defined in Webster's New International Dictionary, second edition, 1936, thus: "To originate and secure the permanent existence of; to found; to institute; to create and regulate . . . "
>
> Just why the Legislature, in its wisdom, saw fit to prohibit the establishment of cemeteries in cities and towns, and did not see fit to prohibit enlargements or additions, is no concern of ours. Certain it is that language could not be plainer than that employed to express the legislative will. From it we can see with certainty that . . . a cemetery . . . may be added to or enlarged without running counter to the inhibition found in [the statute]. . . . Our duty is to construe the statute as written.[7]

Judges, like Justice Gregory, who cling to the words fail to appreciate that the dictionary staff did not sit in Virginia's

[7]*Temple v. City of Petersburg,* 182 Va. 418 (1944), pp. 423–424. Responding to the vague words of the Mann Act (quoted in Chapter II), Justice Day wrote in his majority opinion in *Caminetti,* "Where the language is plain and admits of no more than one meaning the duty of interpretation does not arise. . . . " Was the language of the Mann Act plain?

legislature. By sticking to the words, the judges prevent themselves from asking what problem the legislature sought to address. Just why the legislature might purposely allow enlargement but not establishment of cemeteries in cities and towns *is* Justice Gregory's concern. Unless he tries to solve that puzzle, we can have no confidence that he has applied the statute to achieve its purpose.

Second Actuality: The Golden Rule

Of course, Lord Atkinson could have solved his problem another way, by sticking to the words *except* when they produce absurd results. The Golden Rule of statutory interpretation holds that judges should follow

> the grammatical and ordinary sense of the words . . . unless that would lead to some absurdity, or some repugnance or inconsistency with the rest of the instrument, in which case the grammatical and ordinary sense of the words may be modified, so as to avoid the absurdity and inconsistency, but no farther.[8]

The Golden Rule solves the problem of the clever intoxicated driver. It would be absurd and possibly dangerous to require that the officer ride with him and collect the specimen while weaving down the road.

But the Golden Rule, unfortunately, does not solve much more because it does not tell us how to separate the absurd from the merely questionable. To test this weakness in the rule, ask yourself two questions: (1) Is it absurd to allow expansion of existing graveyards while prohibiting the creation of new ones, or only questionable? (2) Is it absurd to use the Mann Act to prevent the transporation of willing girlfriends and mistresses across state lines along with unwilling "white slaves" and prostitutes, or merely questionable? The Golden Rule provides no answer.

Both the literal approach and the superficially more sensible rejection of absurdity in the Golden Rule fail. They de-

---

[8]*Grey v. Pearson,* 6 H.L. Cas. 61 (1857), 106, quoted in Cross, p. 15.

ceive judges into believing that words in isolation can be and usually are clear and that the words communicate by themselves. But they don't. The word "establish" in *Temple* (the graveyard case), the phrase "immoral purpose" in *Caminetti* (our first Mann Act case), and the word "vehicle" in *McBoyle* (the airplane theft case) simply are not clear, and no blunt assertion to the contrary will make them so. Even when words in isolation do seem unambiguous, the process of coordinating them with the facts of a particular case may make them unclear. The judge who simply examines the words by themselves and asserts that they are clear seeks only an easy exit. Taking Webster's definition of "establish" as an example, the responsible judge would at least have to explain why the city of Petersburg was not originating and securing "the permanent existence of" the new acre for a cemetery. Justice Gregory did not explain this. Interpreting words in isolation rather than in context, then, is a danger because it leads judges to believe that they have thought a problem through to its end when they have only thought it through to its beginning.

To summarize, words become meaningful only in context. In statutory interpretation, judges must analyze two contexts, the legislative context—what general problem exists and what kind of policy response to it the legislature has created; and the case context—what the litigants are disputing and whether their dispute involves the problem the statute addresses. To say that words are clear or unclear depending on the context really means that the words would become clear if we could imagine a *different* case or context arising under each of the same statutes this book has mentioned so far. If Mr. McBoyle had stolen a car, or if Mr. Caminetti had abducted a Mexican-American immigrant girl, judges would have had no difficulty concluding that the statutory words clearly and unambiguously determine the case. Judges would similarly not have hesitated to prohibit Petersburg from opening a brand new cemetery within the city limits.

Justice Holmes once wrote, "A word is not a crystal, transparent and unchanged, it is the skin of a living thought and may vary greatly in color and content according to the circumstances and the time in which it is used."[9] Despite his mangled metaphor, Holmes advances our understanding. The words of statutes contain ideas—policy ideas with the force of law—and judges must articulate these ideas.

Third Actuality: Legislative Intent and Legislative History

Idle Armchair Speculation

One common way in which judges try to articulate the meaning of statutes is to try to discover what the legislature "intended" its statutory words to mean. I shall try in a moment to persuade you that "legislative intent" is a most slippery and misleading concept. For now, think carefully about the following use of legislative intent. How much more comfortable are you with Chief Justice Rugg's reasoning in the next case than you were with Lord Atkinson's literal approach or Justice Gregory's reasoning in the cemetery case or Justice Day's argument in *Caminetti?*

Shortly after it became a state, and long before the Nineteenth Amendment to the United States Constitution enfranchised women, Massachusetts passed a statute providing that "a person qualified to vote for representative to the General Court [the official name of the Massachusetts legislature] shall be liable to serve as a juror." Ten years after the passage of the Nineteenth Amendment, one Genevieve Welosky, a criminal defendant, found herself facing a Massachusetts jury that excluded all women. Welosky protested the exclusion, appealed, and lost. Under the literal or Golden Rule approaches she would surely have won, for "person" includes women, and women were "qualified to vote." Even before the days of women's liberation, we would hardly label it absurd to allow female jurors.

But Massachusetts Chief Justice Rugg invoked the intent of the legislature:

---

[9] *Towne v. Eisner,* 245 U.S. 418 (1917), p. 425.

> It is clear beyond peradventure that the words of [the statute]
> when orginally enacted could not by any possibility have
> included or been intended by the General Court to include
> women among those liable to jury duty. . . . Manifestly,
> therefore, the intent of the Legislature must have been, in
> using the word "person" in statutes concerning jurors and
> jury lists, to confine its meaning to men.[10]

The legislature didn't intend women to become jurors when
they passed the statute because at that time women could not
vote. Despite the literal meaning of the words, women cannot
therefore sit on juries.

The title of this section offered the hope that judges can
find statutory truth by discovering legislative intent. The Massachusetts court has identified an uncontested social background fact—that women could not vote when the statute was
passed—and concluded logically that the legislature did not
intend women to sit on juries. This logic is straightforward
enough, but the *Welosky* opinion is a virtual fraud. Rugg says
the simple sequence of historical events reveals the legislature's intent; because the statute came before the amendment,
the legislature did not intend to include women. But Rugg's
first quoted sentence sends us on a wild goose chase. It is plausible that the legislature did not consider the possibility of
women—or for that matter immigrant Martians—becoming
jurors. But, it is simultaneously plausible that the Massachusetts legislature "intended" to settle the problem of who may
sit as a juror once and for all by simply gearing jury liability
automatically to all future changes in the voting laws. A legislature that did so would hardly act absurdly. Rugg completely
fails to show that it did not so act.

Does the hope that legislative intent will reveal the meaning of statutory language hence fail? Ultimately it does fail,
but not because of poorly reasoned cases like *Welosky*. The
quest for legislative intent is a search for hard evidence. It is
detective work in the legal field, not Rugg's idle armchair speculations, so we should not abandon the field of legislative intent so quickly.

---

[10]*Commonwealth v. Welosky*, 276 Mass. 398 (1931), pp. 402–406.

Judges have many sleuthing techniques for discovering "hard evidence" of intent, of which we now review three of the most prominent. What do you think of them?

Other Words in the Statute

The brief excerpt from the cemetery case may have treated Justice Gregory unfairly, for he did not simply rest his opinion on Webster's dictionary. He continued by pointing out that another section of the cemetery statute of Virginia

> affords a complete answer to the question of legislative intent in the use of the word "established" in Section 56, for the former section [Section 53] makes a distinction between "establish" and "enlarge" in these words: "If it be desired at any time to establish a cemetery, for the use of a city, town, county, or magisterial district, or to enlarge any such already established, and the title to land needed cannot be otherwise acquired, land sufficient for the purpose may be condemned. . . . "
>
> The foregoing language, taken from Section 53, completely demonstrates that the legislature did not intend the words "establish" and "enlarge" to be used interchangeably, but that the use of one excluded any idea that it embraced or meant the other.[11]

Similarly, Justice McKenna, dissenting in *Caminetti,* found support in the official title of the Mann Act:

> For the context I must refer to the statute; of the purpose of the statute Congress itself has given us illumination. It devotes a section to the declaration that the "Act shall be known and referred to as the 'White Slave Traffic Act.'" And its prominence gives it prevalence in the construction of the statute. It cannot be pushed aside or subordinated by indefinite words in other sentences, limited even there by the context.[12]

The title of the statute tells Justice McKenna that Congress did

---

[11]*Temple v. City of Petersburg,* p. 424.
[12]*Caminetti v. United States,* p. 497.

not intend to police the activities of willing girlfriends. Willing girlfriends are not white slaves; the conclusion sounds sensible.

The Expressed Intent of Individual Legislators and Committee Reports

Like Justice Gregory, Justice McKenna made more than one argument to support his conclusion.[13] In fact, he went directly to the words of the bill's author and quoted extensively from Representative Mann:

> The author of the bill was Mr. Mann, and in reporting it from the House committee on interstate and foreign commerce he declared for the committee that it was not the purpose of the bill to interfere with or usurp in any way the police power of the states, and further, that it was not the intention of the bill to regulate prostitution or the places where prostitution or immorality was practiced, which was said to be matters wholly within the power of the states, and over which the Federal government had no jurisdiction. . . . [Mann stated]:
>
> "The White Slave Trade—A material portion of the legislation suggested and proposed is necessary to meet conditions which have arisen within the past few years. The legislation is needed to put a stop to the villainous interstate and international traffic in women and girls. The legislation is not needed or intended as an aid to the states in the exercise of their police powers in the suppression or regulation of immorality in general. It does not attempt to regulate the practice of voluntary prostitution, but aims solely to prevent panderers and procurers from compelling thousands of women and girls against their will and desire to enter and continue in a life of prostitution." *Congressional Record,* vol. 50, pp. 3368, 3370.
>
> In other words, it is vice as a business at which the law

---

[13]Appellate judges often give multiple arguments for the conclusions in their opinions, but they rarely articulate whether one argument, by itself, would justify the same result. They don't, in other words, spell out the relative importance of the arguments they use.

is directed, using interstate commerce as a facility to pro-
cure or distribute its victims.

Judges rarely argue that the expressed views of any one
legislator necessarily convey legislative intent, but they frequently cite committee reports and statements of authors as
proof of intent. This is a curious practice, for it seems to allow
a minority of legislators to determine what the law holds in
spite of the fact that in a legislature the majority rules.

Other Actions, Events, and Decisions in the Legislature

To establish legislative intent, judges may also look at how the
legislature handled related legislation. In *Welosky*, Chief Justice
Rugg noted that the Massachusetts legislature had in 1920
changed several laws relating to women in order to make them
conform to the Eighteenth and Nineteenth Amendments, but
said nothing about the problem of female jurors. He argued
regarding the 1920 legislation:

> It is most unlikely that the Legislature should, for the first
> time require women to serve as jurors without making pro-
> vision respecting the exemption of the considerable num-
> bers of women who ought not to be required to serve as
> jurors, and without directing that changes for the conven-
> ience of women be made in court houses, some of which
> are notoriously overcrowded and unfit for their accommo-
> dation as jurors.

Judges may even find in the physical evidence presented
to committees the key to intent. In the 1940s the postmaster
general refused to grant the preferential lower postage rate to
books, like workbooks and notebooks, that contained many
blank pages. Congress then amended the relevant statute to
grant books with space for notes the preferential rates. However, the postmaster general continued to refuse the rate to
so-called looseleaf notebooks with blank pages on the basis
that they were not permanently bound. A shipper of such

notebooks eager for the cheaper postage rate sued for an or-der granting the preferential rate.

The opinion of Judge Groner concluded that Congress *did* intend to give the preferential rate to looseleaf notebooks because the many physical exhibits placed before the com-mittee that handled the bill included some such notebooks. Groner wrote, "[I]t follows logically that textbooks of the make and quality of those of appellant were considered and pur-posely included by Congress in the list of publications entitled to the book rate."[14]

The list of possibilities in this category could continue for pages. For example, judges are fond of finding legislative intent by discovering that one house's version of a bill con-tained a clause that does not appear in the final law, approved by both houses. They conclude from this discovery that the legislature intended that the remaining words *not* mean what the dropped clause meant. Superficially, these discoveries of "hard evidence" of legislative intent appeal to us because they seem to reveal the purpose of the statute. But comparing the examples of sleuthing with our "first principles" of statutory interpretation reveals that legislative intent fails as badly as our other two approaches. Only the statute, the words for which the majority of both houses of the legislature voted, has the force of law.

When Judge Groner concludes "logically" that the legis-lature intended to include looseleaf notebooks for the prefer-ential rate, he is logically completely incorrect. He does not give one shred of evidence that any legislator, much less the majority, actually thought about the physical exhibits when they voted. Of course, Representative Mann's thoughts give us some clue to *his* intent, but we do not know that a majority heard or read his thoughts. Even if a majority in the House and Senate did know what Mann intended, we don't know that they agreed with him. After all, the statute uses the word "Prostitution" without Mann's qualifications. Maybe the ma-

---

[14]*McCormick-Mathers Publishing Co. v. Hannegan,* 161 F.2d 873 (D.C. Cir. 1947), p. 875. See Arthur Phelps, "Factors Influencing Judges in Interpreting Stat-utes," 3 *Vanderbilt Law Review* 456 (1950).

jority voted for the act because they wanted a tougher response than did Mann. Finally, when Justice Gregory pointed out the Virginia legislature's distinction between establishing and enlarging cemeteries for condemnation purposes, he did not prove that the legislators ever thought about the distinction with respect to what is essentially a zoning problem.

Why then, precisely, does legislative intent fail as a tool of statutory interpretation? A legislature is an organizational unit of government. By itself a legislature can no more intend something than can a government car or office building. *People* intend things, and, because the elected representatives in a legislature are people, they may intend something when they vote. If all members of the voting majority intended the same thing, then that might well provide the meaning of the statute. Here three difficulties fatal to the cause of legislative intent arise.

First, intent is subjective. It is usually impossible to tell with 100 percent centainty what anyone, ourselves included, intends. Thus, if a majority of legislators were fortunate enough to intend the same thing, it is highly unlikely that judges could actually discover what that thing was.

Second, we know enough about politics to know that in all likelihood the individuals making up the voting majority do not intend the same thing. Most will not have read the statute they vote on. Some will intend to repay a debt, or to be a loyal follower of their party leaders, or to encourage a campaign contribution from a private source in the future. If we want to deduce collective intent on anything, we must take a poll, and the only poll we ever take of legislators is when the presiding officer of the house calls for the vote to enact or defeat a bill. That much intent we might presume, but no more.

The third and most serious difficulty is that if by a miracle we overcome the first two difficulties, so that we actually know that the majority intended the same thing about a statute, it is highly unlikely, if not absolutely impossible, that they intended anything about the unique facts of the case before the court. In all probability the facts of cases such as *Mortensen* or *Cleveland* arose long after the law-making legislature disbanded. Just as in the *Repouille* case, a general feeling about an issue in the abstract does not necessarily resolve concrete cases, yet legislators at best intend only such general directions. Pose for the Mann Act Congress problems of migrating Mormons or vacationing prostitutes and you would probably get a gruff instruction to "ask a judge about the details." And of course by the time those cases actually arose, the majority of the makers of the Mann Act were, if not in their graves, surely no longer in Congress.

We shall see later that the evidence we falsely ascribe to legislative intent can sometimes help define the purpose of the statute, the problems the statute tries to solve. But this evidence is rarely decisive alone.

WHY DO JUDGES SO OFTEN INTERPRET STATUTES POORLY?

This chapter provides as powerful a group of illustrations of judicial confusion as any to be found in this book. Hart and Sacks have written, "The hard truth of the matter is that American courts have no intelligible, generally accepted, and consistently applied theory of statutory interpretation."[15] Three characteristics of the reasoning process help explain the high frequency of unpersuasive statutory interpretations.

The Disorderly Conduct of Words

Linguistics and the philosophy of language are abstruse and difficult subjects. Much of our knowledge of the complexity of

[15]Henry M. Hart, Jr., and Albert M. Sacks, *The Legal Process* (Cambridge: Harvard Law School, 1958), p. 1201. In a sense the problem is even worse, for scholars of legal reasoning are themselves confused about the confusion. Many writers discuss at length the "plain meaning rule" of interpretation. But each scholar (as well as each judge) tends to define this "rule" of statutory interpretation his own way, so that the plain meaning rule has no plain judicial or scholarly meaning. See Dickerson, pp. 229–233. And see Arthur Murphy, "Old Maxims Never Die: The 'Plain Meaning Rule' and Statutory Interpretation in the 'Modern' Federal Courts," 75 *Columbia Law Review* 1299 (1975), p. 1308. Murphy asserts, "[T]he courts have no clear idea about what the plain meaning rule is and, what is more, . . . they really do not care."

language is quite recent. Few lawyers—hence few judges—study the disorderly conduct of words, and this is the first characteristic that helps to explain interpretive confusion. To understand this we must master generality, vagueness, and ambiguity in language.

First, words are often necessarily *general.* General language allows us to think of many specific possibilities simultaneously. Advertisers often use generalities to good advantage. An advertisement that says "Dynamic Motors cars over the last five years have needed fewer and less costly repairs than Universal Motors cars," wants us to believe that all Dynamic Motors (DM) cars perform more reliably than all Universal Motors (UM) cars. Of course, even if the ad is completely true, it does not mean that. It certainly does not mean that DM's bottom line models perform more reliably than UM's top line models. But this is a helpful generalization, especially if you are debating whether to invest in DM or UM stock. Statutes necessarily speak in general language in order to control the wide variety of specific cases that are part of the social problem with which the statute copes, but judges must take care to discover what the generalization does *not* mean.

Second, language can be *vague.* The Dynamic Motors ad may be general (it may also be factually wrong!), but it is not vague because we can easily tell DM-built cars from UM-built cars. But consider this statement: "Bigger cars are safer than little cars." Vagueness in language refers to uncertainty about how much or of what degree of something a statement encompasses. We do not know how much car is enough to make it big, and we don't know whether bigness is size, weight, or both.

Third, and most important, words turn out to communicate *ambiguous* ideas; that is, words allow us to think of two simultaneously inconsistent concepts. Sometimes ambiguity in language arises when one or just a few words have mutually inconsistent meanings, because the dictionary itself permits such a clash of meanings. What does this statute mean? "It shall be a misdemeanor to sleep at a railway station." Does the word "at" include those comfortably asleep in their upper berths while their train rests at the station? Sleep can mean (1) being in a state of unconscious repose or (2) deliberately bedding down and spending the night. The first definition would cover both the hobo sprawled on a bench and the tired commuter dozing upright while waiting for the delayed train. The second meaning would spare the commuter but not the hobo.[16]

Language may also possess syntactic ambiguity. In this case, it is the ordering of the words, not varying dictionary definitions, that causes a problem. A statute regulating bank loans might say, "The banker shall require the borrower promptly to repay the loan." Does this mean the banker shall require the borrower to repay as soon as the law permits the banker to do so, or does this mean that the borrower must repay quickly once the banker begins requiring repayment, whenever that might be? Relocating the position of the word "promptly" in the sentence would have avoided the ambiguity.[17]

This chapter has emphasized the importance of interpreting the meaning of words by examining their context.[18] If the sentence proscribing sleeping in train stations augments a statute controlling vagrancy, the context of vagrancy solves the problem. If the neighboring language in the bank statute governs bankers on one hand or borrowers on the other, that ambiguity would disappear. But, despite this chapter's lecture about the importance of context, context can create as well as eliminate ambiguity. This was one of the problems created by

---

[16]Linguists call this semantic ambiguity. See Dickerson, pp. 45–46. It may help you to understand these distinctions if you figure out why the general and vague statements about cars are not semantically ambiguous, or syntactically or contextually ambiguous either, as the next few paragraphs define these concepts.

[17]Dickerson, pp. 46–47. The meaning of "ambiguity" here is much narrower than in Chapter II, where it encompassed all sources of imprecision in law.

[18]The classical illustration in the literature is from Wittgenstein, one I have modernized here. Suppose a father takes his child to Las Vegas, hires a croupier, and says, "Teach the kid some games." Would the father be disappointed to find the croupier taught the boy the fine points of Monopoly? If the father had uttered the same sentence to a baby sitter at home, he could be equally disappointed to discover the child gambling his college savings on the chance of drawing to an inside straight in seven-card stud. The context—Las Vegas versus living room—makes all the difference.

the wording of the Mann Act. While "prostitution" normally carries a fairly clear meaning, placing it in the context of the "White Slave" act potentially changes the word's interpretation. While prostitutes as a rule need not be unwilling, maybe *these* prostitutes must be unwilling before the statute applies.

Once we realize that the context of statutes can render them ambiguous, we must face this reality: The linguistically honest judge will, from time to time, have to admit that the statute does not, through its words, communicate any clear-cut solution to the case and context before him. We'll see later what this judge must then do.

The Booming Canons of Statutory Construction

In the past, judges have defended themselves against the imprecision of words by arming themselves with interpretive weapons called "canons of construction." Judges have often used these weapons unwisely, and this unwise use of the canons is another source of confusion in statutory interpretation.

A canon of construction or interpretation (they are, for our purposes, the same), is really a rule for interpreting rules, a device designed to make vague or ambiguous words appear precise. Here is an example:

> Where general words follow a statutory specification, they
> are to be held as applying only to persons and things of
> the same general kind or class of thing to which the speci-
> fied things belong.

This canon, called *ejusdem generis,* may not mean much to you until you apply it in the context of a specific case. Fortunately, we have already covered two legal problems to which this canon could apply.

In the first, *McBoyle,* which involved the theft of an airplane, the relevant statute forbade transportation across state lines of a stolen "automobile, automobile truck, automobile wagon, motorcycle or any other self-propelled vehicle not designed for running on rails." Is an airplane such a vehicle? By invoking the *ejusdem generis* canon ("of the same kind"), a judge could conclude that the general words "or any other self-propelled vehicle" refer only to items *like* (in the same genus as) the objects the statute specifically mentions (the species). In this case, all the specific items run on land. Therefore, an airplane is not a vehicle.

Similarly, Justice Day invoked the ejusdem generis canon in reaching the conclusion that the Mann Act did cover concubines. He said that the general words "other immoral purposes" refer only to sexual immorality because all the specific examples fit that genus. If you take your mother or a female friend across a state line to gamble illegally or rob a bank, you will not violate the Mann Act.

Before we consider why the canons represent a vice rather than a virtue in statutory interpretation, it will help to review a few more examples from among dozens of canons that judges utilize. One frequently cited canon instructs judges to interpret criminal statutes narrowly. This means that, when a judge finds that the statute does not clearly resolve his case, he should resolve it in favor of the defendant. Again *McBoyle* can illustrate. Justice Holmes wrote for the Supreme Court in that case:

> [I]t is reasonable that a fair warning should be given to the world in language that the common world will understand of what the law intends to do if a certain line is passed. To make the warning fair, so far as possible the line should be clear.

Holmes argues, in other words, that unless judges interpret criminal statutes narrowly, judges will send to jail people who had no clear notice that they had committed a crime.[19]

Holmes's concern for fairness in *McBoyle* reminds us that the canons are not totally ineffective or undesirable weapons. Felix Frankfurter said that "even generalized restatements from time to time may not be wholly wasteful. Out of them

---

[19]*McBoyle v. United States,* p. 27. A narrow interpretation may produce a very different decision from that of a literal interpretation. A literal interpretation of the words "other immoral purposes" in the Mann Act *would* make the act cover my taking my wife to another state to rob a bank. A narrow interpretation would not.

may come a sharper rephrasing of the conscious factors of interpretation; new instances may make them more vivid but also disclose more clearly their limitations."[20] Nearly every canon that judges have created contains at least a small charge of sensibility. Canons exist to support each of the principles of proper interpretation that this chapter covers. For example, the canon *noscitur a sociis* ("it is known by its associates") states that words are affected by their context. One British court used this canon to confine a statute regulating houses "for public refreshment, resort and entertainment" only to places where people received food and drink and excluded musical and other theatrical places, refreshing though their shows might be. The statute bore the title Refreshment House Act.[21] Again we must ask why the canons are part of the problem rather than part of the solution.

By making disorderly words appear orderly, canons deceive judges into thinking they have found a sensible and purposeful application of the statute to the case. In fact, the canons often allow judges to evade the difficult task of untangling statutory purpose. One example of this judicial evasion of purpose occurred after Congress passed a statute in 1893 designed to promote railway safety.[22] In part, Section 2 of the statute read:

> [I]t shall be unlawful for any ... common carrier [engaged in interstate commerce] to haul or permit to be hauled or used on its line any car ... not equipped with couplers coupling automatically by impact, and which can be uncoupled without the necessity of men going between the ends of the cars.

Section 8 of the Act placed the right to sue for damages in the hands of "any employee of any such common carrier who may

[20]Felix Frankfurter, "Some Reflections on the Reading of Statutes," 2 *Record of the Association of the Bar of the City of New York* 213 (1947), p. 236.

[21]Cross, p. 118. The list of canons is lengthy. Karl Llewellyn cites and provides judicial citations for 56 canons in "Remarks on the Theory of Appellate Decision and the Rules or Canons about How Statutes Are to Be Construed," 3 *Vanderbilt Law Review* 395 (1950), pp. 401–406.

[22]27 Stat. c. 196, p. 531.

be injured by any locomotive, car or train in use contrary to the provisions of this act.... " At common law, the injured employee often had no right of action against his employer; Section 8 created that right. Additionally, the act imposed criminal penalties on railroads that failed to comply.

A workman was injured while positioned between a locomotive and a car. He had tried to couple them by hand because the locomotive did not possess a coupler that coupled automatically with the car. He sued for damages and lost both in the trial court and in the U.S. Court of Appeals, the latter holding that the statute did not require locomotives to possess the same automatic couplers. Judge Sanborn fired canon after canon in defense of his conclusion that the statutory word "cars" did not include locomotives:

- "The familiar rule that the expression of one thing is the exclusion of the others leads to [this] conclusion."
- "A statute which thus changes the common law must be strictly construed."
- "This is a penal statute, and it may not be so broadened by judicial construction as to make it cover and permit the punishment of an act which is not denounced by the fair import of its terms."
- "The intention of the legislature and the meaning of a penal statute must be found in the language actually used."[23]

Do any of these canons convince you that this statute does not require locomotives to have automatic couplers? Again, the canons are not themselves absurd; the damage occurs when they seduce judges so easily into applying them simplistically and into thinking the canon gives *the* answer when the canon only justifies *an* answer. Does not Judge Sanborn's reasoning at least create the suspicion in your mind that he wanted, for whatever reasons, to rule for the railroads, and that the easy availability of canons only provided convenient camouflage for his personal preferences?

---

[23]*Johnson v. Southern Pacific Co.,* 117 Fed. 462 (C.C.A. 8th 1902). Fortunately the United States Supreme Court reversed, 196 U.S. 1 (1904).

The vice of the canons resembles the familiar law of mechanics. For each and every canon there is an equal and opposite canon. Llewellyn organizes his 56 canons noted in footnote 21 into 28 sets of opposing canons: "THRUST BUT PARRY," he calls them. The judge who, for whatever reason, reaches any conclusion can find a canon to defend it.

Consider this example of Llewellyn's point: A federal statute prohibits the interstate shipment of any "obscene . . . book, pamphlet, picture, motion-picture film, paper, letter, writing, print or other matter of indecent character." One Mr. Alpers shipped interstate some phonograph records that, admitted for the sake of argument, were obscene. On the basis of ejusdem generis and "strict construction of criminal statutes," two canons, we might expect Mr. Alpers to win his case. After all, the genus to which all the species belong is "things comprehended through sight." Instead, Justice Minton, for the Supreme Court, alluded to noscitur a sociis, another canon, and upheld the conviction.[24]

In short, the canons themselves are at war. In *Caminetti,* ejusdem generis pushes toward conviction, but "narrow construction" pushes toward acquittal. Shall judges flip coins?

Judicial Naiveté about the Legislative Process

The last and most serious source of judical confusion in statutory interpretation involves the naive assumptions judges often make about how legislatures make laws. An old political aphorism holds: "There are two things that the public should never see being made: sausages and laws." Judges often ignore the mundane realities of legislative life. The frequent judicial discoveries of the intent of the legislature, when in all probability the legislature intended nothing with respect to the unique factual situation before the court, best illustrate the problem.

Much can be (and has been) said for abandoning the concept of legislative intent permanently. The ever-skeptical Holmes wrote, "I don't care what their intention was, I only

---

[24]*United States v. Alpers,* 338 U.S. 680 (1950).

want to know what the words mean." And Frankfurter added, "You may have observed that I have not yet used the word 'intention.' All these years I have avoided speaking of the 'legislative intent' and I shall continue to be on my guard against using it."[25] A few pages back I introduced the reasons that the concept of intent fails. Let me expand those observations in three directions here.

First, legislatures respond to public problems by creating general public policies. The problem is nearly always an accumulation of many different specific instances, like vehicle thefts, white slavery, juror selection, or controlling of the location of cemeteries. Legislatures simply do not confront the concrete and always unique factual case. In this sense, as former Attorney General Levi once said, "Despite much gospel to the contrary, a legislature is not a fact-finding body. There is no mechanism, as there is with a court, to require the legislature to sift facts and to make a decision about specific situations."[26] In all probability no one in the legislature foresaw the precise problem facing the judge, and it is even less likely that the legislature consciously intended to resolve the case one way or another.

The candid judge looking for firm evidence of intent often won't find it. A candid Rugg would, for example, have concluded, "I simply can't say whether the Massachusetts legislature thought about women becoming jurors or not." The names Holmes and Frankfurter endure more prominently than Rugg because they were especially able to make such candid judgments.[27]

For further illustration of this point, consider one final problem. A federal immigration statute requires that immigrants receive an immigration permit prior to leaving their home country and that they present the permit on arrival be-

[25]Frankfurter, pp. 227–228.

[26]Edward H. Levi, *An Introduction to Legal Reasoning* (Chicago: University of Chicago Press, 1949), p. 31.

[27]The eminent jurisprudent John Gray wrote, "The fact is that the difficulties of so-called interpretation arise when the Legislature has had no meaning at all; when the question which is raised on the statute never occurred to it. . . ." *The Nature and Sources of the Law* (New York: Macmillan, 1927), p. 173.

fore being allowed to enter and move about the United States. Imagine that on a voyage of immigrants from China a woman with a permit gives birth to a child. While the mother can present her permit and enter, her new infant cannot. There is no shred of evidence in the legislative history of the immigration law that Congress ever once thought about this problem. Must the infant (and presumably its mother) return to China?[28]

Second, although the United States government prints reams of information about legislation in Congress—committee hearings, committee reports, speeches, and so forth—judges often have no access to this kind of information about how state legislatures operate. Even if we could count on this information to reveal the true intent of legislators (which we can't), much of the time judges won't get the information in the first place.

The *third* and most important set of reasons that judges misunderstand the legislative process is that they hide from the mundane facts of political life; legislatures are very practical and political places. Consider:

- We saw earlier (on pg. 68) that Judge Groner could not logically conclude that the Congress intended to include looseleaf notebooks in the preferential rate just because one committee's exhibits contained samples of them. The conclusion appears even shakier once we acknowledge that a lobbyist, with or without conscious help from a busy committee chairman, might have deliberately planted that evidence before the committee. The lobbyist may not aggressively try to influence the committee, but he would hope to persuade the judge later in litigation that the planted evidence proves legislative intent and thereby win a favorable judicial ruling for the lobbyist's client. As long ago as 1947, Archibald Cox wrote that "it is becoming

---

[28]Charles Curtis, "A Better Theory of Legal Interpretation," 3 *Vanderbilt Law Review* 407 (1950), p. 413.

increasingly common to manufacture 'legislative history' during the course of legislation."[29]

- Both houses of a bicameral legislature must approve the identically worded bill before it becomes law. Often when the two houses disagree, special joint committees form to negotiate the compromise. Whatever force committee reports and speeches might have had on the passage of the original bill in each house, it is difficult, if not impossible, to discern the grounds on which the two houses compromise. Often the compromise package includes a decision to leave a question deliberately unanswered simply to avoid stalemate. The process of deciding on a compromise also often means, in practice, that one house may ratify without debate a bill containing provisions it never considered one way or another when it debated and passed its own bill.

- Judges often claim to distill congressional intent from the formal speeches and remarks of legislators printed in the *Congressional Record,* as if the entire body of legislators sat in rapt attention, devouring and ultimately approving the tenor of the remarks. But the bulk of the *Record's* comments simply appear there at the request of the legislator. Even when debate precedes the vote, the floor usually contains virtually no one but debaters and a very few listeners. The *Record* tells nothing about how many rushed in to record their votes without hearing the floor debate.

- Most voting legislators never read the bill on which they vote at all; more likely, they hurriedly glance at the committee report. Most often, the voting legislator relies on party leadership, or on the advice of an aide

[29]Archibald Cox, "Some Aspects of the Labor Management Relations Act, 1947," 61 *Harvard Law Review* 1 (1947), p. 44. See also Garth Mangum, "Legislative History in the Interpretation of Law," *Brigham Young University Law Review* (1983), p. 281. Professor Mangum, a participant in the passage of the Job Training Partnership Act of 1982, documents how the official House and Senate documents regarding this legislation bear only slight resemblance to the issue under debate and left "fuzzy" in the final statute.

who has reviewed the problem, or on the record of public opinion, or on the private urging of a lobbyist. They may do any or all of these without giving any detailed thought to the bulk of the words and sentences in the act (drafted most likely by administrators, aides, and lobbyists in combination—not by legislators) that lawyers piously debate later in court.[30]

- Finally, judges often ignore the possibility that the lawmaking process might purposely create unclear law because legislatures *want* the courts to fill in the details. This may amount to buck-passing in the hope that the courts will take the pressure for an unpopular result. But legislators may also believe that case-by-case judicial action is the best way to decide precisely what the statute should include and exclude. The judge who fails to look for that purpose evades his own judicial responsibilities.

These examples of legislative realities should make judges wary of concluding that the legislature ever intended anything. "Legislative intention," Professor Horack wrote,

is useful as a symbol to express the gloss which surrounds the enacting process—the pre-legislative history, the circumstances and motivations which induced enactment.... Society cannot act effectively on subjectivity of intent; and, therefore, legislative intention becomes not what the legislature in fact intended but rather what reliable evidences there are to satisfy the [judicial] need for further understanding of the legislative action.[31]

---

[30]On his retirement late in 1986, long-time senator (and 1964 presidential candidate) Barry Goldwater told an interviewer, "We don't work.... Monday. We don't work Friday or Saturday. So we work a three-day week.... People don't get here for 9 o'clock meetings until 9:15 AM, and 9:30 PM.... We were elected to serve our country and yet we don't do it very well." "Retiring Goldwater fires parting shots, says Congress doesn't serve nation well," *Atlanta Journal and Constitution,* November 27, 1986, p. 2N. See also the comments of a former congressman, Judge Abner Mikva, "How Well Does Congress Support and Defend the Constitution," 61 *North Carolina Law Review* 587 (1983).

[31]Frank E. Horack, Jr., "The Disintegration of Statutory Construction," 24 *Indiana Law Journal* 335 (1949), pp. 340–341.

The ultimate danger in all of these methods of statutory interpretation—the literal and Golden Rule approaches, the use
of canons, and the search for legislative intent in legislative
history—is that each allows the judge to reach a conclusion
without ever struggling with the fundamental question
whether one interpretation or another actually copes with social problems effectively. These methods, in other words, perpetuate decisions that may not promote law's basic goal, that
of social cooperation. The next section describes a better way
for judges to interpret statutes.

HOW JUDGES SHOULD INTERPRET STATUTES IN THE FIRST INSTANCE

Statutory interpretation so frequently seems inadequate because judges face an unavoidable necessity. Judges must say
what the law "is" in order to resolve the case before them. I
call this a necessity for judges because our society, our culture,
believes that judges act unfairly when they do not decide on
the basis of what the law says and is. Judges cannot hear a
case and then refuse to render a decision because they cannot
determine the legal answer.[32] We do not pay judges to say,
"Maybe the law is X. Maybe the law is Y. I'll guess Y. You lose!"
(Or worse, "I don't care if it's X or Y. You still lose!") In order
to render justice in our culture, judges must persuade us to
believe with certainty that which is inherently uncertain.

Making the uncertain appear certain (the *art* in judging
and in everything else) is particularly difficult in statutory
interpretation. In common law and in constitutional law, the
courts know that they have authority to make law. In these
realms judges can say, "The law ought to be X, not Y. Therefore the law is X." But legislative supremacy bars judges from
interpreting statutes so boldly. They must try to find the
"oughts" somewhere in the legislative process, an uncertain

---

[32]This is true of most formal legal systems. For example, the French Civil
Code dating from 1804 states, "A judge who refuses to enter judgement on
the pretext of silence, obscurity, or inadequacy of the statute is subject to
prosecution for the denial of justice."

and distant process in which judges themselves play little part. It is like sending forth a knight with orders to find the Holy Grail, requiring him to return in a week with anything he finds as long as he can persuade us that what he found is the Grail, and repeating this order week after week.

Judges will continue to make uncertain statutes certain in their application by creating and asserting that certainty can and does emerge from the generality, the vagueness, and the ambiguity in words, and from the disorderly world of politics. How can judges create certainty out of uncertainty persuasively?

The Centrality of Statutory Purpose

Judges should believe, almost as an article of faith, that words by themselves *never* possess a plain or clear or literal meaning. Statutes become meaningful only to the extent that their words fit some intelligible purpose. The problem the statute addresses always gives direction to the search for purpose. A dictionary never does.

Judges must satisfy themselves that their application of a statute to the case before them serves the statute's purpose. Sometimes a statute seems automatically to determine a case. We saw that this would occur if McBoyle had transported a stolen automobile instead of an airplane. But judges must understand that no conclusion is totally automatic. We can imagine that an individual could transport an automobile across state lines, knowing the car to be stolen, and yet not violate the act: an FBI agent driving the car back to its owner. The agent does not violate the act because he is not part of the problem the act tries to solve—he is part of the solution.

Let me explain this a slightly different way. The questions people ask determine the answers they receive. The key to legal reasoning is asking the right question. The right answer to the wrong question should never satisfy a judge. In statutory interpretation, the right questions always begin with a question about statutory purpose. Think of the difference it can make in *Johnson* (the locomotive coupling case) to ask (1) "Is a locomotive a railroad car?" versus (2) "Is protecting the safety of workers coupling locomotives to cars as well as cars to cars a sensible part of the problem this law tries to cope with?" Notice that whenever a judge inquires into the purpose of the legislation he must *inevitably* inquire into the background facts that reveal the nature of the social problems involved in the case and how the statute tries to cope with them.

Determining Purpose: Words Can Help

It is the language of a statute that alone has the force of law. Nothing else that individual legislators or legislative bodies say or do legally binds a judge. Some legislation includes specific definitions of key words. These definitions in statutes may or may not agree with a dictionary definition, but they are law and they bind the judge. Legislation, though lacking an internal dictionary, always contains words whose ordinary definitions unambiguously shape its purpose. By including the word *prostitution,* the Mann Act unambiguously covers more than white slavery because by no ordinary definition are prostitutes necessarily enslaved in that occupation. Judges must never give words a meaning that the words, in their context, cannot bear. Except for its euphemistic title, the "White Slave Act" contains not one word to indicate that the women whose transportation it forbids must be unwilling. It is in this context that the word *prostitution* unambiguously shapes the Mann Act's meaning.

Context is always crucial. Some contexts require courts to decide precisely the opposite of the literal command of words. If, through some printing error, the officially published version of a statute omits a key word, judges properly include the word if the context makes such a purpose clear. Suppose that a statute prohibiting some very undesirable behavior omits in its official version the key prohibitory word "not." Although the statute would then literally permit or even require the unwarranted behavior, judges may apply the statute as if it contained the missing and critical "not."

Canons of interpretation may help reassure judges that a given word, phrase, or sentence has a certain meaning in a specific context. They may serve as shorthand reminders of ways of thinking about purpose. But a canon should never dictate to a judge that words must have one meaning regardless of context. The canons of ejusdem generis and of narrow construction of criminal statutes may help a judge exclude airplanes and obscene records from the reach of those two statutes, but they do not compel that conclusion, as the next section illustrates.

Noscitur a sociis can also be a helpful reminder for a way of thinking about purpose. The context of neighboring words may crystallize the meaning of an ambiguous phrase. What, for example, is "indecent conduct"? In the abstract, we might agree that it depends on individual perceptions and moralities and that we can't really tell what it is. But consider two statutes, one that prohibits "indecent conduct at a divine service of worship" and another that prohibits "indecent conduct at a public beach or bathing place." The contexts of worship and beach could both classify total nudity as indecent conduct, but only one context would classify playing a game of volleyball in string bikini bathing suits as indecent.

Determining Purpose: The Audience

Legislatures direct different statutes to different kinds of audiences. Some statutes, especially criminal statutes, communicate to the community at large. Criminal statutes thus have the purpose of communicating general standards of conduct to large populations containing people of widely varying degrees of literacy and local customs and habits. Judges properly interpret such words according to the common meanings they may expect these words to convey to this diverse population. Other perhaps highly technical laws may communicate only to special classes of people, such as commercial television broadcasters or insurance underwriters. Here the words may assume technical meanings that only the special audience understands. Similarly, judges should hold that a statute purposely changes a long-held principle of common law or the legality of a behavior widely believed proper in the past only when they think a statute makes that purpose unambiguously clear.

Determining Purpose: The Assumption of Legislative Rationality and the Uses of Legislative History

In determining whether an issue in a lawsuit is part of the problem that a statute purposely tries to address, judges should treat the people who make laws and the process of law-making as rational and sensible, "reasonable persons pursuing reasonable purposes reasonably," as Hart and Sacks put it.[33] This assumption helps judges determine purpose because it forces them to determine what portion of the law, prior to the enactment of the statute, worked so poorly that a rational legislature wanted to change it.[34] Again, think about how the result in the locomotive coupling case would differ if the court had approached the problem this way. Finally, what purposes would a rational legislator have for inserting the "good moral character" test in our nationalization laws? Is such a purpose well served by making moral judgments about incest or mercy-killing in the abstract?

The judge who thinks about lawmaking as a logical process also recognizes that no statute exists in isolation, for rational lawmakers understand that no one act can completely define where its policy stops and another competing policy ought, instead, to govern. Congressmen realize (and the courts grasp that they know) that state law, not federal law, assumes the major responsibility for defining and policing criminal behavior. Knowing that state laws purposely define and prohibit sexual immorality limited the purpose the Court attributed to the Mann Act in *Mortensen.*

Courts can generate sensible conclusions about the purpose of statutes from the statements of legislative committees, sponsors of the bill, and so forth. This history may allow a judge to understand what aspects or consequences of prior

[33]Hart and Sacks, p. 1415.

[34]Lord Coke originated this helpful approach, sometimes labeled the *mischief rule,* in 1584. Occasional judicial attention to history can prove surprisingly profitable. For a lucid discussion of the concept of statutory purpose and its modern applications see Julian B. McDonnell, "Purposive Interpretation of the Uniform Commercial Code: Some Implications for Jurisprudence," 126 *Pennsylvania Law Review* 796 (1978).

law failed to cope with a social problem so that the legislature needed to create a new law. Legislative history may also clarify where one policy should give way to another. Legislative history relating to specific applications of the statute, as in the looseleaf notebook case, only helps the judge to the extent that it provides good evidence of the legislation's general purpose. (You should recall that the physical presence of looseleaf notebooks bore virtually no relationship to the purpose of that statute—the statute did not attempt to create a standard definition of the word *book* for postage purposes. Judge Groner should therefore have ignored that evidence.) In sum, where isolated examples of legislative intent don't mesh with sensible statutory purpose, judges should ignore them.

Illustrations

Three Easy Cases

You should now have little difficulty resolving comfortably some of this chapter's cases. Despite the ambiguities in the statutory language, you should not hesitate (1) to allow the officer to collect the breath specimen from a driver standing on the shoulder of the road, not while the driver weaves down the highway; (2) to prohibit the liquor store from reopening at 10:01 (see footnote 6); and (3) to allow the sleepy commuter to doze upright on the bench while prohibiting the hobo from encamping in a corner. The words don't require these conclusions and judges probably lack any legislative history for these state and local laws, but judges can still reach sensible results. The words can bear these interpretations, and our knowledge of social problems and purposes compels these conclusions. Notice, by the way, how the wise solution to each of these three cases hinges on the judge's realistic assessment of social background facts.

Of course, other cases could arise under these same statutes in which the words themselves would not bear the interpretation claimed for them. Our officer cannot collect breath specimens in parking lots and driveways outside cocktail parties at midnight, even if he safely assumes that many will soon drive home and even if we believe it a highly wise social policy to prevent intoxicated drivers from driving in the first place. This action might be an effective preventive, but it is not found in the meaning and purpose of this law because the words make "driving" a prerequisite for demanding the specimen.

The Case of the Lady Jurors, or Why Legislative Intent Does Not Necessarily Determine Statutory Purpose

Recall briefly Chief Justice Rugg's justification for excluding women from jury liability despite the fact that they could vote and despite the fact that the statute required jury duty of "persons" (not "men") qualified to vote. The legislature did not intend "person" to include females because females could not then vote.

Like the case of the automatic couplers, *Welosky* offers a classic example of a judge reaching the right answer to the wrong question. Of course the legislature did not intend to include women, but that doesn't answer the right question. The proper question is, "What purpose does legislation serve that gears jury liability to voter eligibility?"

Efficiency is one possible answer because this policy spares the legislature from repeatedly rehashing the issue. Quality is another, for this policy provides a test of qualifications that will insure at least the same degree of responsibility, competence, education, and permanence of residence for both jurors and voters. Both voting and jury duty are general civic functions of citizens. Gearing the right to practice medicine, for instance, to voting eligibility would not make much sense, but gearing these two similar civic functions sounds reasonable. But where does turning the problem around leave us? Does it serve a purpose to pass a statute saying, in effect, "If you are qualified to vote, you are qualified to serve as a juror; however, any changes in voter eligibility hereafter enacted won't count because we haven't thought of them yet"? If the legislation had this purpose, why didn't it simply list the desirable qualifications for jurors? Read the statute as Rugg did and the gearing loses purpose. Rugg did not treat the policy process as rational and sensible. He did not admit that juror qualifications could have been purposely designed to change with the times.

The difference between a search for legislative intent and a search for purpose, then, is the difference in the evidence judges seek. A judge who believes he must show intent will examine reports, speeches, and prior drafts of bills. This evidence probably won't give clear meaning to the statute because it will contain internal inconsistencies or raise issues only in general terms. Moreover, the judge who thinks he must find intent to do his work can fool himself into believing that he has found it in the evidence. On the other hand, the judge who feels he must articulate a sensible statement of purpose will necessarily search much further, into dictionaries, canons, verbal contexts, and competing social policies as well as history itself. He will coordinate the materials in order to reach a confident articulation of purpose. He will perform the judicial function as Benjamin Cardozo described it. (See the epigraph that opens this book.) He will work harder than will the judge who stops when he has found a nugget of legislative history, which is why so many judges, possessing the all-too-human tendency to laziness, are satisified with the nugget.

Statutory Purpose in the Cases of Criminal Commerce: Caminetti, McBoyle, and Alpers

In each of these three cases, Congress, under the authority of the commerce clause of the U.S. Constitution, forbade citizens from moving what Congress deemed evil from one state to another. Let us assume that every state had laws to deal with each of the evil things—stolen vehicles, women on whom evil designs were made, and pornography. What purpose, then, does additional *federal* legislation on these matters serve? For each of the federal statutes we possess records of committee reports, floor speeches, and other legislative history. In no case, however, does the solid data of legislative history reveal whether the purpose of the statute does or does not include the cases of our defendants. After a delightfully detailed review of the House and Senate reports on the Mann Act and of the discussions reported in the *Congressional Record* showing, if not total confusion about the act, at least much disagreement about its specific meaning, Levi concludes, "The Mann Act was passed after there had been many extensive governmental investigations. Yet there was no common understanding of the facts, and whatever understanding seems to have been achieved concerning the white-slave trade seems incorrectly based. The words used were broad and ambiguous."[35]

These cases resemble each other not only in their constitutional origins but also because the canons of construction could resolve each of them. The canon dictating narrow construction of criminal statutes could allow a judge to reverse the three convictions, since the law does not unambiguously apply to any of these special factual situations. A judge who adopted Holmes's belief that criminal laws must communicate to a general lay audience with a clarity the average man can understand would reach the same result. Following ejusdem generis, however, Mr. Caminetti might go to jail, but McBoyle, the airplane thief, and Alpers, the seller of obscene records, would still go free.

Despite these similarities, these cases do not come out this way. The smut peddler and the boyfriend go to jail. McBoyle goes free. The three judicial opinions together articulate no coherent linkages between purposes and outcomes. To link purposes and outcomes, we must begin with the right question: Why would Congress, "reasonable persons pursuing reasonable purposes reasonably," pass laws making actions crimes when all the states already have, through their criminal laws, expressed a policy? Does not the purpose lie in the fact that movement from state to state makes it difficult for the states to detect or enforce the violation? A car owner who has his car stolen may have trouble tracking it in another state. The prosecutor in the state where citizens receive wanted or unwanted pornography cannot reach the man who peddles by mail from another state. Men who hustle girls far from home may make both detection and social pressure to resist prostitu-

[35]Levi, p. 40, and see pp. 33–40.

tion impossible. Movement has consequences. It makes objects and behaviors physically harder to locate. It makes apprehension and prosecution more difficult because police and prosecutors in one jurisdiction don't have authority in another. The presence of physical movement thus helps to reveal purpose.

In *McBoyle*, then, the proper questions ought to look something like this: (1) Do airplanes, because they are movable, complicate the task of catching people who steal them? (2) Does it, secondarily, serve any purpose to assume that McBoyle thought flying a stolen airplane to another state was legal because of the ambiguities in the word *vehicle*? Is it, in other words, unfair to McBoyle to convict him under this act because the act does not unambiguously include airplanes? You should reach your own conclusion, but I would answer the first question with a yes, the second with a no, and respectfully dissent from Justice Holmes.

You should ask one other question about *McBoyle*. Suppose McBoyle's lawyer had argued that when the Motor Vehicle Theft Act was passed air travel was in such infancy that Congress probably did not intend to include airplanes. Notice that this argument should matter to you only if you think it important to ask what Congress intended. If you instead consider legislation as policy designed to adjust to technological and other changes, and if you ask instead what kind of crimes call for the kind of law enforcement help that this act provides, you would find McBoyle's lawyer's argument trivial.

Is *Alpers* any different? It might be, particularly if you see the case as presenting a constitutional problem of free expression. The purpose of this statute might be said to be to prevent exposing children or unwilling people, people who open mail or see magazines left around, to visual pornography. Is this purpose served by prohibiting the shipment of obscene records?

I find *Alpers* an especially difficult case. Unlike Mr. McBoyle, Mr. Alpers could reasonably have interpreted the act as not banning records for two reasons. First, the competing principle of free expression does set limits on government interference with the communication of ideas. No such principle limits governmental interference with the movement of property known to be stolen. Second, the purpose of the Motor Vehicle Theft Act specifically seems to apply to airplanes. They are very transportable. The act's purpose may therefore especially apply to airplanes. However, one reading of the purpose of the satute in *Alpers*—visual pornography left around may offend but a phonograph record lying around does not—reduces its applicability to *Alpers*. But, although it reduces it, it doesn't eliminate it. The recipient might play the dirty record to an unwilling person and cause that person great offense. However, does not the *McBoyle* example provide a strong argument for excusing Alpers? Isn't transporting stolen property at least as morally ambiguous as pornography?

Finally, consider the man who brings in a willing girl-friend from out of state for a night or for the big game weekend. Conceivably, the Mann Act could purposely try to police all forms of sexual immorality, involving, somehow, interstate transportation. But what are the probabilities that this legislation has such purpose in light of (1) the title of the act; (2) the canons of narrow construction of and clear communication in criminal statutes; (3) the problem arousing public concern at the time; (4) the fact that states are just as able, if they so choose, to discover and crackdown on noncommercial illegal sex as the FBI; (5) Representative Mann's report and the wide-spread belief that the general police powers reside in state and not federal hands?

Notice how only by using many different techniques of interpretation together do we begin to develop confidence about the purpose of the Mann Act.

A Final Complication

This summary of sensible judicial approaches to statutes may, I fear, have misled you in one critical respect. You may now feel that in every case the "right-thinking" judge will find the one "right" solution simply by uncovering a single purpose of the statute. This chapter's illustrations all make sense when we analyze them in terms of purpose. *We may, however, still honestly disagree about purpose.* Justice does not reside in judges who find the one right solution as much as it resides in judges who do their best to discern purpose and decide cases in terms of purpose. The task of judging is choosing among plausible alternative possibilities, not solving an algebra problem. Even judges who work to discover purpose may disagree about the resolution of a specific case.

To illustrate, suppose Holmes had said in *McBoyle,*

> The purpose of this act is to permit federal assistance to states in finding easily moved and hidden vehicles. But airplanes, while easily moved, are really like trains, which the act expressly excludes, because, like trains, they are tied to places where they cannot be hidden—airports. What goes up must come down, and only in certain places. One black Ford may look like a thousand other black Fords almost anywhere, but an airplane is much more like a train in this respect. Therefore, since we believe states, not the federal government, possess primary police powers, this act does not cover airplanes.

Finally, suppose Justice Gregory argued,

> Establishment and expansion of cemeteries differ because the people near an expanded cemetery are already used to its presence, but to create a new cemetery in a place where residents had not planned on seeing funeral processions and graves and other unwanted reminders of life's transience is another matter.

Whether we agree or disagree with these analyses, at least these analyses rest on purpose. We should prefer them to the automatic citation of a canon, a quotation from a dictionary, or to any technique of interpretation that allows judges to evade the difficult task of determining statutory purpose.

STARE DECISIS IN STATUTORY INTERPRETATION

This chapter has reviewed some of the most enticing problems in legal reasoning. These problems and their solutions appeal to our instinctive quest for sensibility, not just in law but in all our affairs. They show us that reason, our reason, can give us the confidence to assert that some judicial choices are wiser than others. The discovery that we can make sense of important and apparently complex legal issues can give us, more generally, a feeling of independence and competence in an increasingly complex society. Democracy will not survive in conditions of high complexity if most citizens conclude that government and politics have become too complicated for them to understand and influence.

These materials illustrate a serious error in the way many judges think they should do their jobs. It is an erroneous view of the role of courts with respect to legislative institutions and to government generally. Worse, it is an error based on a false view of law, of language, and of the nature of man. The error should worry us.

To bring this error and its remedy into sharper focus, we must start by recognizing that in nearly all of this chapter, we have thus far studied an atypical occurrence in statutory interpretation, interpretation *in the first instance.* This may already have puzzled you, for in Chapter II I stated that reasoning by example—using precedents as guides for resolving legal conflicts—is central to legal reasoning. So far, however, this chapter has not mentioned reasoning by example at all. In the interpretation of statutes in the first instance, courts by definition have no precedents with which to work. In this chapter, we have examined some methods for interpreting statutes in the first instance, but these methods do not resolve the more typical problem: Once a court has given direction and meaning to a statute by interpreting it in the first instance, when should courts in the future follow that interpretation? When, conversely, should courts prefer a different interpretation and ignore or overrule an earlier court's first effort to make sense of the statute's meaning?

Let me make this point more sharply. Assume that the *McBoyle* decision wrongly interpreted the National Motor Vehicle Theft Act because its purpose does cover the theft of airplanes. Or assume that *Caminetti* wrongly applied the Mann

Act to include the transportation of girlfriends. Should a court facing a new airplane or girlfriend case feel bound to accept that interpretation? Once a precedent or series of precedents gives a clear answer on a point of law, should courts leave it to legislatures to change that questionable interpretation by statutory amendment? In what circumstances should judges adhere to stare decisis in statutory interpretation?

It might seem sensible to you to answer these questions by referring to the justifications for stare decisis that appeared near the end of Chapter II. When adherence to a prior interpretation or series of cases interpreting a statute promotes stability in law and this stability in turn allows citizens to plan their affairs on the basis of certain and stable law—in short, when stability promotes the paramount social goal of cooperation—courts should not abandon stare decisis. Similarly, if a citizen now deserves to receive the same treatment a citizen in a precedent did, or if we feel stare decisis would preserve efficient judicial administration or a positive public image of justice, then courts should honor it. When stare decisis does not promote these goals, courts should freely ignore it. Thus, assuming a court felt that both *McBoyle* and *Caminetti* were wrongly decided, normal stare decisis theory would permit overruling *Caminetti* but not *McBoyle*. It injures no citizen to declare that something once held criminal is no longer so, but it does seem unfair to convict someone after declaring that his actions were not crimes.

Unfortunately, some judges and legal scholars believe that judges should invariably follow the first judicial attempt to find statutory meaning even when they have doubts about the wisdom of the first attempt and, worse, when the characteristics of the problem do not call for stare decisis. We shall first review an example of this "one-shot theory" of statutory interpretation in action. Then we shall evaluate its shortcomings. We shall see that, in part, it fails because it depicts judges once again misunderstanding how legislatures operate and how courts should reason from legislative action and inaction. We shall also see in this example considerable judicial ignorance about stare decisis itself.

Major League Baseball, Haviland's Dog and Pony Show, and Government Regulation of Business

The power of the federal government to regulate business derives from the constitutional clause empowering Congress to make laws that regulate commerce "among the several states." Armed with this authority Congress has passed many statutes regulating wages, hours of work, safety and health standards, and so forth in businesses. Such laws apply not only to businesses and businessmen that physically cross state lines or transact business among states. They also apply to businesses operating within one state entirely, on the theory that these businesses nevertheless may compete with and affect businesses operating from other states.[36] Modern economic and political theory also suggest that the collective health of small businesses and of labor can and does affect the national welfare.

Among the many such statutes regulating business, we shall consider only two. The more substantial of the two, the federal antitrust laws, responded to the huge cartels and monopolies that emerged in the nineteenth century by prohibiting certain activities that restrain competition in business. (See page 57.) They authorize criminal and civil proceedings by government and by citizens privately when they feel they are damaged by anticompetitive business practices. The Animal Welfare Act of 1970, our second statutory example, specifies a variety of requirements for handling animals in a humane manner.[37] The statute requires "exhibitors" of animals "purchased in commerce or the intended distribution of which affects commerce or will affect commerce" to obtain an exhibitor's license. The statute explicitly includes carnivals, circuses, and zoos. It empowers the Agriculture Department to administer its regulatory provisions.

---

[36]*United States v. Darby,* 312 U.S. 100 (1941), and *Wickard v. Filburn,* 317 U.S. 111 (1942).

[37]15 U.S.C. 1 et seq. and 7 U.S.C. 2131 et seq.

Within the context of these two statutes, we shall now observe a truly wondrous phenomenon in contemporary law. Within the past twenty years courts have held: (1) that the multimillion-dollar industry of professional baseball, with all its national commercial television coverage and travel from state to state and to foreign countries, *is not* a business in interstate commerce such that the antitrust laws govern the owners of baseball clubs; and (2) that "Haviland's Dog and Pony Show," consisting of a maximum of two ponies and five dogs traveling the rural byways of the American Midwest and earning a handful of dollars weekly, *is* a business in interstate commerce that must therefore meet the requirements of the Animal Welfare Act.[38]

We need say little more about the *Haviland* case. Haviland refused to obtain an exhibitor's license. The court held that he was wrong to refuse. Given the current legal definition of commerce, the interpretation is entirely defensible constitutionally. This interpretation and result also make sense in terms of the presumed purpose of the statute. Owners of dog-and-pony shows, we can assume, are no less likely to abuse their animals than is the staff of the San Diego Zoo; rather more likely, I should think.

But why don't antitrust statutes regulate major league baseball? Rigid adherence to stare decisis in statutory interpretation provides the answer, as the following chronology of decisions illustrates.

> 1922 The "Federal Baseball Club of Baltimore," a member of a short-lived third major league, sued the National and American Leagues claiming that the two leagues had, in violation of the antitrust laws, bought out some Federal League clubs and induced other owners not to join the league at all. The Baltimore franchise found itself frozen out

[38]*Flood v. Kuhn*, 407 U.S. 258 (1972); *Haviland v. Butz*, 543 F.2d 169 (D.C. Circuit 1976).

and sued to recover the financial losses caused by the anticompetitive practices of the other leagues. The case reached the United States Supreme Court, where Justice Holmes's opinion held that the essence of baseball, playing games, did not involve interstate commerce. The travel from city to city by the teams, Holmes thought, was so incidental that it did not bring baseball within the scope of the act. Thus, without reaching the question whether the defendants did behave anticompetitively within the meaning of the statute, Holmes ruled that the act did not apply to professional baseball any more that it would apply to a Chautauqua lecturer traveling the circuit.[39]

Comment: We should not hastily condemn Holmes's reasoning. His opinion predated by 20 years the final shift in the legal meaning of commerce that solidified in the holding of *Wickard v. Filburn,* so we cannot blame him for an antiquated definition. Also, to his credit, Holmes did not try to discover whether Congress intended to include baseball within the scope of the antitrust laws. There is nothing in the opinion that stamps its results with indelibility, nothing that says if the commercial character of baseball changes, baseball club owners would nevertheless remain free to behave monopolistically. For its time, *Federal Baseball* rested on defensible if not indisputable reasoning

1923 A year later Justice Holmes addressed the applicability of the antitrust laws in the field of public entertainment. In this case, the plaintiff, a Mr. Hart, acted as a booking agent and manager for a variety of actors. He specialized in negotiating contracts between vaudeville performers, on one hand, and large theater chains sponsoring vaudeville shows on the other. Hart sued the Keith Cir-

[39]*Federal Baseball Club of Baltimore v. National League of Professional Baseball Clubs,* 259 U.S. 200 (1922).

cuit, the Orpheum Circuit, and other theatrical chains, claiming that, in violation of the antitrust laws, they colluded to prevent any of his actors from obtaining contracts in their theaters unless Hart granted them what we would today call kick-backs. Holmes noted that some of these contracts called for the transportation of performers, scenery, music, and costumes. Distinguishing *Federal Baseball*, he held that "in the transportation of vaudeville acts the apparatus sometimes is more important than the performers and . . . the defendant's conduct is within the [antitrust] statute to that extent at least."[40]

Comment: Note fact freedom at work here. Holmes does not, despite vaudeville's obvious resemblance to baseball, find that the two are factually similar enough to govern vaudeville by baseball's precedent. There was, he said, a difference. Some of the disputed contracts did involve transportation itself. Holmes could have chosen to follow the previous year's precedent. The travel is still incidental to local performance of either baseball or vaudeville. Compare this with what happened 30 years later.

1953 Baseball again, but not an alleged attempt to prevent the formation of a third league. Now it was the players' turn to allege violation of the antitrust laws. The violation took the form of the well-publicized reserve clause,[41] or so players claimed. The players contended that the clause prevented open competition for better salaries. In *Toolson v. New York Yankees* the Supreme Court ruled in an unsigned *(per curiam)* opinion that baseball still did not fall under the coverage of the antitrust laws. It so held despite the efforts of Justices Burton and Reed, who dissented, to marshall extensive evi-

[40]*Hart v. B. F. Keith Vauderville Exchange*, 262 U.S. 271 (1923), p. 273.
[41]*Toolson v. New York Yankees*, 346 U.S. 356 (1953), pp. 362–363.

dence of baseball's dramatic growth since 1922. The majority opinion stated:

> Congress has had the [*Federal Baseball*] ruling under consideration but has not seen fit to bring such business under these laws by legislation having prospective effect. The business has thus been left for thirty years to develop, on the understanding that it was not subject to existing antitrust legislation. The present cases ask us to overrule the prior decision and, with retrospective effect, hold the legislation applicable.... Without reexamination of the underlying issues, the judgments below are affirmed on the authority of *Federal Baseball* ... so far as that decision determines that Congress had no intention of including the business of baseball within the scope of the federal antitrust laws.

Questions: Did Justice Holmes conclude in 1922 that "Congress had no intention of including the business of baseball within the scope of the federal antitrust laws"? Do you believe that, because Congress has not legislated on the subject of baseball and the antitrust laws, therefore professional baseball does not fall within the act? Remember that not only had baseball become more businesslike since 1922, but the definition of commerce had also changed so that travel or movement from state to state did not have to be an essential part of a business's activities in order to put it under the act. Why is it necessary to follow the 1922 precedent? Why could not the *Toolson* opinion simply say that both the law and the sport have changed and the owners have no justified expectation to rely on an outdated judicial ruling? Do you think, in other words, that because in 1922 the Court told the established leagues they could try to prevent the formation of a third league, they therefore rightly planned in 1946 to deal with their players by contracts that prevented free competition in that business?

1955 In *United States v. Shubert*, Chief Justice Warren, speaking for the Supreme Court, upheld the government's claim that theater owners who monopolized the booking of theater attractions violated the antitrust laws.[42] The Court acknowledged *Hart*, though only in passing. It refused to follow *Toolson*, calling it "a narrow application of the rule of *stare decisis.*"

Question: One purpose of stare decisis is to promote equality. On what basis should the law treat actors and baseball players unequally, as this case concludes the law must?

Chief Justice Warren, in a companion case to *Shubert*, held that professional boxing did fall within the scope of antitrust laws.[43] He distinguished *Toolson* for the same reasons he gave in *Shubert*.

Questions: How equally do you think baseball players felt the courts applied the law in 1955? If you had managed the Boxing Club, would you have relied on the *Toolson* decision? Would you think of boxing as any more a business than baseball? Would the new boxing decision possibly surprise you?

1957 In *Radovich v. National Football League*, the lower appellate court, mystified by the distinction between baseball and boxing that the Supreme Court had created, decided that football did not fall under the antitrust laws because football, like baseball but unlike boxing, was a team sport. The Supreme Court reversed.[44]

Comment: "Foolish consistency is the hobgoblin of little minds."

1971 The Supreme Court held that the antitrust laws did govern professional basketball.[45]

[42]*United States v. Shubert*, 348 U.S. 222 (1955).
[43]*United States v. International Boxing Club of New York, Inc.*, 348 U.S. 236 (1955).
[44]*Radovich v. National Football League*, 352 U.S. 445 (1957).
[45]*Heywood v. National Basketball Association*, 401 U.S. 1204 (1971).

> *Question:* By now do you think the Court could safely overrule *Federal Baseball?*

1972 Fifty years after *Federal Baseball,* Curt Flood's challenge to the reserve clause reached the Supreme Court. After a panegyrical review of baseball's history, replete with references to Thayer's "Casey at the Bat," and a long and curious list of baseball's greats (the list includes such immortals as Three-Finger Brown and Hans Lobert but omits Stan Musial, Joe DiMaggio, Ted Williams, and Hank Aaron), Justice Blackmun refused to abandon *Toolson* or stare decisis. Flood lost. Blackmun wrote:

> [W]e adhere once again to *Federal Baseball* and *Toolson* and to their application to professional baseball. We adhere also to *International Boxing* and *Radovich* and to their respective applications to professional boxing and professional football. If there is any inconsistency or illogic in all this, it is an inconsistency and illogic of long-standing that is to be remedied by the Congress and not by this Court. If we were to act otherwise, we would be withdrawing from the conclusion as to congressional intent made in *Toolson* and from the concerns as to retrospectivity therein expressed. Under these circumstances, there is merit in consistency even though some might claim that beneath that consistency is a layer of inconsistency.[46]

Justice Douglas dissented. He wrote, "The unbroken silence of Congress should not prevent us from correcting our own mistakes.[47]

That's enough of the chronology of judicial decisions. In the wake of judicial and congressional failure to deal with the reserve clause, the baseball players struck in the early 1970s. The strike successfully freed the players from the clause, and

---

[46]*Flood v. Kuhn,* p. 284.

[47]For an update on what continues to be a troubled body of law, see Gary R. Roberts, "Sports League Restraints on the Labor Market: The Failures of Stare Decisis," 47 *University of Pittsburgh Law Review* 337 (1986).

recent increases in players' salaries can be creditied to this change.

What went wrong here? In the immediate case of sports and the antitrust laws, *Toolson's* utterly inaccurate insistence that *Federal Baseball* means that Congress did not intend to include baseball wreaked the most havoc. *Toolson*, to paraphrase, says, "The highest lawmaking body in the country, Congress, has determined that the antitrust laws should not apply to professional baseball. Therefore the owners of baseball teams have made many business arrangements in reliance on this state of the law. It would be wrong to upset these expectations legitimized by the intent of Congress." This position is pure nonsense. Congress did not intend to exclude baseball. Holmes in *Federal Baseball* never said Congress so intended. As my questions at the end of the *Toolson* excerpt imply, the baseball owners had no reason to rely on *Federal Baseball,* at least not in 1953, given intervening precedents. Stability and reliance do *not* in this instance require the Court to invoke stare decisis and follow *Federal Baseball. Toolson* reached that different result by merely saying, without supporting evidence, that Congress so commanded.

Unfortunately, the Supreme Court's reasoning in these cases is worse than that. At least, you might say, baseball owners probably did honestly believe that they had a good chance of escaping the antitrust laws and acted on that basis. There is some merit in the reliance argument. But if stare decisis seeks to assist people to make plans in reliance on stable law, then surely owners of football, basketball, and boxing franchises and athletes had every bit as much reason for relying on *Federal Baseball* or *Toolson* as did the baseball owners. After all, in terms of the antitrust law, there is no difference among these sports that ought to induce baseball owners to rely on the original precedent while preventing those in the other sports from doing so.

In the name of stare decisis, then, we have a series of decisions that hardly seems stable, that violates reliance expectations to the extent that there are any, and that does not treat equals equally. To complete the list of justifications for adhering to precedent, do these decisions strike you as efficient judicial administration? What image of justice do these cases flash in your mind? Oafish, perhaps?

Fortunately, I have deliberately chosen an extreme example. Faced with statutory precedents, courts do not invariably invoke stare decisis in order to wreak havoc on the very justifications for stare decisis. Nevertheless, this critical question remains: *If* a judge feels that an existing judicial interpretation of a statute is erroneous and *if* the judge also feels that he may overrule it without doing violence to the five justifications of stare decisis, do *any* aspects of the court's relationship to the legislature nevertheless compel adherence to the questionable interpretation? I believe the proper answer to this question is no. However, on two analytical levels, judges and legal scholars have at times reached a different conclusion. Let us review their reasons for doing so on both levels.

The Case Against Increased Adherence to Precedent in Statutory Interpretation

The first, and more superficial, analytical level holds that the legislature may take certain actions that compel the courts to adhere to precedent. In *Toolson,* for example, the Supreme Court seemed to say that, since Congress had not passed a statute to cover baseball by the antitrust laws, Congress had somehow converted *Federal Baseball* into statutory law. Would any of the following events in Congress, or in any legislature, strengthen such a conclusion?

- Many bills were introduced to cover baseball, but none of them passed.
- Many bills were introduced to exempt baseball, but none of them passed.
- Congress re-enacted the relevant antitrust provisions, with some modifications, none of which attempted to cover or exempt baseball specifically.
- Congress passed a statute explicitly placing, say professional boxing prior to 1955, under the antitrust laws but makes no mention of baseball's status.
- Congress passed a joint resolution that officially states

that baseball is hereinafter to be considered "The National Pastime of the United States."

Judges often buttress their adherence to precedents on
such grounds, but these grounds are insufficient. Congress
possesses no power to make law other than by passing statutes.
Statutes are, among other items, subject to presidential veto
power. Not even joint resolutions, which escape presidential
veto, therefore create law. To say that any of the legislative acts
I just listed create law is to give Congress a law-making power
not found in the Constitution.

Furthermore, consider these reasons that a legislature
might not, in fact, directly respond to a judicial interpretation
by law.[48]

- Legislators never learn of the judicial interpretation in
  the first place.
- Legislators don't care about the issue the interpretation raises.
- Legislators care but feel they must spend their limited
  time and political resources on the other more important matters.
- Legislators like the proposed new statute or amendment but feel it politically unwise to vote for it.
- Legislators decide to vote against the bill because they
  do not like another unrelated provision of the bill.
- Legislators feel the bill does not go far enough and
  vote against it in hopes of promulgating more comprehensive law later.
- Legislators don't like the bill's sponsor personally and
  therefore vote negatively.
- Legislators believe, in the words of Hart and Sacks,
  "that the matter should be left to be handled by the
  normal process of judicial development of decisional
  law, including the overruling of outstanding decisions

[48]Hart and Sacks, pp. 1395–1396.

to the extent that the sound growth of the law requires. . . ."[49]

Do not all these possibilities, especially the last, convince you that courts should not speculate about the meaning of a statutory interpretation by guessing at why the legislature didn't pass a law affecting the interpretation?

The second analytical level is more complex. Sophisticated proponents of the "one-shot" theory of statutory interpretation admit that legislative silence is meaningless.[50] They worry instead about the proper apportionment of legislative and judicial responsibilities. Their argument goes this way: Legislatures deliberately use ambiguous language in statutes, not simply to bring many somewhat different specific events under one policy roof but also to allow room for the compromises necessary to generate a majority vote. Once written, the words of a statute will not change, but, because they are general, vague, and ambiguous, courts will certainly have the opportunity to interpret those same words in many different ways.

If, the argument continues, words have different meanings at different times and places, the legislature's power to make law becomes pointless, or at least quite subordinated to judicial power of interpretation. Courts must find one meaning. They do so by determining legislative intent. The judiciary insults the legislature if it says that at one time the legislature intended the words to carry one meaning and at another time another meaning. To say this is to say of the legislature that it had no intent and that it did not understand its actions. That assertion would embarrass the legislature, to say the least.

---

[49]Ibid, p. 1396. Professor Beth Henschen writes, "Congress rarely responds to the statutory decisions of the Court in at least . . . labor and antitrust policy. . . . Over a 28 year period, Congress considered legislation constituting reactions to only 27 of 222 cases in which the Court interpreted labor and antitrust statutes. . . . Moreover, only 9 of those decisions . . . were modified by the enactment of a bill that was signed into law." "Statutory Interpretations of the Supreme Court: Congressional Response," *American Politics Quarterly,* 441 (1983), p. 453.

[50]See especially Levi, pp. 31–33.

The argument thus holds that part of the judicial responsibility to the legislature is to reinforce the concept that the
legislature did in fact have a specific intention because that is
what the public expects of legislatures. The first half of this
chapter has, I trust, revealed why this argument fails.

Fortunately, the argument does not stop there. Levi asserts:

> Legislatures and courts are cooperative law-making bodies. It
> is important to know where the responsibility lies. If legis-
> lation which is disfavored can be interpreted away from
> time to time, then it is not to be expected, particularly if
> controversy is high, that the legislature will ever act. It will
> always be possible to say that new legislation is not needed
> because the court in the future will make a more appropri-
> ate interpretation. If the court is to have freedom to rein-
> terpret legislation, the result will be to relieve the legislature
> from pressure. The legislation needs judicial consistency.
> Moreover, the court's own behavior in the face of pressure
> is likely to be indecisive. In all likelihood it will do enough
> to prevent legislative revision and not much more. There-
> fore it seems better to say that once a decisive interpreta-
> tion of legislative intent has been made, and in that sense a
> direction has been fixed within the gap of ambiguity, the
> court should take that direction as given. In this sense a
> court's interpretation of legislation is not dictum. The
> words it uses do more than decide the case. They give broad
> direction to the statute.[51]

Levi's argument cuts too deeply. Indeed, there are instances in which legislators breathe sighs of relief that courts
have taken delicate political problems from them. (Curiously
enough, courts most often do so by applying constitutional
standards to legislation, and in this area Levi does not demand
similarly strict stare decisis.) But Levi's position is simply inaccurate in its assumption that most questions of interpretation
raise highly charged public issues that legislatures ought to
deal with but won't if the Court does it for them. For the most
part, judicial errors in statutory interpretation involve border-

---

[51]Ibid., p. 32.

line application of statutes. The interpretations may do considerable injustice to the parties who find themselves in borderline situations without, in any significant way, damaging the central purposes of the statutory policy as a whole. In the large bulk of cases, then, it is wholly unrealistic to assume that either overruling or adherence will affect how legislators perform. Try to imagine, for example, how Congress would have reacted had the Supreme Court held in 1946 that the traveling bigamous Mormons did not violate the Mann Act. I suspect with a yawn.

To conclude, notice how many of the problems that courts have created for themselves regarding the place of stare decisis in statutory interpretations would evaporate if only judges convinced themselves to seek the purpose of a statute and not to speculate about legislative intent from inconclusive legislative evidence. The inadequate conclusions that judges reach when they reason on the first and more superficial analytical level would disappear altogether. At the more sophisticated level, the concept that the courts embarrass legislatures by implying the rather obvious truth that the legislators probably had no intent with respect to the precise issue before the court would also disapear. Is this truth so awful? Of course not. That statutes speak in general terms is a simple necessity in political life. Such generality explains and justifies the existence of courts.

A SUMMARY STATEMENT OF THE APPROPRIATE JUDICIAL APPROACH TO STATUTORY INTERPRETATION

Judges should follow precedents when the justifications of stare decisis so dictate. Their primary obligation to the legislature is to apply the statutes it creates so as to achieve, as best judges can determine it, the intelligible solution of problems the statute exists to solve. Judges should try to determine purpose accurately, but they will err from time to time. It is no embarrassment to the legislature for judges to admit that they erred in determining statutory purpose and applying it to cases properly before them. They should therefore give stare decisis no special weight in statutory interpretation. They should do so with the confidence that to the extent that they can predict legislative behavior at all, they can predict that the legislature is no less likely to correct them if they err today than if they erred yesterday. Of course, legislation needs judicial consistency. Affixing proper legislative responsibility will occur only when courts consistently discern sensible statutory purposes.

SUMMARY

- What are statutes?
- What is statutory interpretation "in the first instance"?
- What characteristics of words prevent statutes from resolving all legal cases arising under them?
- What are the strengths and weaknesses of the canons of statutory interpretation?
- In what ways does the statute-making process in legislatures differ from judicial assumptions about it?
- How and why do legislative intent and statutory purpose differ?
- Do reasoning by example, fact freedom, and stare decisis operate in unique ways in statutory interpretation? Should they? Why have some judges and scholars insisted that judges should follow precedents more rigidly in statutory interpretation than in other areas of law? Does not this point of view rest on essentially the same naive assumptions about politics and legislating that infect the search for legislative intent?

ILLUSTRATIVE CASE

The next opinion's format will seem unfamiliar to you because the case comes from England over a century ago. Note that this report summarizes the positions of the attorneys as well as the opinions of each of the judges. The reference at the very beginning is the citation to the statute that the court must interpret. Also, the word "personate" is the same as our modern "impersonate." Hart and Sacks used this case to good advantage in their materials, cited frequently in this book.

Whiteley v. Chappell
L.R. 4 Queen's Bench 147 (1868)

The following is the substance of the case:—

By 14 & 15 Vict. c. 105, s. 3, if any person, pending or after the election of any guardian [of the poor], shall wilfully, fraudulently, and with intent to affect the result of such election. . . . "personate any person entitled to vote at such election," he is made liable on conviction to imprisonment for not exceeding three months.

The appellant was charged with having personated one J. Marston, a person entitled to vote at an election of guardians for the township of Bradford; and it was proved that Marston was duly qualified as a ratepayer on the rate book to have voted at the election, but that he had died before the election. The appellant delivered to the person appointed to collect the voting papers a voting paper apparently duly signed by Marston.

The magistrate convicted the appellant.

The question for the Court was, whether the appellant was rightly convicted.

Mellish, Q.C. (with him *McIntyre*), for the appellant. A dead person cannot be said to be "a person entitled to vote;" and the appellant therefore could not be guilty of personation under 14 & 15 Vict. c. 105, s. 3. Very possibly he was within the spirit, but he was not within the letter, of the enactment, and in order to bring a person within a penal enactment, both must concur. In Russell on Crimes . . . under a former statute, in which the words were similar to those of 2 Wm. 4, c. 53, s. 49, which makes it a misdemeanor to personate "a person entitled or supposed to be entitled to any prize money," &c., *Brown's Case* (1) is cited, in which it was held that the personation must be of some person primâ facie entitled to prize money. In the Parliamentary Registration Act . . . the words are "any person who shall knowingly personate . . . any person whose name appears on the register of voters, whether such person be alive or dead;" but under the present enactment the person must be entitled, that is, could have voted himself.

Crompton, for the respondent. *Brown's Case* is, in effect, over-ruled by the later cases of *Rex v. Martin,* and *Rex v. Cramp,* in which the judges decided that the offence of personating a person "supposed to be entitled" could be committed, although the person, to the knowledge or belief of the authorities, was dead. Those cases are directly in point. The gist of the offence is the fraudulently voting under another's name; the mischief is the same, whether the supposed voter be alive or dead; and the Court will put a liberal construction on such an enactment; *Reg. v. Hague.*

Mellish, Q.C., in reply. "Supposed to be entitled" must have been held by the judges in the cases cited to mean supposed by the person personating.

LUSH, J. I do not think we can, without straining them, bring the case within the words of the enactment. The legislature has not used words wide enough to make the personation of a dead person an offence. The words "a person entitled to vote" can only mean, without a forced construction, a person who is entitled to vote at the time at which the personation takes place; in the present case, therefore, I feel bound to say the offence has not been committed. In the case of *Rex v. Martin,* and *Rex. v. Cramp,* the judges gave no reason for their decision; they probably held that "supposed to be entitled" meant supposed by the person personating.

HANNEN, J. I regret that we are obliged to come to the conclusion that the offence charged was not proved; but it would be wrong to strain words to meet the justice of the present case, because it might make a precedent, and lead to dangerous consequences in other cases.

HAYES, J., concurred.

Judgment for the appellant.

QUESTIONS

1. If a student attends class one day dressed in a 10-gallon hat, Western boots, and chaps, is it linguistically possible to say that he is "impersonating" a cowboy? Is it linguistically possible to define "impersonation" as any act in which someone pretends to be someone other than his or her real self?
2. If it is possible to impersonate a general type of character, or a fictitious character, is it not linguistically possible to violate the statute simply by pretending to be a voter entitled to vote?

3. Does not the question in *Whiteley* inescapably boil down to what purpose it would serve, if any, for the legislature to make it a crime to impersonate a live person but not a dead person at an election?

4. What important background facts does your determination of the purpose of this statute depend on? Is it not true that impersonating a live registered voter might deprive such a person of his right to vote, whereas this plaintiff did not so deprive anyone? But the statute does not distinguish between an attempt to vote in the name of a living person before, rather than after, that person successfully votes. Or does it? Do we not suspect that the main purpose is to protect the integrity of the voting system, rather than an individual right to vote? If so, what conclusion should the court have reached in this case?

5. If you were a member of the legislature making the statute in this case, how carefully do you think you could anticipate all the situations that might arise under this law? In what spirit would you want a judge to interpret your law? Would you want a judge to appreciate that you were trying to state general policy to solve a problem at the polls and that you would not be able to anticipate and cover in statutory language every quirky factual situation that might arise under it? You should be able to think of at least a half-dozen other quirky situations that might or might not be covered under this statute, depending on the technique you choose to use to interpret it.

6. The Alabama school prayer case, *Wallace v. Jaffree,* 105 S. Ct. 2479 (1985), presents a question of constitutional law that in turn depends on principles of statutory interpretation for its resolution. Alabama's statute—§ 16-1-20.1—which the Court struck down in this case, authorized a period of silence "for meditation or voluntary prayer" in public schools. Under *Lemon v. Kurtzman,* 403 U.S. 602 (1971), the First Amendment "establishment clause" has permitted statutes that incidentally or secondarily advance religion if the statute's primary purpose is secular. Alabama passed § 16-1-20.1 in 1981. Earlier, in 1978, Alabama had passed § 16-1-20, which approved one minute of silent meditation in the classroom, and the Court assumed that this provision, by itself, was constitutionally acceptable. Then in 1982, Alabama added § 16-1-20.2, which authorized teachers to lead willing students in a prescribed prayer to "Almightly God . . . the Creator and

Supreme Judge of the world." The Supreme Court had, prior to *Wallace,* held that §16-1-20.2 violated the *Lemon* principle. Here are excerpts from Justice Stevens's opinion in *Wallace.* Does this opinion claim to have discerned the actual intent of the Alabama legislature, or does evidence of intent help shape Justice Stevens's vision of §16-1-20.1's purpose?

Appellee Ishmael Jaffree is a resident of Mobile County, Alabama. On May 28, 1982, he filed a complaint on behalf of three of his minor children; two of them were second-grade students and the third was then in kindergarten.... The complaint ... alleged that two of the children had been subjected to various acts of religious indoctrination "from the beginning of the school year in September, 1981"....

On August 2, 1982, the District Court held an evidentiary hearing on appellees' motion for a preliminary injunction. At that hearing, State Senator Donald G. Holmes testified that he was the "prime sponsor" of the bill that was enacted in 1981 as § 16-1-20.1 He explained that the bill was an "effort to return voluntary prayer to our public schools ... it is a beginning and a step in the right direction." Apart from the purpose to return voluntary prayer to public school, Senator Holmes unequivocally testified that he had "no other purpose in mind." A week after the hearing, the District Court entered a preliminary injunction. The court held that appellees were likely to prevail on the merits because the enactment of § 16-1-20.1 and 16-1-20.2 did not reflect a clearly secular purpose.

In November 1982, the District Court held a four-day trial on the merits. The State did not present evidence of any secular purpose....

The legislative intent to return prayer to the public schools is, of course, quite different from merely protecting every student's right to engage in voluntary prayer during an appropriate moment of silence during the school day. The 1978 statute already protected that right, containing nothing that prevented any student from engaging in voluntary prayer during a silent minute of meditation. Appellants have not identified any secular purpose that was not fully served by § 16-1-20 before the enactment of § 16-1-20.1. Thus, only two conclusions are consistent with the text of § 16-1-20.1: (1) the statute was enacted to convey a message of State endorsement and promotion of prayer; or (2) the statute was enacted for no purpose. No one suggests that the statute was nothing but a meaningless or irrational act.

We must, therefore, conclude that the Alabama Legislature intended to change existing law and that it was motivated by the same purpose that ... Senator Holmes' testimony frankly described. The Legislature enacted § 16-1-20.1 despite the existence of § 16-1-20 for the sole purpose of expressing the State's endorsement of prayer activities for one minute at the beginning of each school day. The addition of "or voluntary prayer" indicates that the State intended to characterize prayer as a favored practice. Such an endorsement is not consistent with the established principle that the Government must pursue a course of complete neutrality toward religion. ...

On June 19, 1987, by a 7–2 vote, the Supreme Court rejected Louisiana's "Creationism Act," which forbade teaching evolutionary theories in public schools without also teaching "creation science." The case, like *Wallace,* turned on a reading of the legislature's motives. In dissent, Justice Scalia insisted that the Court must accept the claim, made in the legislative record, that the Creationism Act served a secular purpose. For the majority, Justice Brennan concluded that the statute could not have a secular purpose because it required teaching only one alternative to evolution, which was based on religious teaching.[52]

7. The Iran-Contra scandal, which first surfaced in 1986, revealed, among other things, that in 1985 President Reagan and the National Security Council took direct measures to get military aid to the Contra rebels in Nicaragua. But the Boland Amendment, enacted on October 12, 1984 commanded that:

> During fiscal year 1985, no funds available to the Central Intelligence Agency, the Department of Defense, or any other agency or entity of the United States involved in intelligence activities may be obligated or expended for the purpose or which would have the effect of supporting, directly or indirectly, military or paramilitary operations in Nicaragua by any nation, group, organization, movement, or individual.

---

[52]*Edwards v. Aguillard,* 107 S.Ct. 2573 (1987).

How might different methods of statutory interpretation discussed in this chapter lead to differing conclusions about its coverage? How might we define an "intelligence activity"? What if the only expenditure of "funds" by the White House consisted of long-distance phone calls? We can imagine at least two different purposes of the Boland Amendment. The first purpose, to forbid the expenditure of tax dollars to help the Contras, would make the violations technical at best, since the bulk of funds supplied came from private and foreign sources. But if the purpose was to withdraw support from the Contra effort, do not the violations become more substantial?

Chapter IV

COMMON LAW

> *The life of the law has not been logic; it has been experience. The felt necessities of the time, the prevalent moral and political theories, intuitions of public policy, avowed or unconscious, even the prejudices which judges share with their fellow-men, have had a good deal more to do than the syllogism in determining the rules by which men should be governed.*
> *—Oliver Wendell Holmes, Jr.*

Near its beginning this book urged you to treat reason in law as a puzzle that may achieve its full significance only as the last pieces fit into place. One of the sections of the still-incomplete picture that may now puzzle you is the large group of pieces called common law. Common law is judge-made law, a process distinct from statutory interpretation and constitutional law. However, the examination of reason in statutory interpretation reveals that judges inevitably make law when they interpret statutes. Chapter V will explain how courts inevitably exercise even broader constitutional lawmaking power. How then is common law any more judge-made than any other kind of law?

The short, and therefore inadequate, answer lies in our legal tradition, which empowers judges to resolve conflicts when no statute or constitutional provision addresses the problem. When a statute speaks to the issue, the judge must look to the statute for his solution. But, when no statute speaks, the judge resolves the conflict by reasoning from common law cases that judges have decided in the past and from the doctrines that emerge from them.

The origins of a better answer come from the complex history of English law.[1] To make sense of this history, let me ask you to start by joining in a role play.

ORIGINS OF COMMON LAW

Put yourself in the position of William the Conqueror. You are, like many of your Norman kin, a shrewd politician. You have just managed the remarkable political feat, at least for the eleventh century, of assembling thousands of men and the necessary supporting equipment to cross the English Channel and to win title to England in battle. In these feudal days title means ownership, and in a real sense you own England as a result of the Battle of Hastings.

However, your administrative headaches have just begun. On the one hand you must reward your supporters—and your supporters must reward their supporters—with grants of your land. On the other hand, you don't want to give up any of the land completely. You deserve to and shall collect rents—taxes are the modern equivalent—from the landholders beneath you. You must give away with one hand but keep a legal hold with the other.

---

[1]Plucknett's "concise" history of the subject is over 700 pages long. Theodore F. T. Plucknett, *A Concise History of the Common Law,* 5th ed. (Boston: Little, Brown, 1956). For real conciseness try Frederick G. Kempin, *Historical Introduction to Anglo-American Law in a Nutshell,* 2nd ed. (St. Paul: West, 1973). To contrast common law systems with the deductive or "code-based" systems of law on the European continent I recommend John Henry Merryman, *The Civil Law Tradition* (Stanford: Stanford University Press, 1969).

Furthermore, you must keep the peace, not only among the naturally restless and resentful natives but also among your supporters. As time goes on and their personal loyalty to you dwindles, they will no doubt fight more readily over exactly who owns which lands. And, of course, you have a notion that you and your successors will clash with that other group claiming a sort of sovereignty, the Church.

You must, in short, develop machinery for collecting rents, tracking ownership, and settling disputes.

Fortunately, you have conquered a relatively civilized land. At the local level some degree of government already exists on which you can build. In what we would call counties, but which the natives call shires, a hereditary *shire reeve* (our sheriff) cooperates with a bishop representing the Church to handle many of the problems of daily governance. These shires have courts, as do the smaller villages within them. You hope that, in the next century at least, your successors will be able to take control of them.

Meanwhile you take the action of any good politician. You undertake a survey, a sort of census, of who owns what lands—the *Domesday Book*. You organize all the lords, to whom you granted large amounts of land, church leaders, and many of the major native landlords who swear allegiance to you, into a Great Council. They advise you (and you thus co-opt their support) on the important policy questions before you. You start appointing the local sheriffs yourself. You also create a permanent staff of bureaucrats, personal advisors who handle and resolve smaller problems as they arise.

You succeed in creating a new political reality, one in which it soon becomes somehow right to govern in the name of the ultimate landlord, the king.

So much for the role play.

William in no sense developed the contemporary common law system, but he did create the political reality in which that development had to happen: governing in the king's name—settling land disputes, collecting rents, and keeping the peace—meant rendering justice in the king's name. William's personal advisors, his staff, often traveled about the country administering *ad hoc* justice in the king's name. Additionally, many of the more serious offenses, what we would today call crimes, came directly to the Great Council for decision because they were offenses against the king's peace.

One hundred years later, Henry II began the actual takeover of the lower local courts. Initially, the king insisted on giving permission to the local courts before they could hear any case involving title to his land. A litigant would have to obtain from London a *writ of right* and then produce it in court before the court could hear the case. Shortly thereafter the king's council began to bypass the local courts altogether on matters of land title. Certain council members heard these cases at first, but, as they became more and more specialized and experienced, they split off from the council to form the king's Court of Common Pleas.

Similarly, the council members assigned to criminal matters developed into the Court of the King's Bench. The Court of the Exchequer, which handled rent and tax collections, evolved in similar fashion.

Only three problems remained. The first concerned the law these judges should use. One solution, ultimately adopted in many continental jurisdictions, was simply to use the old Roman codes. In England, however, partly because it was easy and partly because it possessed considerable local political appeal, the king's judges adopted as far as possible the practice of the pre-Conquest local courts. This practice of the lower courts consisted of adopting as far as possible the local customs of the place and time and applying to daily events what people felt was fair. We might call this the custom of following custom.

The custom of following custom, however, produced the second problem. In a sparsely populated area, a primitive area by today's standards of commerce and transportation, customs about crimes, about land use, and about debts and so forth varied considerably from shire to shire, village to village, and manor to manor. But the king's judges could hardly decide each case on the basis of whatever local custom or belief happened to capture the fancy of those living where the dispute arose. To judge that way would amount to judging on shifting and inconsistent grounds. It would not judge in the

king's name but only in the name of the location where the
dispute arose. Following local custom would undercut William's long-range political objectives.

Hence the royal courts slowly adopted some customs and
rejected others in an attempt to rule consistently in the king's
name. Because justice in England rested on the custom of customs, the customs that the royal courts adopted and attempted
to apply uniformly became the customs *common* to all the
King's land. Thus the royal courts did not just follow custom.
They created new common customs by following some and
rejecting others and combining yet others into new customs.

Of course, by doing this the courts no longer ruled by
custom, strictly speaking. Because they sought to rule in the
king's name, they sought to rule consistently. In doing so, the
courts rejected some customs. Although judges no doubt felt
that what they decided was right because it had its roots in
some customs, it would be wiser to say they created not common custom but common law, law common throughout England.

With the solution of the third problem as follows, the
story of the origins of common law ends. If judges adopt today
a custom by which to govern other similar cases before the
royal courts tomorrow, then tomorrow the judges must have
some way of remembering what they said today. By the year
1250, the problem of faulty judicial memory so bothered one
judge, Henri de Bracton, that he wrote a huge treatise attempting to solve it. Plucknett describes the work this way:

> [Bracton] procured, for his own private use, complete tran-
> scripts of the pleadings in selected cases, and even referred
> to the cases in the course of his treatise. This great innova-
> tion gives to his work in several places a curiously modern
> air, for like modern law writers he sometimes praises and
> sometimes criticises his cases. At the beginning of his book
> he explains, however, that the contemporary bench is not
> distinguished by ability or learning, and that his treatise
> is, to some extent, a protest against modern tendencies. He
> endeavours to set forth the sound principles laid down by
> those whom he calls "his masters" who were on the bench
> nearly a generation ago; hence it is that his cases are on

the average about twenty years older than his book. Of really recent cases he used very few. It must not, therefore, be assumed that we have in Bracton the modern conception of case law. He never gives us any discussion of the authority of cases and clearly would not understand the modern implications of *stare decisis*. Indeed, his cases are carefully selected because they illustrate what he believes the law ought to be, and not because they have any binding authority; he freely admits that at the present moment decisions are apt to be on different lines. Bracton's use of cases, therefore, is not based upon their authority as sources of law, but upon his personal respect for the judges who decided them, and his belief that they raise and discuss questions upon lines which he considers sound. Although it is true that the use of cases as a source of law in the modern sense was still far in the future, nevertheless Bracton's use of cases is very significant. He accustomed lawyers of the thirteenth and early fourteenth centuries to read and to discuss the cases which he put in his book, and this was a great step towards the modern point of view.[2]

Bracton's great work, together with smaller pamphlets of other judges and lawyers, were followed within half a century by "year-books," annual reports of court proceedings and decisions that heavily emphasized procedure. Procedure in England, the correct way and the incorrect way to proceed in court, had rapidly become rigid, and lawyers who could not master it and who could not remember all the strict technicalities lost their cases. They needed to write the technicalities down to remember them. Bracton and his successors, of necessity, began the tradition, very much expanded today, of writing down the essential conclusions of the courts and using these writings as guides for future judicial choices.

As Plucknett reminds us, however, Bracton and his followers did not create the practices of reasoning by example and stare decisis as we know them. Indeed, until the American Revolution, men actively rejected the notion that judges actually made law as they decided cases. Men believed rather in

[2]Plucknett, pp. 259–260.

natural law, if not God's law at least nature's own. To them the proper judicial decision rested on true law. The decision that rested elsewhere was in a sense unlawful. This was, after all, the problem facing Bracton. Prior to and throughout most of the eighteenth century, lawyers and judges thought of common law as a collected body of correct legal doctrine, not the process of growth and change that reasoning by example makes inevitable.

Additional reasons explain why common law only rather recently began to emphasize reasoning from precedents. Bracton's treatise and the many that followed it did not reliably report the factual details of each and every case. These were unofficial, incomplete, and often critical commentaries. Not even a judge who wanted to follow the examples of precedents could use them with confidence. Only the radical and recent change in viewpoint and the recognition that law comes from politicians and not from God or nature, coupled with accurate court reporting, permitted reasoning by example and staré decisis to flourish.[3]

It is time to close this historical circle. In calling common law judge-made law we mean that, for a variety of historical reasons, a large body of legal rules and principles exist because judges without legislative help have created them. As long as judges continue to apply them, they continue to re-create them with each application. The fact that judges for most of this history thought they simply restated divine or natural law matters relatively little to us today. What matters is that the twentieth-century United States has inherited a political system in which, despite legislative supremacy, judges constantly and inevitably make law. How they do so—how they reason, in other words—thus becomes an important question in the study of politics and government themselves; one of the

---

[3]Kempin, p. 85, suggests that as late as 1825 in the United States and 1865 in England stare decisis rested on very shaky ground. Anthropologists are quite comfortable with the conclusion that rules of law in contrast to imperfectly articulated customs and interpersonal understandings play a relatively insignificant role in many if not most of the world's justice systems. See Stanley Diamond, "The Rule of Law vs. the Order of Custom," 51 *Social Research* 387 (1984).

central questions in this book is not *whether* courts should make law but *what* law to make, and *how.*

COMMON LAW REASONING ILLUSTRATED

Much of the everyday law around us falls into the category of common law. Although modern statutes have supplanted some of it, particularly in the important area of commercial transactions, even these statutes for the most part preserve basic definitions, principles, and values articulated first in common law. One of the most important common law cate-gories, also probably the one least touched by statute today, concerns the law of tort. Tort law wrestles with these problems: What limits a person's liability to compensate those he hurts? When does law impose liability on me if I threaten someone with a blow (assault)? If I strike the blow (battery)? If I publicly insult another (libel and slander)? If I do careless things that injure other people (negligence)? These questions may sound like questions of criminal law to you, but they are not, for the law of torts does not expose the lawbreaker to punishment by the state. The law of torts, while much of it overlaps criminal law, defines at what times people who hurt other people's bod-ies, their property, their reputations, or their freedom must compensate them for their hurt.

In this section, indeed for the bulk of the chapter, we illustrate common law in action with problems of tort law, mostly of negligence. But we do not discuss tort law in its en-tirety, of course, for it would take books triple the size of this one to review all the subtleties and uncertainties in the law of tort. We shall instead focus in some detail on an important and perennial problem in the law of tort: To what extent may we hurt other people without incurring a legal liability to com-pensate those we hurt *because we hurt them on our own land?*

Let us begin with a review of the basic rules of common law that seemed to govern this situation in the middle of the last century. First, the common law of negligence required one to act in a way a reasonable and prudent person would act and to refrain from acting in a way a reasonable and prudent person would refrain from acting. Lawyers would say that a "standard of care" existed. Second, the law defined the classes of persons to whom a "duty" to act carefully was and was not owed. Third, law imposed liability upon those who in fact carelessly violated the "reasonable man" standard. Whether a person in fact acted negligently in a specific case is one of those legal history questions juries often decide. Fourth, someone to whom a duty is owed must actually suffer an injury as a result of the hurt. Juries often make this factual decision also. Thus the critical *legal* questions in negligence cases involve the definition of the standard and the duty.

Similarly, the law of battery commands us not to strike another deliberately unless a reasonable person would do so, as in self-defense. If we strike another unreasonably, then we become liable as long as we owe a duty to the injured person not to strike.

As you may already suspect, the requirement of a duty before liability attaches can make a great difference. One of the common law principles of the last century quite plainly said that people do not owe a duty to avoid injuring, carelessly or deliberately, people who *trespass* (encroach without express or implied permission) on their property.

We shall examine three common law cases to illustrate some of the main features of reasoning in common law. These cases provide evidence, or clues, that support some basic truths about the common law process:

- General principles, including the rules of negligence and battery just described, do not neatly resolve legal problems.
- Precedents do not neatly resolve legal problems, either.
- In reasoning from precedents, judges do make choices, do exercise fact freedom, and it is this exercise that best describes how and why they decide as they do.
- Social background facts often influence case outcomes more powerfully than the facts in the litigation itself.
- The beliefs and values of individual judges do influence law.

- The precise meaning of common law rules—here of trespass and of duty—changes as judges decide each new case.
- Over time, as fundamental social values change, common law also changes in a fundamental way to reflect these changes in social values.
- Judges have shifted their conception of their role, have shifted from a belief that their role requires them to apply divine or natural law toward a recognition of the inevitability of judicial lawmaking and its consequences.

Here are the three cases.

The Cherry Tree

It is summer in rural New York. The year is 1865. The heat of midday has passed. Sarah Hoffman, a spinster living with her brother, a country doctor, sets out at her brother's request to pick ripe cherries for dinner.

A cherry tree stands on her brother's land about two feet from the fence separating his land from that of his neighbor, Abner Armstrong. Sarah's previous cullings have left few cherries on Hoffman's side of the fence. Hence, nimbly enough for her age, Sarah climbs the fence and from her perch upon it begins to take cherries from the untouched branches overhanging Abner's yard.

Angered by this intrusion, Abner runs from his house and orders her to stop picking his cherries. She persists. Enraged, he grabs her wrist and strongarms her down from the fence. Ligaments in the wrist tear. She cries from the pain and humiliation. She sues at common law for battery. The trial jury awards her $1,000 damages.

Abner appealed. He claimed that *he,* not Sarah or her brother, owned the cherries overhanging his land. Because he owned the cherries, he had every right to protect them, just as he could prevent Sarah from pulling onions in his garden with a long-handled picker from her perch. In other words, Sarah was not a person to whom Abner owed a duty. By her trespassing and her interference with Abner's property, Sarah exposed herself to Abner's legal battery committed in defense of his property.

Abner's lawyer cited many legal sources in support of his argument. He began with the maxim, *cujus est solum, ejus est usque ad coelum et ad inferos,* sometimes translated as "he who has the soil, has it even to the sky and the lowest depths." He then referred the appellate judge to the great English commentator, Blackstone, quoting: "Upwards, therefore, no man may erect any building, or the like to overhang another's land." He also cited *Kent's Commentaries,* the Bouvier *Institutes, Crabbe's Text on Real Property,* and seven cases in support of his position. One of these, an English case titled *Waterman v. Soper,* held "that if A plants a tree upon the extremest limits of his land and the tree growing extends its roots into the land of B next adjoining," then A and B jointly own the tree.[4]

Sarah's lawyer responded that, in law, title to the tree depends on who owns title to the land from which the tree grows. Sarah did not trespass; therefore, Abner owed her the duty not to batter her. In support he cited several commentaries, Hilliard's treatise on real property, and four cases. Sarah's lawyer relied especially on a case, *Lyman v. Hale,* decided in Connecticut in 1836.[5] In *Lyman* the defendant picked and refused to return pears from branches overhanging his yard from a tree the plaintiff had planted four feet from the line. The *Lyman* opinion explicitly rejected the reasoning of the English precedent, *Waterman.* Despite the antiquated language, *Lyman* is a remarkably sensible, unlegalistic opinion. The court held that *Waterman's* "roots" principle is unsound because of the practical difficulties in applying it:

> How it may be asked, is the principle to be reduced to practice? And here, it should be remembered, that nothing depends on the question whether the branches do or do not overhang the lands of the adjoining proprietor. All is made to depend solely on the enquiry, whether any portion of the roots extend into his land. It is this fact alone, which creates the [joint ownership]. And how is the fact to be ascertained?

[4]*Waterman v. Soper,* 1 Ld Raymond 737 (opinion undated).
[5]*Lyman v. Hale,* 11 *Conn. Rep.* 177 (1836).

Again; if such [joint ownership] exist, it is diffused over the whole tree. Each owns a certain proportion of the whole. In what proportion do the respective parties hold? And how are these proportions to be determined? How is it to be ascertained what part of its nourishment the tree derives from the soil of the adjoining proprietor? If one joint owner appropriate . . . all the products, on what principle is the account to be settled between the parties?

Again; suppose the line between adjoining proprietors to run through a forest or grove. Is a new rule of property to be introduced, in regard to those trees growing so near the line as to extend some portions of their roots across it? How is a man to know whether he is the exclusive owner of trees, growing, indeed, on his own land, but near the line; and whether he can safely cut them, without subjecting himself to an action?

And again; on the principle claimed, a man may be the exclusive owner of a tree, one year, and the next, a [joint owner] with another; and the proportion in which he owns may be varying from year to year, as the tree progresses in its growth.

It is not seen how these consequences are to be obviated, if the principle contended for be once admitted. We think they are such as to furnish the most conclusive objections against the adoption of the principle. We are not prepared to adopt it, unless compelled to do so, by the controuling force of authority. The cases relied upon for its support, have been examined. We do not think them decisive.[6]

In effect the *Lyman* opinion says property titles must be clear to help us plan our affairs, to help us know whether we can or can't cut down a tree for winter firewood, for example. Given the inescapable background facts about trees, the roots rule introduces inevitable uncertainty. We must therefore reject it.

Sarah won.[7] The appellate court in New York found *Lyman* most persuasive and followed it.

Abner appealed again, to the state's highest court of appeals. In 1872 (court delays are not a uniquely modern phe-

---

[6]*Lyman v. Hale*, pp. 183–184.
[7]*Hoffman v. Armstrong*, 46 Barbour 337 (1866).

nomenon) Abner lost again. The attorneys presented the same arguments. Perhaps surprisingly, however, the highest court did not mention *Lyman*. Instead it seemed to say that *Waterman* does correctly state the law, but Abner's lawyer forgot to prove that the cherry tree's roots actually extended across the property line:

> We have not been referred to any case showing that where no part of a tree stood on the land of a party, and it did not receive any nourishment therefrom, that he had any right therein, and it is laid down in Bouvier's Institutes . . . that if the branches of a tree only overshadow the adjoining land and the roots do not enter into it, the tree wholly belongs to the estate where the roots grow.[8]

Therefore Abner lost.

This simple case, occupying only a few pages in the reports of the two New York appellate courts, richly illustrates many essential features of common law:

1. Note first that none of the judges either in *Hoffman* or in *Lyman* questioned their authority to decide these cases without reference to statutes. The laws, both of assault and battery and of the more fundamental problem of ownership, come from the common law heritage of cases, commentaries, and treatises. The judges automatically assumed the power to make law governing a very common human conflict, overlapping claims to physical space on this planet. Surely a legislature could legislate on the subject, but judges have no guilt feeling about doing so themselves in the face of legislative silence.

   In this connection, recall that legislatures pass statutes addressing general problems. How likely is it that a legislature would ever pass a statute regulating tree ownership on or near property lines? Is it not better that our government contains a mechanism, the courts, that must create some law on this subject once the problem turns out to be a real one?

[8]*Hoffman v. Armstrong*, 48 N.Y. 201 (1872), pp. 203–204.

2. The general common law definitions of battery and of property ownership do not resolve this case. Neither do specific precedents. Instead, both sides cite conflicting principles and inconsistent precedents and urge from them contradictory conclusions. The judge must find some justification, some reason, for choosing, but nothing in either side's argument, at least in this case, compels the judge to choose one way rather than another. Judges possess the freedom to say that either *Lyman* or *Waterman* expresses the right law for resolving this problem.

Consider specifically the matter of the Connecticut precedent, *Lyman*. Judges possess the freedom to say, as the first appellate court said, "We find the facts of *Lyman* much like those in Abner's conflict with Sarah. We also find *Lyman*'s reasoning persuasive, therefore we apply the rule of *Lyman* to this case and rule for Sarah." But judges also possess the freedom to say, as did the second court, "Connecticut precedents do not govern New York. Older common law precedents and principles from England conflict with Connecticut's law. We choose the older tradition. Abner would win if only he could show that the roots really grew on his property."

The New York courts in *Hoffman* had other options. The second court could have easily assumed that, since roots underground grow about the same distances as do branches above ground, that the roots did cross the line and that their nourishment probably supported the cherries Sarah tried to pick. Or they could take judicial notice of the fact that any reasonably sized tree grows roots in all directions more than two feet from its base. But they didn't.

Judges must decide which facts in the case before them matter and what they mean. They must simultaneously decide what the facts in the often inconsistent precedents mean in order to reach their legal conclusion. The two appellate courts reached the same conclusion but by emphasizing different facts.

The first court found that roots shouldn't matter. Even though legal authorities sometimes mention them, the court believed the location of roots should have no legal significance. To give root location legal significance suddenly makes our knowledge of what we own more uncertain. Before we can cut down a tree we must trespass on our neighbor's land and dig a series of holes in his yard looking for roots. And what if the neighbor has flowers growing in a bed that he doesn't want dug up? The root rule leaves us out on a limb.

3. To understand how these two courts choose differently to reach the same result, examine the difference in their basic approach to the problem. The first appellate court seems eager to assume the responsibility to shape law, to acknowledge relevant background facts and hence to make laws that promote human cooperation in daily affairs. The second court approaches the problem much more cautiously. It seems to say: "We admit the precedents conflict. Fortunately we do not really need to choose between them. As long as Abner failed to prove the roots grow on his side of the fence, he loses either way. Therefore we choose the path that disturbs common law the least. The lower appellate court explicitly chose to reject *Waterman,* but we don't have to do that, so we won't."

This judicial caution is very common, but it is not particularly wise. Without realizing it, the highest New York court (whose opinion therefore overrides the precedential value of the better opinion of the court below) has made new law. Now we have New York precedent endorsing *Waterman.* Future courts will have to wrestle with the problem of overruling it or blindly follow it and produce all the practical problems against which *Lyman* rightly warned.

The reason these two sets of judges ruled differently, therefore, rests precisely on the fact that they are different people with different values and beliefs about what judges ought to do. Their values help determine the law they create.

4. At a deeper level, the difference reflects much more than a difference in judicial beliefs. These two approaches illustrate two common law styles. The final higher court opinion in *Hoffman* views common law as fixed, stable, and true. It wants to avoid upsetting Bouvier's *Institutes* and Blackstone's maxims if it possibly can. The court thinks these are the common law. The lower court's *Lyman* approach, though it predates *Hoffman* by nearly 40 years, observes the spirit rather than the letter of common law. It views common law as a tradition in which judges seek to adapt law so that it improves our capacity to live together peacefully and to plan our affairs more effectively. It retains the capacity to change with changing conditions. This more modern style comes closer to helping law foster social cooperation, that basic legal goal identified in Chapter II.

5. Finally, the case of the cherry tree illustrates a fundamental difference between statutory interpretation and common law. In statutory interpretation we saw that many judges often try to determine the intent of the legislature. Since in practice legislative intent proves slippery at best, we prefer interpretation based on determinations of statutory purpose. In either case of statutory interpretation, however, we saw that judges must attempt to see the legal problem through the eye of the lawgiver. Once the court determines a statute's purpose, it has no need to second-guess the wisdom of that purpose.

In common law, on the other hand, the judge who reasons from a precedent does not care about what the prior judge intended or about the purpose of the announced rule of law. In common law, the judge is always free to decide on his own what the law ought to say. The prior judge's intent or purpose does not dictate how his opinion will bind as precedent.

Put another way, the legislature's classification of what does and does not belong in its legal category, a classification created by the words of the statute, does bind the judge. In common law, the judge deciding the case creates the classification. He sets his own goals.

This goal-setting occurred in both the first and second *Hoffman* opinions. The first court wanted to make workable and practical law, not because *Lyman* or any other precedent commanded it to but because the court wanted to achieve that goal. The second court ruled as it did not because Bouvier's *Institutes* or *Waterman* commanded it to do so but because that court preferred the goal of changing past formal statements of law as little as possible.[9]

The Pit

Five years after Sarah's final victory, New York's highest court faced a related common law problem. A Mr. Carter, along with several other citizens of the town of Bath, maintained an alley running between their properties: "Exchange Alley," people called it. The public had used the alley for 20 years as a convenient way to travel from one long block to another, but the town never acknowledged Exchange Alley as a public street nor attempted to maintain it. In May 1872, Carter began excavating to erect a building on his land. The construction went slowly, so slowly in fact that on a gloomy night the next November an open pit still remained on Carter's property. That night a Mr. Beck passed through the alley on his customary way to supper when, rather suddenly, a carriage turned down the alley and rushed toward him. Beck stepped rapidly to his left to avoid the carriage, tripped, and fell headlong into the pit, injuring himself. Although the evidence was never totally

[9]By contrast, the words of the Mann Act do command the courts to include at least the transportation of willing prostitutes, and the courts could not properly ignore that command.

clear, since the alley had no marked border, it appeared that the pit began no less than seven feet away from the outermost possible edge of the "public" alley.

The lawsuit that followed brought much the same kind of problem to the court as had Sarah's problem. Lawyers for Carter cited the common law rule that landowners have the right to use their property as they please. They have no duty to avoid harming trespassers negligently. The lawyers cited English cases to show that travelers who were hurt falling into pits 5, 20, and 30 feet from a public way could not recover damages because the danger must "adjoin" the public way.

Despite these arguments the court held for Beck. It had no difficulty whatsoever determining that, even though Carter and others together privately owned Exchange Alley, allowing the public to use the property over time created a duty to the users not to hurt them negligently.[10]

But the pit excavated truly private property. Is a seven-foot distance from a public alley sufficient to exempt the owner from liability to the public, or does the pit legally "adjoin" the alley, thereby creating a duty of care?

The court ruled that the alley did adjoin. It approved the idea that if the hole was "so situated that a person lawfully using the thoroughfare, and, in a reasonable manner, was liable to fall into it, the defendant was liable."[11]

The court did not have to rule this way. It could have defined adjoining pits as pits that literally border on public land. Or it could have said that seven feet was simply too far away to make a landowner liable. But the court offered a better decision. As in *Lyman,* it produced a workable distinction between injuries to deliberate trespassers and to those who reasonably attempt to use either their own space or the public's space. Just as in the *Lyman* and *Hoffman* decisions, the judges in *Beck v. Carter* chose as they did because their values, their beliefs about desirable and undesirable social relations,

[10]As an aside, you might try at this point to define property. You should observe from this example that, legally speaking, property is not so much what people hold title to as it is what the law says they can and cannot do with a thing, whether they hold title to it or not.

[11]*Beck v. Carter,* 68 N.Y. 283 (1876), p. 293.

led them to this conclusion. If they deeply believed in the absolute sanctity of private property, ambiguity in common law would certainly have given them freedom to say, "Land owners must be free to do what they wish with their land. Carter's pit was entirely on his private land, separated from the thoroughfare. Therefore Carter owed Beck no duty of care."

The Diving Board

Before you proceed, note how these two principal cases, reduced to their simplest terms, combine to form a seemingly comprehensive statement of law: When the plaintiff's deliberate act is not proved a trespass on the defendant's property, then the defendant owes the plaintiff a duty of care *(Hoffman)*. Furthermore, when the plaintiff accidentally but conclusively does trespass on the defendant's property, but the defendant should have foreseen the injury from such accidental trespass, the defendant is also liable *(Beck)*. Thus arises the final question: What result should a court reach when the plaintiff deliberately and unambiguously trespasses on the defendant's property and is injured?

On another summer day in New York, July 8, 1916, Harvey Hynes and two friends had gone swimming at a favorite spot along the Bronx bank of the then relatively unpolluted Harlem River. For five years they and other swimmers had dived from a makeshift plank nailed to the wooden bulkhead along the river.

The electrified line of the New York Central Railroad ran along the river. The power line was suspended over the track between poles, half of which ran between the track and the river. Legally the railroad owned the strip of river bank containing track, poles, wires, and bulkhead. Hence, about half of the 16-foot diving board touched or extended over the railroad's land while the rest reached out, at a height of about three feet, over the surface of the public river.

As Harvey prepared to dive, one of the railroad's overhead supports for the power line suddenly broke loose from the pole, bringing down with it the writhing electric line that powered the trains. The wires struck Harvey, throwing him from the board. His friends pulled him dead from the waters of the Harlem River.

Harvey's mother sued the railroad for the damages caused by its alleged negligence in maintaining the supports for the wire. Conceding that the New York Central's mainte-nance of the supports failed to meet the "reasonable man" standard of care, the trial court and the intermediate appel-late court nevertheless denied her claim. Harvey was a tres-passer, a deliberate trespasser, and property owners have no duty to protect such trespassers from harm.

Before proceeding further, reflect on the cases of the cherry tree and the pit because you are about to see these rather distantly related cases, two cases among thousands that had tried to thrash out the borderline between property and tort, merge as key precedents in the final *Hynes* decision.

The lawyers for the railroad presented a battery of cases in their favor. They cited *Hoffman* to show that, while perched on the board, even if he was over the river, Harvey trespassed, because the board was attached to the railroad's land. They also cited cases, *Beck* among them, to establish the point that the trespass was not a temporary and involuntary move from a public space but a sustained series of deliberate trespasses onto the defendant's land.

Three of the justices on New York's highest court agreed. The railroad had no duty of care to this trespasser. But a ma-jority of four, led by Cardozo, supported Harvey's mother and reversed.

Cardozo cited relatively few precedents. He did, how-ever, cite *Hoffman* and *Beck,* but not in the way the railroad's lawyers had hoped. The lawyers tried to convince the judges that a mechanical rule commanded a decision for the railroad. Anything, a cherry tree or a diving board, belongs to the rail-road if it is affixed to the railroad's land, regardless of what it overhangs. Therefore, Harvey, at the time the wires struck him, trespassed. Since the trespass was deliberate, *Beck* com-mands a decision for the railroad.

Cardozo, however, appealed to the deeper spirit of these cases, a spirit that rejects mechanical rules like the root rule for determining ownership of cherry trees. He cited *Hoffman*

not for its reasoning but for its result: There was no real trespass. The spirit requires enunciating policy—law—that corresponds to a deeper sense of how society ought to regulate
rights and responsibilities in this legal, as well as physical,
borderland. He wrote:

> This case is a striking instance of the dangers of "a jurispru-
> dence of conceptions" (Pound, "Mechanical Jurispru-
> dence," 8 *Columbia Law Review*, 605, 608, 610), the extension
> of a maxim or a definition with relentless disregard of con-
> sequences to . . . "a dryly logical extreme." The approximate
> and relative become the definite and absolute. Land-
> owners are not bound to regulate their conduct in contem-
> plation of the presence of trespassers intruding upon pri-
> vate structures. Landowners *are* bound to regulate their
> conduct in contemplation of the presence of travelers
> upon the adjacent public ways. There are times when there
> is little trouble in marking off the field of exemption and
> immunity from that of liability and duty. Here structures
> and ways are so united and commingled, superimposed
> upon each other, that the fields are brought together. In
> such circumstances, there is little help in pursuing general
> maxims to ultimate conclusions. They have been framed *alio
> intuitu*. They must be reformulated and readapted to meet
> exceptional conditions. Rules appropriate to spheres which
> are conceived of as separate and distinct cannot, both, be
> enforced when the spheres become concentric. There must
> then be readjustment or collision. In one sense, and that a
> highly technical and artificial one, the diver at the end of
> the springboard is an intruder on the adjoining lands. In
> another sense, and one that realists will accept more readily,
> he is still on public waters in the exercise of public rights.
> The law must say whether it will subject him to the rule of
> the one field or of the other, of this sphere or of that. We
> think that considerations of analogy, of convenience, of pol-
> icy, and of justice, exclude him from the field of the de-
> fendant's immunity and exemption, and place him in the
> field of liability and duty. . . .[12]

[12]*Hynes v. New York Central R.R.*, 231 N.Y. 229 (1921), pp. 235–236. How
should a judge, following *Hynes*, rule in a case identical to *Hoffman* except that
Abner picks cherries from the branches overhanging his yard and that, to stop
him, Sarah shoots him in the leg with a .22 pistol?

Note again the effect of fact freedom on judicial choices. Although they wrote no dissenting opinion, we can make an intelligent guess that the dissenters in *Hynes* reasoned from *Hoffman* this way: "The fact is that the diving board grew from the railroad's land. If the cherry tree growing from Hoffman's land belongs to him, then the board belongs to the railroad." But Cardozo in effect responds, "The important fact is that Sarah didn't really trespass. Just as she used what didn't clearly belong to Abner, so these boys diving into the river from a board over the river didn't really interfere with the railroad's property." Reason in law does not allow us to call one approach legally right and the other legally wrong. After all, with a switch in one vote, *Hynes* would produce a very different legal precedent. However, by recognizing that ethics and values determine choices, we do free ourselves to say that one choice is better, another worse, and to justify why we feel that way.

These cases reveal the inevitability of ambiguity, fact freedom, and choice in the legal process. They teach at least three additional lessons about the analysis of cases, about changing judicial styles, and about the way law itself changes.

Analyzing Cases

For the better part of a century, students of law, both in law schools and in college courses, have paid special attention to the opinions of appellate courts. In 1930 Professor Arthur L. Goodhart published what has turned out to be one of the more popular methods for reading an opinion and discerning its meaning. I shall paraphrase his statement of the method for locating what he calls the principle or *ratio decidendi* of the case. Think about the preceding cases as you read, and you will see why Goodhart's well-known method gives a very misleading view of legal reasoning. I shall explain why in a moment. Here is the paraphrase of Goodhart:[13]

[13]Arthur L. Goodhart, "Determining the *Ratio Decidenci* of a Case," 40 *Yale Law Journal* 161 (1930).

1. We cannot determine the principle, the essential legal meaning of a case, simply by examining the reasons the judge gives in the opinion. Sometimes judges state reasons that don't logically relate on close examination to the legal issue; sometimes judges never state the reasons that produce the result.
2. We cannot determine the principle only by articulating the rule of law set forth in the case. This is because judges often state legal rules in very general terms—landowners have no duty to trespassers—when the facts of the case raise a much more precise and delimited question.
3. We cannot, moreover, find the principle by looking at all the facts in the case, for some of the facts have no legal significance. Had Sarah Hoffman's parents instead christened her Griselda or if Harvey had been a girl, the result, we devoutly hope, would not have been different.
4. We *can* find the principle of a case by examining the facts that the deciding judge treats as material and his rulings of law based on these material facts.
5. In doing so we must also take account of the facts the judge determines do not matter, facts the judge determines to be immaterial.

Think about how Cardozo treated *Hoffman* and *Beck*. Does Goodhart's method accurately describe how Cardozo found the meaning, the precedential value, in these cases? The basic problem with Goodhart's method is that it asks us to determine the principle of a case in the abstract, by reading it. But a judge starts from a very different place. The judge starts always with a new case, a legal conflict he must resolve. He inevitably looks at any precedent from the frame of reference provided by the new facts before him. By Goodhart's method the principle of the final *Hoffman* opinion would look something like this: To collect the fruit of a tree overhanging your property you must introduce evidence that the roots also intrude into your land. Neither Cardozo nor the dissenters, confronted with the problem of liability for Harvey's death, saw the case that way at all. The meaning of cases, then, emerges only as judges compare them and use them.

Professor Julius Stone has, crisply if rather primly, criticized the Goodhart method this way:

> The assumption that "the material facts" will thus yield only one *ratio* would imply, if true, that there is only one set of such "material facts" which is to be related to the holding. And this immediately confronts the theory with a main difficulty. This is that, apart from any explicit or implicit assertion of materiality by the precedent court, there will always be more than one, and indeed many, competing versions of "the material facts"; and there will therefore not be merely one but many *rationes,* any of which will explain the holding on those facts, and no one of which therefore is strictly *necessary* to explain it. For apart from any selection by the precedent court, all the logical possibilities remain open; and in the logician's sense it is possible to draw as many general propositions from a given decision (each of which will "explain" it) as there are possible combinations of distinguishable facts in it. It is in these terms that, it has been said, the question—What single principle does a particular case establish? is "strictly nonsensical, that is, inherently incapable of being answered." . . .
>
> Yet these are not the most crucial difficulties with Professor Goodhart's system. The crucial ones arise rather from the several alternative *levels of statement* of each "material fact" of the precedent case, ranging from the full unique concreteness of that actual case, through a series of widening generalisations. In this series only the unique concreteness is *firmly* anchored to the precedent court's view that a given Fact A is "material"; and *ex hypothesi* that level of unique concreteness can scarcely figure as a part of the binding *ratio* for other cases. By the same token the reach of the *ratio,* even after each "material fact" seen by the original court is identified, will vary with the level of generalisation at which "the fact-element" is stated. How then is the "correct" level of statement of each fact-element to be ascertained by the later court?[14]

[14]Julius Stone, *Legal System and Lawyers' Reasonings* (Stanford: Stanford University Press, 1964), pp. 269, 272.

The distinction between letter and spirit that separates Cardozo from his dissenters in *Hynes* perfectly illustrates Stone's point about indeterminate levels of factual meaning.

How then, does one analyze cases? One analyzes them only on an incremental, comparative basis, only through reasoning by example.

Changing Judicial Styles

We can detect a shift in style—the basic sense of what common law is all about—in these cases. We might label this style change with the question, "Whatever happened to Bouvier's *Institutes?*" Judges are today more conscious of their responsibility to shape the law so as to promote cooperation and of the importance of social background facts. They are less likely to hide behind a formal statement of law in a treatise, a commentary, or a common law principle. Do they indeed carry this style too far in the discretionary direction? We shall return to this question in the final section of this chapter.

Change in Law Itself

Before reading further in this subsection, consider the general change in the borderline law of property and tort the preceding cases describe.

Do they not narrow the freedom one has for doing as one pleases with one's land and expand our obligation to avoid hurting others? The shift in the last 50 years from a legal philosophy whose principles emphasize property rights and individualism to a system that promotes social caring and cooperation is as major a change as our legal system has ever experienced, at least in so short a time. The case at the end of this chapter will illustrate the trend further. Do you believe that, if such a change is occurring in our law, it corresponds to a more fundamental shift in public sentiments recognizing interdependence and acknowledging our collective obligation to share and help rather than compete? If so, then common law here has passed at least the minimal test of changing to reflect changing social values.

But how, over a period of time, does change in law occur? Some legal scholars say that law changes in a circular way. Basic concepts, much less crisp and precise than legal rules, build up in law as cases accumulate, but then disappear when, as they become rigid, they prove too inflexible to accommodate new ideas. Levi describes it this way:

> In the long run a circular motion can be seen. The first stage is the creation of the legal concept which is built up as cases are compared. The period is one in which the court fumbles for a phrase. Several phrases may be tried out; the misuse or misunderstanding of words itself may have an effect. The concept sounds like another, and the jump to the second is made. The second stage is the period when the concept is more or less fixed, although reasoning by example continues to classify items inside and out of the concept. The third stage is the breakdown of the concept, as reasoning by example has moved so far ahead as to make it clear that the suggestive influence of the word is no longer desired.[15]

Levi illustrates the point by describing the emergence and later decay of the legal concept known as the "inherently dangerous" rule. The courts had, for several decades in the beginning of this century, held manufacturers of products legally liable to people who were hurt by *negligently* manufactured items only if (1) the injured person was the one who actually contracted the purchase of the product or (2) the product was "inherently dangerous."

No doubt, legal concepts do move in and out of law in much the way Levi describes. The history of the inherently dangerous rule, studied carefully, makes fascinating reading.[16] Many texts in legal process have reprinted it. I must, however, voice two related cautionary notes.

First, the neatness of Levi's thesis and illustration that

---

[15]Edward H. Levi, *An Introduction to Legal Reasoning* (Chicago: University of Chicago Press, 1949), pp. 8–9.

[16]Not too surprisingly, the hero in the dispatch of the inherently dangerous rule was Benjamin Cardozo, writing in *MacPherson v. Buick,* decided in the year of Harvey's death, 217 N.Y. 382 (1916). Cardozo's principal tactic for discrediting the concept was to deny that it ever really existed in the first place.

makes it such an appealing addition to textbooks also makes the model seem universal when it is not. The more typical model of legal change must accommodate the fact that common law can evolve by a process of fumbling from one half-formed concept to another without ever moving through Levi's crystallized stage. The second *Hoffman* opinion's deliberate ignoring of *Lyman* and Cardozo's creative use of *Hoffman* in *Hynes* to recover the spirit of *Lyman* illustrate my point.

Second, do not lose sight of Levi's own qualification of the model. Even when concepts in law do crystallize, they do not automatically resolve cases. The facts of the case, as we have seen, may permit the judge to invoke a variety of different concepts, some of them crystallized and some of them created spontaneously. Which one he chooses, and hence the impact of his decision on change in law, is still very much a function of fact freedom.

In summary, concepts do exist in law. Often they turn out to be sufficiently fixed and stable so that lawyers can engineer from them secure plans for their clients. At any given time for any given problem, however, lawyers must initially be prepared to contend with changing, uncertain, or competing concepts rather than fixed law.

KEEPING THE COMMON LAW TRADITION ALIVE

The preceding section introduces the most typical common law judicial problem, one in which precedents provide some guidance but do not automatically resolve problems. In the typical situation, the judge faces an array of precedents, some of which may seem inconsistent, some seem imaginative, and others wedded to past "truths" in common law. None of them necessarily controls, so the judge must make a choice. Sometimes the precedent or principle he chooses gives him no more than a point of departure from which to justify the unexpressed beliefs and values that determine the result. Precedents in many cases are vehicles for rationalizations.

Sometimes, however, a genuinely new problem arises,

one to which precedents prove so remote, so factually different, that the judge cannot build his rationalizations on them.
He must then realize that a decision for either party in the
case will create not a new variation on older law but a new
and different law, a new and different definition of how
people should relate to one another. In other situations, the
reverse happens. The judge faces a precedent so factually similar to the one before him that he cannot distinguish or ignore
it. If he chooses to reach a new result, he must overrule the
precedent.

This section answers questions involving these less typical judicial problems: How should judges proceed when they
cannot find common law cases that seem to apply to the case
before them? When should they make common law from
whole cloth? In what circumstances should courts choose deliberately to reject a case or principle that controls the case
before it? How, in other words, does stare decisis operate in
common law?

Answers to these questions depend, as did much of the
analysis in Chapter III, on what we think about the proper
balance between judicial and legislative lawmaking. What
kinds of problems require the kind of fact-gathering and
value-balancing techniques available to legislatures but not
courts? What types of problems require, for their solution, the
creation of complex administrative planning and enforcement apparatus that only legislatures can create, fund, and
supervise?

You may have already discerned my own general approach to the problem of judicial-legislative balance. Let me
make it explicit here. Courts and legislatures have much in
common. They both gather evidence in a systematic way,
courts through witnesses at trial and through the briefs of the
parties on appeal, and legislatures through committee hearings and the many other efforts of lobbyists. Both institutions
do so, at least formally, in an open-minded way. Courts hear
both sides. Our adversary system requires it. Legislatures also
hear competing arguments in committee hearings and in the
vying efforts of lobbies. Furthermore, we acknowledge that
both courts and legislatures possess lawmaking power. People

who look to law to plan their affairs know they should look to both institutions to find final answers. Finally, politics influences both branches of government. Many state judges win office by election. Politicians appoint federal judges and those state judges in nonelective posts, so political restraints affect both.

In Chapter V, we will address some important political differences. Nevertheless, *judges should always presume themselves competent to take the lawmaking initiative when the legislature has not spoken clearly to them.* In other words, because as a general matter courts and legislatures have a similar authority and competence, the burden of proof always rests on the party that argues for the court to remain silent because the legislature is better qualified to speak.

Keeping the Tradition Alive: Making New Common Law

In early March 1928, two seagoing tug boats towing barges of coal set out in good weather from Norfolk, Virginia, bound for New York. About midnight on March 8, under fair skies but with the barometer falling slightly, the tugs passed the Delaware Breakwater, a safe haven for tugs and barges caught in bad weather. The next morning, however, the wind began to freshen. By noon, gale force winds blew up heavy seas. Early in the afternoon two barges sprung leaks. Their crews signaled the tugs that they would proceed to anchor the barges and ride out the storm. They did so, but conditions steadily worsened. The Coast Guard heroically rescued the crews of both barges late in the day. The dawn light on March 10 revealed no trace of the barges. By then, both the barges and their cargoes rested on the ocean floor.

The coal owners sued the barge company alleging both that the company had breached its contract of carriage and that the unseaworthiness of the barges made it liable for the loss of the coal. The barge company in turn sued the tug boat owners for the loss of both the coal and the two barges. The barge owners claimed that the two tugs had not properly handled the cargo. More precisely, they claimed that the tug owners should bear the total loss because they had not provided their tugs with conventional AM radio receivers.

At trial, the barge owners established several critical facts. On March 8 the Arlington weather bureau broadcast a 10:00 a.m. prediction calling for shifting and increasing winds the following day. Another ship in the vicinity of the tugs and barges had received this report on its AM radio. At 10:00 p.m. on the same day, the Arlington bureau predicted "increasing east and southeast winds, becoming fresh to strong Friday night and increasing cloudiness followed by rain on Friday." On the basis of the morning report, one tug owner towing cargo in the vicinity had anchored at the Delaware Break-water. Even the captain of the defendant tug conceded at trial that, had he heard the evening report, he would have done the same.

Place yourself in the position of a judge resolving this case. In your first step, aided by the arguments of the lawyers, you try to discover how much, if any, of this problem the law already makes clear. You soon find that the law of admiralty—a branch of common law for our purposes—imposes an abso-lute liability on ship owners for the loss of cargoes in their ships if unseaworthiness of the ship caused the loss. Note that this unseaworthiness doctrine does not simply extend the law of negligence to the sea. The ship owner may have no knowl-edge of the faulty condition. It may have been impossible even for a reasonable and prudent man to prevent the unseaworthy condition—hidden rot in some of a hull's wooden planking, for example. The rule creates a guarantee of seaworthiness.

But is a ship that does not carry a radio in 1928 therefore unseaworthy because it won't receive weather reports? On this point the law gives no help. You find that Congress has passed a statute requiring steamers carrying more than 50 passengers to carry two-way radios so that they can call for help and re-ceive information, but the statute does not include tugs and barges. You find no precedents whatsoever linking seaworthi-ness with possession of radios or any other new invention. At this point you have several choices.

CHOICE ONE:

Congress in its wisdom chose not to require two-way short-wave radios of tugs and barges. Furthermore, Congress has made no law requiring AM radios. Therefore, Congress has

intended that tugs without AM radios are seaworthy and
the tug owners are not liable for the loss.

CHOICE TWO:
I find no law requiring receiving sets. Since legislatures, not
the courts, are the lawmakers in our democratic nation, I
have no legal authority to find the tug owners liable. Therefore they are not liable.

You can, I trust, reject both these choices immediately.
Choice one possesses many of the evils described in Chapter
III. We have no evidence whatsoever that Congress thought
about AM receivers, much less intended or decided to pass a
statute calling tugs without them nevertheless seaworthy. We
could just as easily conclude that the statute recognizes the
general importance of radios in improving navigation safety.
Therefore, the statute gives ship owners a positive signal that
they should seriously examine whether radios can help them
navigate better. If you have any further doubts about the weakness of the first choice, consider the fact that no congressional
statute required tugs to carry compasses.

The second choice conflicts with the common law tradition. Courts do continue to make law as conditions change;
courts have specifically fashioned the principles of admiralty
and of seaworthiness within admiralty law over the years.

CHOICE THREE:
I admit that judges retain their general lawmaking power in
admiralty. In this case, however, only a legislature can decide whether ships must carry radios. Only through legislative hearings could we learn, for example, how common it
was in 1928 for people to own radios. It would hardly be
fair to hold the tug owners liable if, in 1928, radios were
only novel. Similarly, only legislative hearings can learn
whether shipowners themselves carry radios and think it
wise or necessary to do so. If they do, then the fact dictates
a new policy of seaworthiness, but we can't tell. As in ancient common law, custom may hold the key to justice, but
only a legislature today is equipped to find the key.

The third choice may sound like an improvement, but
it's not. Its major premise, that courts can't obtain the facts, is

false. The actual case, from which this example is derived, shows that the courts were able to make the necessary factual determinations.[17] The brief for the cargo owners documented the phenomenal growth in the sales of radios, over 1,000 percent between 1922 and 1928. It quoted Frederick Lewis Allen's *Only Yesterday* (1931): "At the age of three and a half years, radio broadcasting had attained its majority. Behind those figures of radio sales lies a whole chapter of the life of the Postwar Decade: radio penetrating every third home in the country; giant broadcasting stations with nation-wide hook-ups. . . ."[18] The cargo owners also elicited testimony on the witness stand from one tug captain to the effect that, although only one tug line required radios, at least 90 percent of the tugs had them, if only for entertainment.

The lesson here is critically important. As a rule, courts can find background facts as effectively as can legislatures. We applaud the adversary system in courts precisely because we believe it gives lawyers the incentive to present the fullest possible range of facts to support their position. Legislatures may prove superior lawmakers where complex problems require a simultaneous set of solutions and the means to coordinate them, but well-established judicial practices allow courts in cases like this one to determine the background facts that determine whether a given legal choice is wise and fair.

> CHOICES FOUR AND FIVE:
>
> Custom is a time-honored source of common law. In this case it has been convincingly shown that tugs customarily carry radios. Radio has become a part of our everyday lives. The absence of the radios in this case caused the loss.
>
> Custom is a time-honored source of common law. In this

---

[17]*The T.J. Hooper,* 60 F.2d 737 (2nd Cir. 1932). As is customary in admiralty law, the name of the ship whose seaworthiness is questioned provides the name of the case.

[18]Quoted in Henry M. Hart and Albert M. Sacks, *The Legal Process* (Cambridge: Harvard Law School, 1958), pp. 432–433. My selection of illustrative cases in this section draws heavily upon the much larger variety of cases that Hart and Sacks provide. Although I use these cases for somewhat different purposes, I cannot improve upon their choice of working materials; here, as elsewhere, I am much indebted to them.

case it has been convincingly shown that a majority of tug owners do not customarily require radios. Since we cannot say that the customs of the sea require radios, we cannot conclude that the absence of a radio in this case caused the loss.

Choices four and five are improvements over earlier choices. They are better judicial choices because they do not shrink from judicial responsibility for lawmaking. They succeed where the other choices failed in that they create a clear rule to guide future conduct. But, of course, you should still feel unsatisfied, for custom appears to produce two contradictory results. How should you choose between them?

CHOICE SIX:

Is it then a final answer that the business had not yet generally adopted receiving sets? There are, no doubt, cases where courts seem to make the general practice of the calling the standard of proper diligence. . . . Indeed, in most cases reasonable prudence is in fact common prudence; but strictly it is never its measure; a whole calling may have unduly lagged in the adoption of new and available devices. It may never set its own tests, however persuasive be its usages. Courts must in the end say what is required; there are precautions so imperative that even their universal disregard will not excuse their omission. . . . We hold the tugs . . . had they been properly equipped . . . would have got the Arlington reports. The injury was a direct consequence of this unseaworthiness.

The language of choice six speaks with a power and persuasiveness the other choices lack because it is Judge Learned Hand's, taken from his opinion finally disposing of the case.[19]

---

[19]*The T.J. Hooper*, p. 740. The problem illustrated in this case is a perennial one in law. It has recently appeared in a case in which the victim of a nighttime mugging in the parking lot of a private shopping center sued the owners, claiming the parking lot was not adequately illuminated. And should Johnson & Johnson, the makers of Tylenol, be held liable for the deaths caused in the first known "tampering" case (in 1982) because Tylenol was not packaged in tamper-proof containers? Tamper-proof technology had been available for many years. The simple paper tax seal on a liquor bottle, although it served a different purpose initially, is such a technology.

Hand's choice sets a clear standard, one that, anticipating the certain further growth of the radio industry, would occur sooner or later. Note, however, that with the exception of choice four, any other choice could well have created a precedent that would delay considerably any judicial decision requiring tugs to carry radios. These choices say tugs don't need to carry radios. Judicial change would require overruling any of these alternative decisions. In short, the timid and deferential judge potentially creates a common law precedent with just as much policy impact as does the active judge.

Above all, Hand's choice avoids the problem of lawmaking by default. Judges can never know whether or when or how Congress will act on any but dramatic national issues. Courts that wait for better legislative solutions may wait for a solution that never comes. Do you disagree with Hand's choice? Is it not the court's proven capacity to establish the facts about the use of radios, coupled with Hand's sound ethical judgment that tugs ought to carry radios, that makes his opinion persuasive?

Keeping the Tradition Alive:
Horizontal Stare Decisis in Common Law

There remains the final common law problem category of horizontal stare decisis. How should judges respond to precedents that seem completely to cover and control the outcomes of cases before them? Lawyers label these precedents "precisely in point" or "on all fours with the case at bar." The existence of these precedents does not, however, contradict the concept that law remains ambiguous. Judges always choose the results. Some judges, faced with a precedent that produces an unwanted conclusion, will choose to ignore it, much to the anger of the losing lawyer. A judge always retains the choice to overrule or to refuse deliberately to follow a precedent, even when he doesn't choose to ignore it. Choices remain. However, they no longer resemble choices reasoned by example. Instead, ideally, they rest on choices of purpose much like those discussed in Chapter III. The purposes of stare decisis, as we have seen, are to promote legal stability, to protect honest reliance, to preserve efficient judicial administration, to maintain similar treatment of persons similarly situated, and to promote public confidence in courts. The judge must always decide whether adherence to a precedent will accomplish any of these values.

Chapters II and III detailed the theory of stare decisis. We may here proceed to illustrations of the same theory in the common law context.

First Illustration:
Rightly Adhering to Precedent Because
the Need for Stability and Reliance Is Present

The law of tort, especially the law of negligence, creates enticing moral questions because, almost by definition in the case of negligence, courts apply the law only when it has in fact failed to control how people behave. The negligent driver simply does not plan to have or avoid an accident based on his knowledge of negligence law, even if he has some understanding of it. As a result, negligence law does not, unless the expectations expressed in an insurance contract are thwarted, confront a judge with the problem of upsetting someone's expectations if he changes the law. Negligence law defines when someone owes someone else a remedy for a past wrong, and this focus leads inevitably to the moral question of how man ought to relate to his fellow man.

The need for stability in law more often exists with respect to laws that deal with people's business and contractual relations and with their related planning of the use and disposition of their property. Here we may not reach ultimate moral questions so quickly. When plans depend on law, the law's philosophical shortcomings may not justify changing it. We therefore temporarily abandon tort law and turn to one very small problem in a very complicated subject, the law of business contracts.

Contracts, among many other items, are agreements among businesspeople that allow them to formalize their buying and selling of each other's goods and services. Plans involving millions or even billions of dollars can rest on such agreements. For example, a construction company specializing in high-rise office buildings may conditionally contract with a supplier of steel to buy steel at a given price in order to know what to bid on a construction project. If the company receives the award, its entire profit margin could disappear if its steel supplier at the last minute insisted on a higher price for the steel.

But what legal rules convert an ordinary agreement— He: "Can you come to dinner at my place at 8:00?" She: "I'd love to! See you then."—into a legally binding contract? In early common law, if a written agreement contained the impression of a promise-making person's seal in wax, then the beneficiary of the promise could hold him to his promise. Men wore signet rings etched with their sign, their seal, with which to impress the wax. The only exception for a time was the king. He sealed the wax on his agreements with the impression of his front teeth. Gradually the use of wax, seals, and front teeth declined, to the point where printing the word "seal" or the letters "L.S." (for the Latin *locus sigilli*) created the contractual tie.

Today, seals do not make agreements legally binding: half the American states have passed statutes abolishing the seal. But, in many jurisdictions in the past and in some today, when people have sealed their contract (perhaps simply by adding at the end "Seal" or "L.S."), the law has made it very difficult for the contracting parties to dispute it. The law has rendered it difficult if not impossible to argue that the contract has been made fraudulently or to prove that the promisor has already performed the act he promised.

Long after agreements became enforceable in law without a seal, the law preserved some of the special rigidities for those contracts with seals. In one specific example, unlike an unsealed contract, only the person named in a sealed contract can be held to it. When, for example, a buyer seeks to disguise his interest by having another contract for him, using the agent's name but remaining the interested party, he along with the agent may find himself bound, but only if the contract of sale bears no seal. The sealed purchase contract, on the other hand, would only bind the agent named in it, not the interested party.

Businesspeople regularly transact business through agents. Sometimes, and this is particularly true in commercial real estate transactions, a businessperson will fund another to buy or sell property for him. He will fund the agent but insist that the agent assume all the responsibilities of the contract. The legal name for such a backer is "undisclosed principal." This technique of preserving anonymity is not necessarily unfair to the other side. If someone buys up various lots in an area in order to build a factory in his own name, the owners approached last may insist on a highly inflated price, knowing that if the buyer fails to get the last lot in order to proceed, all his other purchases will become meaningless.

Beginning in the nineteenth century, by both statute and judicial decision, the legal gap between the protections of sealed and unsealed contracts began to narrow. However, in the 1920s, this New York case arose. In a contract under seal, an agent agreed to buy land without naming an undisclosed principal. The seller agreed, but the agent shortly thereafter withdrew from the agreement. The seller, having learned the name of the principal, sued the principal. He asked the judge to order the principal to pay for the land and accept the deed.

The court ruled for the defendant. It noted many New York precedents limiting the significance of a seal on a contract. Nevertheless it concluded:

> We find no authority for the proposition that a contract under seal may be turned into the simple contract of a person not in any way appearing on its face to be a party to or interested in it, ... and we do not feel at liberty to extend the doctrine applied to simple contracts executed by an agent for an unnamed principal so as to embrace this case....
>
> Neither do we find any authority since 1876 in this court for the proposition. *Briggs v. Partridge*[20] has been cited by us many times with no hint of disapproval.... We repeat that we do not feel at liberty to change a rule so well understood and so often enforced. If such a change is to be made it must be by legislative fiat....
>
> .... Thousands of sealed instruments must have been

---

[20]*Briggs v. Partridge,* 64 N.Y. 357 (1876).

executed in reliance upon the authority of *Briggs v. Partridge.* Many times the seal must have been used for the express purpose of relieving the undisclosed principal from personal liability. It may not be unwise to preserve the distinction for this especial purpose. But whether wise or unwise the distinction now exists.[21]

Any doctrine, stare decisis included, has impact only when it leads to action not likely otherwise. Stare decisis affects judicial choices when, because of judges' commitment to it, they reach decisions they might in general terms think to be poorly constructed law.

In many respects it is inequitable to allow the undisclosed principal to avoid contractual responsibility because of a seal. New York's Justice Crane, who did not participate in the *Crowley* decision, wrote:

> Thus, if an unsealed contract to sell real estate is signed by the agent in his own name, and the fact that he is acting for another and not for himself appears nowhere upon the face of it, the real principal can always sue and be sued upon the instrument. But if it should happen that the printed letters "L.S." appear after the agent's name, all would be different. The principal could neither sue nor be sued. The absurdity of this is apparent upon the face of the statement, and the danger and pitfall of such a doctrine in business transactions is realized when we pause to consider how many printed forms of agreements have the letters "L.S." stamped upon them, or how easy it is to make the scroll.[22]

But another justice who joined the *Crowley* opinion, Benjamin Cardozo, later praised the result:

> The rule was settled at common law that an undisclosed principal might not be held to liability upon a contract which had been executed under seal. Much of the law as to seals has small relation in society as now organized to present-day realities. The question came up whether we would

---

[21]*Crowley v. Lewis,* 239 N.Y. 264 (1925), pp. 265–267.
[22]Frederick E. Crane, "The Magic of the Private Seal," 15 *Columbia Law Review* 24 (1915), pp. 34–35.

adhere to the rule that I have mentioned, or hold it to have faded away with the fading significance of seals. The decision was that the old rule would be enforced. Precedents of recent date made departure difficult if *stare decisis* was not to be abandoned altogether, but there were other and deeper grounds of policy. Contracts had been made and transactions closed on the faith of the law as it had been theretofore declared. Men had taken title in the names of "dummies," and through them executed deeds and mortgages with the understanding, shared by the covenantees, that liability on the covenant would be confined to the apparent principal. They had done this honestly and without concealment. Something might be said, too, in favor of the social utility of a device by which the liability of the apparent principal could be substituted without elaborate forms for the liability of another back of him who was to reap the profits of the transaction. The law has like devices for limiting liability in other situations, as *e.g.*, in joint stock associations, corporations, and limited partnerships. In any event retrospective change would be unjust. The evil, if it was one, was to be eradicated by statute.[23]

Both Crane and Cardozo are in a sense correct. The rule may work to an unfair advantage, and it is the place of courts, not just legislatures, to minimize unfair advantages in law. However, the court rightly left legal change to the legislature because it understood that many businessmen, without acting unfairly, regularly employed that legal technique in planning their affairs. Judicial action would upset existing plans made by fair men, but the legislature would make law for the future. This difference, not a difference in lawmaking authority, gives the *Crowley* decision its wisdom.

[23]Benjamin N. Cardozo, *The Paradoxes of Legal Science* (New York: Columbia University Press, 1928), pp. 70–71. More recently, the development of a new golf course by golfer Jack Nicklaus almost failed because land prices surged when news of the development leaked out. See "A Golfer Becomes an Executive," *Wall Street Journal,* 27 January 1987, p. 33.

Second Illustration:
Rightly Overruling Because No Need
for Stability or Reliance Exists

Here we return to and further explore the borderland between tort and property. The common law distinguished between trespassers and guests, invitees in legal language. Had
Carter invited Beck onto Carter's land, Carter would without
question have become liable to Beck for injuries he suffered
by tripping and falling into the hole Carter negligently left
uncovered. The New York Central, had it sponsored a swim-a-
thon on the banks of the Harlem, would have been liable for
Harvey's death.

Common law also created a third category, that of licensee, a person who receives permission to use land or whose
entry upon property the owner expressly or by implication
tolerates. The common law rules of negligence applied equally
to trespassers and licensees: The landowner owed no duty to
protect the safety of either one.

In the early 1880s, a policeman, Officer Parker, entered
a building at night to check suspicious activities. In the gloom
he did not see an open and unprotected elevator shaft. He
fell, suffered serious injuries, and sued the building's owner,
Mr. Barnard, for damages.

In preparing the lawsuit, Parker's attorney obviously
confronted the common law rule, stated in many decisions of
the courts in Massachusetts, where the accident occurred. His
client was a prototypical licensee. Barnard had not invited
him onto the premises, but surely Barnard willingly allowed
policemen to enter the building to protect his property. Fortunately, the lawyer discovered that Massachusetts had a criminal statute imposing a fine and/or jail for any owner of a building whose elevator well was not "protected by a good and
substantial railing." Although the statute said nothing about
civil liability in tort to those who were injured, Parker's lawyer
used the statute to argue that the courts should abandon licensee precedents in such cases.

He argued first that the common law rule denying recovery to licensees was unfair and outdated and that modern notions of one person's obligation to another ought to encompass keeping your property safe for people you want or allow to use it. He urged that, in tort, the main legal question for the court is a moral one: Either Mr. Parker or Mr. Barnard must pay the medical bills for Parker's injuries. Generalizing from this situation, should not the person at fault, the person who could have prevented the injuries in the first place, bear the burden?

Barnard's attorney, of course, had an answer to that question: No. This is simultaneously a problem in property rights, one in which the utility of stare decisis is traditionally recognized. Many property owners decide how to maintain their property and to avoid the expense of eliminating dangers precisely because they do not expect guests to expose themselves to the dangers. It is unfair to Barnard to change the rules. Had he known this rule in advance, he might have arranged for the railing or taken out insurance to cover losses to licensees.

Parker's attorney responded as anticipated: Regardless of the general need for reliance in common law, including such a need regarding the use of property, in this case what Barnard did was a crime. Obviously it cannot be said that the legislature intended Parker to recover, but it can be said that the criminal statute told Barnard to install the railing. Barnard cannot claim he had no duty to erect the railing. He had! Although the criminal statute does not control this civil case, its purpose includes protecting those who enter an unfamiliar building in the dark, a category that certainly includes Officer Parker.

The court agreed with Parker. It said simply:

> The fact that there was a penalty imposed by the statute for neglect of duty in regard to the railing and protection of the elevator well does not exonerate those responsible therefor from such liability. . . .
>
> As a general rule, where an act is enjoined or forbidden under a statutory penalty, and the failure to do the act enjoined or the doing of the act forbidden has contributed to an injury, the party thus in default is liable therefor to

the party injured, notwithstanding he may also be subject to a penalty. . . . [24]

The court thus created a new rule. It did so rightly because, given the criminal statute, the excuse for reliance on the older rule diminished.

Third Illustration:
Wrongly Overruling When Stability Is Preferable

Should a court in the future follow the *Parker* decision? Note this subtle but important point. If we assume that the basic rule of *Parker* is correct, then it would not matter even if the *Parker* decision did wrongly upset reliance interests. If we believe that owners should pay for injuries to licensees as a general matter, then we may want to follow precedents that boldly state such a rule, even if, for reliance reasons, the court's boldness was unwise. The new decision becomes law. It undercuts the support that honest men have for relying on an outdated rule. Similarly, if the *Crowley* court had boldly done away with the ability of businessmen to hide their interests in sealed contracts, we would want courts to follow the decision in the future if we believed that seals should be thus abandoned.

Unfortunately, the Massachusetts courts chose not to follow *Parker*. Instead, they hid behind legislative skirts. Since criminal statutes do not expressly create civil liability, they do not alter common law duties. Thus, in 1936, a police officer injured much in the same manner as Parker failed to recover. The court said:

> Moreover, in this Commonwealth, contrary to the rule prevailing in many jurisdictions, violation of a criminal statute of this general class does not ordinarily in and of itself, independently of common law duties, give rise to a civil cause of action. Such a statute has that effect only when by its express terms or by clear implication that appears to have been the legislative intent. That there was no such intent as to one of the very statutes here involved was decided in *Palmigiani v. D'Argenio*, 234 Mass. 434, and again

[24]*Parker v. Barnard*, 135 Mass. 116 (1883), p. 120.

with full discussion in *Garland v. Stetson,* 292 Mass. 95, 100, a case very similar to this. See also *Richardson v. Whittier,* 265 Mass. 478. In view of these cases, so far as there is in *Parker v. Barnard,* 135 Mass. 116, anything inconsistent with what is now decided, we are unable to follow it.[25]

Perhaps by 1936 this result was justified. After all, one justification for stare decisis is its prompting of courts to treat similarly situated people similarly. If all other licensees (or, for that matter, any person claiming to recover for injuries sustained from another's violation of a criminal law) failed to recover with the one exception of policemen who fell down elevator shafts, the law would not treat similarly situated people similarly. Hence the *Wynn* decision, though weak in its deference to nonexistent legislative intent, is not the main problem. Its predecessors that refused to adhere to the sensible development of *Parker* did the damage.

But perhaps the *Wynn* decision itself was not justified. At least the officer in that case must have felt he didn't receive the treatment that the similarly situated Officer Parker had received. The *Wynn* argument may, however, fail for more substantial reasons. If common law changes and grows, admittedly erratically over time, might not a court, mindful that the old law was inadequate, at least add an incremental move in the right direction? It could do so simply by saying, "We believe *Parker* rightly decided. Without attempting to change the entire relationship of owners and licensees in tort, and without adopting negligence *per se* in all situations, we believe the case for adherence in this instance is compelling." Might not such a result encourage other related changes in law over time? To do so would hardly violate the spirit of the common law tradition.

Fourth Illustration: Wrongly Adhering to Precedent When Stability Is Unnecessary

I hope I have not left the impression that courts should always follow precedents in business, contract, and property matters

[25]*Wynn v. Sullivan,* 294 Mass. 562 (1936), p. 566.

but never in the case of negligence. It is not that simple. Tort law can, for example, influence a person's decision to insure against loss. In this final illustration, however, let us look at a property problem in which a court, in a thoughtless opinion, followed precedent when the reasons for stare decisis did not support adherence. This case involves the laws of wills and of trusts, areas in which stability and reliance normally deserve great respect.

The case involved a section of the will of a New Jersey resident. In it the deceased, Rosa E. Green, stated: "I give and bequeath unto my husband, William L. Green, all of the money which I have on deposit at the Paterson Savings and Trust Company, Paterson, New Jersey, however, any money which is in the said account at the time of my said husband's death, the said sum shall be held by my niece, Catherine King Fox, absolutely and forever." William died without removing the money.

Naturally Ms. Fox attempted to withdraw the money from the bank. However, heirs of William claimed that the conditional gift to Ms. Fox was invalid. Lawyers for the heirs cited many New Jersey precedents stating that an unconditional bequest in a will, like the one to William, gave him unconditional ownership. Any conditional gift of the same property would have to be invalid; otherwise, the first gift would not be absolute. William's heirs won. The court said:

> Appellants ask this Court to explicitly and expressly overrule
> the long established law of this state. This we decline to
> do. Such action would be fraught with great danger in this
> type of case where titles to property, held by bequests and
> devises, are involved. A change of the established law by
> judicial decision is retrospective. It makes the law at the
> time of prior decisions as it is declared in the last decision,
> as to all transactions that can be reached by it. On the
> other hand a change in the settled law by statute is prospec-
> tive only.[26]

Think briefly about this result in terms of the reasons for stare decisis. For whom should this law remain stable? Who

[26]*Fox v. Snow,* 6 N.J. 12 (1950), p. 14.

could plan on the basis of this rule? Certainly not Rosa. She intended to make a conditional gift to Catherine but failed. William, if he wanted the money, had only to withdraw it. Until the moment of his death (or legal incapacitation), no one but William could make any plans based on what might happen to "Catherine's" money. For William to plan, we must suppose some reasoning like this: "I am going to die. I don't want the money, but I don't want Catherine to obtain the money, either. I could prevent her from receiving it by depositing it in another bank, but, since the clause is invalid, I'll leave it there." Such planning is possible, but is it probable? Is it the sort of planning that the law needs to preserve at the expense of carrying out the wishes of the deceased? Many people do not know rules of law of this kind. Is it not more probable that William also intended the money to go to Catherine? Is it plausible that, once William died leaving the money in the bank, Catherine made plans on the assumption that she did have the money?

Consider the other purposes of stare decisis: Is the image of justice improved by defeating Rosa's wishes? How important is equality of treatment in this kind of situation? How important is it to say that because courts have refused to carry out the wishes of past testators (the creators of wills) they must treat current testators in the same way for equality's sake?

Finally, efficiency in the judicial process does matter. Judges should not have to question the wisdom of every point of law that arises, but that hardly means they can never do so.

One judge disagreed with the majority in *Fox*. Chief Justice Vanderbilt's dissent is one of the finest essays from the bench on the subject of stare decisis. It provides a fitting summary of this section:

> VANDERBILT, C. J. (dissenting):
> I am constrained to dissent from the views of the majority of the court, first, because they apply to the case a technical rule of law to defeat the plain intent of the testatrix without serving any public policy whatever in so doing and, secondly—and this seems to me to be even more important—because their opinion involves a view of the judicial process, which, if it had been followed consistently in the past,

would have checked irrevocably centuries ago the growth of
the common law to meet changing conditions and which,
if pursued now, will spell the ultimate ossification and death
of the common law by depriving it of one of its most essential attributes—its inherent capacity constantly to renew its
vitality and usefulness by adapting itself gradually and
piecemeal to meeting the demonstrated needs of the
times. . . .

By the words in the third paragraph, "any money
which is in said account at the time of my said husband's
death, the said sum shall be held by my niece, Catherine
King Fox, absolutely and forever," the testatrix beyond any
doubt intended that her husband could use up the bank account but that if he did not, the plaintiff should take what
was left of it on his death. To hold otherwise is to proceed
on the untenable assumption that the quoted words are
meaningless and to ignore the elementary principle that the
provisions of a will are not to be construed as meaningless
except on the failure of every attempt to render them effective. . . . This principle is an integral part of the most fundamental rule of testamentary construction, *i.e.*, the duty of
the court is to ascertain what the intent of the testator was
and, then, having ascertained it, to give it effect. . . .

The opinion of the majority of the court, like every
other decision in this State on the subject, makes no attempt to justify the rule it perpetuates either in reason or
on grounds of public policy. Despite the deleterious effects
of the rule and the lack of any sound principle to support
it, the majority maintains that it should not be overthrown,
because it has been the long established law of this State
and because overruling it "would be fraught with great
danger in this type of case where titles to property, held by
bequests and devises, are involved" by reason of the retroac-
tive effect of all judicial decisions. This view, if it had been
consistently applied in the past, would have prevented any
change whatever in property law by judicial decisions. . . .
Every change in the law by judicial decision necessarily
creates rights in one party to the litigation and imposes corresponding duties on the other party. This is the process
by which the law grows and adjusts itself to the changing
needs of the times.

The process is necessarily used not only to create new rights and corresponding duties but, where necessary, to strike down old ones. *Cessante ratione legis, cessat et ipsa lex* (the reason for a law ceasing, the law itself ceases) is one of the most ancient maxims known to our law and it is constantly followed by our courts. Of this maxim it was said in *Beardsley v. City of Hartford*, 50 Conn. 529, 47 *Am. Rep.* 677, 682 (1883), "This means that no law can survive the reason on which it is founded. It needs no statute to change it; it abrogates itself." The same thought was enunciated by Lord Coke in *Milborn's Case, 7 Coke 7a* (K.B. 1609): *"Ratio legis est anima legis, et mutata legis ratione, mutatur ex lex"* (the reason for a law is the soul of the law, and if the reason for a law has changed, the law is changed). "It is revolting," says Mr. Justice Holmes, "to have no better reason for a rule of law than that so it was laid down in the time of Henry IV. It is still more revolting if the grounds upon which it was laid down have vanished long since, and the rule simply persists from blind imitation of the past," and "To rest upon a formula is a slumber that, prolonged, means death." *Collected Legal Papers* (1920) 187, 306. . . .

To hold, as the majority opinion implies, that the only way to overcome the unfortunate rule of law that plagues us here is by legislation, is to put the common law in a self-imposed straitjacket. Such a theory, if followed consistently, would inevitably lead to the ultimate codification of all of our law for sheer lack of capacity in the courts to adapt the law to the needs of the living present. The doctrine of *stare decisis* neither renders the courts impotent to correct their past errors nor requires them to adhere blindly to rules that have lost their reason for being. The common law would be sapped of its life blood if *stare decisis* were to become a god instead of a guide. The doctrine when properly applied operates only to control change, not to prevent it. As Mr. Justice Cardozo has put it, "Few rules in our time are so well established that they may not be called upon any day to justify their existence as means adapted to an end. If they do not function they are diseased, . . . they must not propagate their kind. Sometimes they are cut out and extirpated altogether. Sometimes they are left with the shadow of continued life, but sterilized, truncated, impotent for harm." *Nature of the Judicial Process* (1921) 98. All lawyers as well as laymen have a perfectly natural longing to think of the law as being as steadfast and immutable as the everlasting hills, but when we face the realities, we must agree with Dean Pound when he says, "Law must be stable, and yet it cannot stand still," *Interpretations of Legal History* (1923) I, and with Professor Williston when he tells us, "Uniform decisions of 300 years on a particular question may, and sometimes have been overthrown in a day, and the single decision at the end of the series may establish a rule of law at variance with all that has gone before." *Some Modern Tendencies in the Law* (1929) 125. . . .

Particularly in the realm of testamentary construction should the courts feel free to depart from precedent when the dictates of justice and reason demand it. Even Chancellor Kent was of this opinion: "Though we are not to disregard the authority of decisions, even as to the interpretation of wills, yet it is certain that the construction of them is so much governed by the language, arrangement, and circumstances of each particular instrument, which is usually very unskillfully and very incoherently drawn, that adjudged cases become of less authority, and are of more hazardous application, than decisions upon any other branch of the law." 4 *Commentaries on American Law* 535. . . . Even in England where the doctrine of the judicial infallibility of the House of Lords has prevailed for a century, we find Lord Chancellor Simon declaring in the case of *Perrin v. Morgan* (1943) 1 All E.R. 187, 194, when an ancient and well established rule of testamentary construction was urged upon the court: "The present question is not, in my opinion, one in which this House is required on the ground of public interest to maintain a rule which has been constantly applied but which it is convinced is erroneous. It is far more important to promote the correct construction of future wills in this respect than to preserve consistency in misinterpretation."

The dangers that the majority fear, it is submitted, are more apparent than real. The doctrine of *stare decisis* tends to produce certainty in our law, but it is important to realize that certainty *per se* is but a means to an end, and not an end in itself. Certainty is desirable only insofar as it operates to produce the maximum good and the minimum harm and thereby to advance justice. The courts have been reluctant to overthrow established rules when property rights are involved for the simple reason that persons in arranging their affairs have relied upon the rules as established, though outmoded or erroneous, and so to abandon them would result sometimes in greater harm than to observe them. The question whether the doctrine of *stare decisis* should be adhered to in such cases is always a choice between relative evils. When it appears that the evil resulting from a continuation of the accepted rule must be productive of greater mischief to the community than can possibly ensue from disregarding the previous adjudications on the subject, courts have frequently and wisely departed from precedent, 14 Am. Jur., Courts, Section 126.

What then, are the relative evils in the instant case? First, we should consider the evils that will result from a perpetuation of the rule here involved. It has already been demonstrated that the rule, in each and every instance in which it is applied, results in a complete frustration of the legitimate intention of the testator. It can only operate to take property from one to whom the testator intended to give it and to bestow it upon another. . . .

Having considered the evils flowing from continuing to follow the rule, let us now inquire into the evils, if any, which might result from its rejection. It is pertinent at this point to recall the words of Mr. Justice Cardozo minimizing the effect of overruling a decision: "The picture of the bewildered litigant lured into a course of action by the false light of a decision, only to meet ruin when the light is extinguished and the decision is overruled, is for the most part a figment of excited brains." *The Nature of the Judicial Process* (1921) 122 [sic.]. The rule in question by its very nature is never relied upon by those who are seeking to make a testamentary disposition of their property, for if the rule were known to a person at the time of the drawing of his will, its operation would and could be guarded against by the choice of words appropriate to accomplish the result desired. This rule is truly subversive of the testator's intent. It is relied upon only after the testator's decease by those who seek, solely on the basis of its technical and arbitrary requirements, to profit from the testator's ignorance and to take his property contrary to his expressed desires. Certainly it is not unjust or inequitable to deny such persons resort to this rule. . . . [27]

[27]*Fox v. Snow,* pp. 14–15, 21–27.

THE COMMON LAW TRADITION TODAY

Chief Justice Vanderbilt's dissent in *Fox* does more than state a sound theory of stare decisis. It also describes the essence of the common law tradition. Judicial choices continue to change common law today. Indeed, only within the past 100 years have judges recognized the inevitability and desirability of choice and change. Thus the full political consequences of choice and change have just come sharply into focus.

By this I mean that understanding the nature of judicial choice has more than academic consequences in law. Common law has in the past changed even when judges *believed* they merely chose the one applicable statute or line of precedents that "correctly" resolved the conflict before them. When judges *think* they solve problems by mechanically finding the one right solution from the past, the slow and erratic developments in law do not occur deliberately. Judges do not grapple with moral and economic aspects of policy choices when judges do not believe they choose policies.

But, when the point of view shifts, when judges begin believing they *do* make policy choices, this consciousness changes the kind and quality of law that judges make in several ways.

The first of these changes we have already studied and condemned. It occurs when judges throw up their hands and say, "In a democracy only the legislature can make new law, not the courts. We must, therefore, deliberately avoid making changes." These decisions, in spite of themselves, do make changes, of course, just as the *Fox* decision, by rejecting Vanderbilt's powerful arguments, more deeply embedded a mechanical view of stare decisis as well as the rule against conditional gifts, in New Jersey's law.

A second modern view of the consequences of acknowledged judicial discretion can avoid this evil. Judges, acknowledging that they can and do make law, pay closer attention, as we are about to see, to the facts and values that help them (and us) decide that some policy choices are wiser than others. Modern decisions do tend to be less mechanistic and more concerned with the consequences for the future of various alternative choices of policy. This quality, after all, gave the *Lyman* case its modern flavor.

There is, however, a third consequence of this shift in viewpoint. Judges may dramatically increase the speed of change and deliberately broaden the lengths of the legal jumps they take from old law to new. When judges realize they rightly possess authority to remake common law, they may overreact and enact what *they* believe are ideal legal solutions without properly honoring competing needs for stability. Similarly, they may ignore the possibility that, while both courts and legislatures share authority to make law, they do not necessarily possess identical institutional characteristics for making wise law.

The problem is so central to reasoning in constitutional law that a thorough canvass of the "judicial limits" territory must be postponed until the following chapter, which deals with reasoning in constitutional interpretation. This problem does, however, arise in common law (and statutory) interpretation.

In this perspective, consider the next case. It illustrates deliberate lawmaking. It exemplifies a dramatic expansion of common law, and it faces squarely the double problem of determining whether a given policy is wise and whether the courts were the wise place to make it. The case, *Tarasoff v. Regents of the University of California,* takes the law of negligence on a substantial jump outward.[28]

Tatiana Tarasoff spent the summer of 1969 in Brazil. She had, with her parents' consent and assistance, left the United States, in part, to escape the almost fanatical affections of one Prosenjit Poddar. During her absence Poddar kept his contact alive. He persuaded Tatiana's brother to share an apartment with him near Tatiana's home in Berkeley, California.

Tatiana returned from Brazil in October. On October 27, 1969, Poddar killed her.

In due course, Tatiana's parents learned that Poddar had, during the summer, received psychological therapy on an outpatient basis from Cowell Memorial Hospital at the Uni-

---

[28]*Tarasoff v. Regents of the University of California,* 551 P.2d 334 (1976).

versity of California, Berkeley. Their further investigation uncovered these facts:

- On August 20, 1969, Poddar told his therapist, Dr. Moore, that he planned to kill his girlfriend when she returned from Brazil.
- When Poddar left, Dr. Moore felt Poddar should be committed for psychiatric examination in a mental hospital. He urgently consulted two of his colleagues at Cowell. They concurred.
- Moore then told two campus police officers that he would request commitment of Poddar. He followed up with a letter of request to the campus police chief.
- Three officers, in fact, took Poddar into custody. Poddar promised them he would leave Tatiana alone in the future. The officers believed Poddar was rational and released him.
- After, and presumably in part because the officers released Poddar, Dr. Moore's supervisor, Dr. Powelson, asked the police to return Moore's letter. Dr. Powelson also ordered destroyed all written evidence of the affair and prohibited any further action to commit Poddar for examination or observation.
- At no point did any members of the hospital staff or the campus police attempt to notify Tatiana, her brother, or her parents of Poddar's threat.
- The staff could easily have determined Tatiana's identity as well as her location and that of her family.

The Tarasoffs sued the doctors, the officers, and university's board of regents, claiming damages for the loss of their daughter. Among other charges, they alleged that "defendants negligently permitted Poddar to be released from police custody without 'notifying the parents of Tatiana Tarasoff that their daughter was in grave danger from Prosenjit Poddar.' "[29] They claimed, in other words, that the defendants had a duty to use reasonable care to protect Tatiana.

The California Supreme Court upheld the legality of this

---

[29]Ibid., p. 341.

claim, but only against the regents and the doctors. Reasoning by example played a major part in its result. The court cited precedents from California and elsewhere holding a doctor liable for the damage caused by illness contracted by people in contact with his patient *if* the doctor negligently failed to diagnose the disease as contagious and to isolate the patient. It also cited a case holding a doctor liable for damages where, following his negligent refusal to admit a mental patient to a hospital, the mental patient assaulted the plaintiff.

The directly relevant case law in California, however, imposed a duty only where the defendant already assumed some responsibility for the victim. If, for example, a mental hospital failed negligently to protect one patient from another's violence, the hospital became liable. In California, no law extended the duty further.

Using fact freedom, however, the court ignored the distinction. It said, "[W]e do not think that the duty should logically be constricted to such situations."[30] Let us review the majority's reasons for the conclusion.

The majority first stated a general framework for determining the existence or absence of a duty, a statement amply supported by recent California precedents. Note above all how different this statement is from earlier mechanical statements like "duty to invitees but no duty to trespassers or licensees." The court, quoting precedents, said the existence of a duty depends

> only upon the "balancing of a number of considerations"; major ones "are the foreseeability of harm to the plaintiff, the degree of certainty that the plaintiff suffered injury, the closeness of the connection between the defendant's conduct and the injury suffered, the moral blame attached to the defendant's conduct, the policy of preventing future harm, the extent of the burden to the defendant and consequences to the community of imposing a duty to exercise care with resulting liability for breach, and the availability, cost and prevalence of insurance for the risk involved."
>
> The most important of these considerations in establishing duty is foreseeability. As a general principle, a "de-

---

[30]Ibid., p. 344.

fendant owes a duty of care to all persons who are foreseeably endangered by his conduct, with respect to all risks which make the conduct unreasonably dangerous."[31]

Having said this much the majority then noted that at common law a duty to warn of foreseeable harm done by a dangerous person existed only when the defendant had a "special relationship" with either the source of danger or the potential victim. The court admitted that the doctors had no special relationship to Tatiana, but it asserted that because they did have such a relationship to Poddar, they therefore owed Tatiana a duty of care.

The court cited no convincing precedent or other authority for this expansion of law, but that did not seem to bother it. The court did pay attention to the arguments sustaining and attacking the practical wisdom and effect of the new policy.

The court had to deal first with the possibility that the harm was not foreseeable in the first place. The issue was made even more difficult because only a few years earlier the court had based an important mental health ruling on the fact that psychological and psychiatric predictions of future behavior are notoriously inaccurate.[32] To this the court responded:

> The role of the psychiatrist, who is indeed a practitioner of medicine, and that of the psychologist who performs an allied function, are like that of the physician who must conform to the standards of the profession and who must often make diagnoses and predictions based upon such evaluations. Thus the judgment of the therapist in diagnosing emotional disorders and in predicting whether a patient presents a serious danger of violence is comparable to the judgment which doctors and professionals must regularly render under accepted rules of responsibility.
>
> We recognize the difficulty that a therapist encounters in attempting to forecast whether a patient presents a seri-

---

[31]Ibid., p. 342.

[32]In this particular case, *People v. Burnick,* 14 Cal. 3rd 306 (1975), the court held that a person could be committed to an institution for mentally disturbed sex offenders only after proof at trial beyond reasonable doubt that the defendant was, in fact, likely to repeat the offense.

ous danger of violence. Obviously we do not require that the therapist, in making that determination, render a perfect performance; the therapist need only exercise "that reasonable degree of skill, knowledge, and care ordinarily possessed and exercised by members of [that professional specialty] under similar circumstances." (*Bardessono v. Michels* (1970) 3 Cal.3d 780, 788 . . .) Within the broad range of reasonable practice and treatment in which professional opinion and judgment may differ, the therapist is free to exercise his or her own best judgment without liability; proof, aided by hindsight, that he or she judged wrongly is insufficient to establish negligence.

In the instant case, however, the pleadings do not raise any question as to failure of defendant therapists to predict that Poddar presented a serious danger of violence. On the contrary, the present complaints allege that defendant therapists did in fact predict that Poddar would kill, but were negligent in failing to warn.[33]

The court then turned to the most complex policy issue of all: Will imposition of the duty to warn discourage patients from seeking the psychiatric help they need, thus preventing not only their own improvement but perhaps increasing the actual incidence of violent harm to others because people don't get help? The court insisted that such a prediction is entirely speculative. It noted that both the California code of evidence and the Principles of Medical Ethics of the American Medical Association permit a doctor to reveal information about a dangerous person if doing so could protect the patient, other individuals, or the community. The court concluded that

the public policy favoring protection of the confidential character of patient-psychotherapist communications must yield to the extent to which disclosure is essential to avert danger to others. The protective privilege ends where the public peril begins.

Our current crowded and computerized society compels the interdependence of its members. In this risk-infested society we can hardly tolerate the further exposure

---

[33]*Tarasoff v. Regents*, p. 345.

to danger that would result from a concealed knowledge of the therapist that his patient was lethal. If the exercise of reasonable care to protect the threatened victim requires the therapist to warn the endangered party or those who can reasonably be expected to notify him, we see no sufficient societal interest that would protect and justify concealment. The containment of such risks lies in the public interest.[34]

Backed by powerful opposition communicated to the court in an amicus curiae ("friend of the court") brief from the American Psychiatric Association, Justice William Clark heatedly disputed the court's policy conclusion.[35] He began by noting that a California statute *prohibits* the release of "all" information about a patient once a person authorized to begin commitment proceedings does so. The majority had avoided that issue by insisting that the pleadings in the case did not state that Dr. Moore was so authorized. Clark insisted he was and further argued that the purpose of the statute applied clearly in the *Tarasoff* case. "The Legislature," he wrote, "obviously is more capable than is this court to investigate, debate, and weigh potential harm through disclosure against the risk of public harm by nondisclosure. We should defer to its judgment."[36]

Clark then turned to common law analysis itself:

Assurance of confidentiality is important for three reasons....

First, without substantial assurance of confidentiality, those requiring treatment will be deterred from seeking assistance. (See Sen. Judiciary Com. comment accompanying Sec. 1014 of Evid.Code; Slovenko, *supra*, 6 Wayne L.Rev. 175, 187–188; Goldstein & Katz, *Psychiatrist-Patient Privilege: The GAP Proposal and the Connecticut Statute* (1962) 36 Conn. Bar J. 175, 178.) It remains an unfortunate fact in our society that people seeking psychiatric guidance tend to become stigmatized. Apprehension of such stigma—ap-

---

[34]Ibid., pp. 347–348.
[35]William Clark later served President Ronald Reagan, first as National Security Advisor and then as U.S. Secretary of the Interior.
[36]*Op. cit.,* p. 358.

parently increased by the propensity of people considering treatment to see themselves in the worst possible light—
creates a well-recognized reluctance to seek aid. (Fisher,
*The Psychotherapeutic Professions and the Law of Privileged Com-
munications* (1964) 10 Wayne L.Rev. 609, 617; Slovenko, *supra,* 6 Wayne L.Rev. 175, 188; see also Rappeport, *Psychiatrist-Patient Privilege* (1963) 23 Md.L.J. 39, 46–47.) This
reluctance is alleviated by the psychiatrist's assurance of
confidentiality. . . .

Second, the guarantee of confidentiality is essential in
eliciting the full disclosure necessary for effective treatment. (*In re Lifschutz, supra,* 2 Cal.3d 415, 431, 85 Cal.Rptr.
829, 467 P.2d 557; *Taylor v. United States* (1955), 95 U.S.
App.D.C. 373, 222 F.2d 398, 401; Goldstein & Katz, *supra,* 36
Conn.Bar J. 175, 178; Heller, *Some Comments to Lawyers on
the Practice of Psychiatry* (1957) 30 Temp.L.Q. 401; Gutt-
macher & Weihofen, *Privileged Communications between Psychiatrist and Patient* (1952) 28 Ind.L.J. 32, 34.* The psychiatric
patient approaches treatment with conscious and unconscious inhibitions against revealing his innermost thoughts.
"Every person, however well-motivated, has to overcome
resistances to therapeutic exploration. These resistances
seek support from every possible source and the possibility of disclosure would easily be employed in the service of
resistance." (Goldstein & Katz, *supra,* 36 Conn. Bar J. 175,
179; see also, 118 Am.J.Psych 734, 735.) Until a patient can
trust his psychiatrist not to violate their confidential relationship, "the unconscious psychological control mechanism of repression will prevent the recall of past experiences." (Butler, *Psychotherapy and Griswold: Is Confidentiality a
Privilege or a Right?* (1971) 3 Conn.L.Rev. 599, 604). . . .

Third, even if the patient fully discloses his thoughts,
assurance that the confidential relationship will not be
breached is necessary to maintain his trust in his psychiatrist—the very means by which treatment is effected.
"[T]he essence of much psychotherapy is the contribution
of trust in the external world and ultimately in the self,

---

*One survey indicated that five of every seven people interviewed said they
would be less likely to make full disclosure to a psychiatrist in the absence of
assurance of confidentiality. (See Comment, *Functional Overlap Between the Lawyer and Other Professionals: Its Implications for the Doctrine of Privileged Communications* (1962) 71 Yale L.J. 1226, 1255). [Asterisk note in original.]

modelled upon the trusting relationship established during therapy." (Dawidoff, *The Malpractice of Psychiatrists,* 1966 Duke L.J. 696, 704). Patients will be helped only if they can form a trusting relationship with the psychiatrist. (*Id.* at 704, fn. 34; Burham, *Separation Anxiety* (1965) 13 Arch.Gen. Psychiatry 346, 356; Heller, *supra,* 30 Temp. L.Q. 401, 406.) All authorities appear to agree that if the trust relationship cannot be developed because of collusive communication between the psychiatrist and others, treatment will be frustrated. (See, e.g., Slovenko (1973) *Psychiatry and Law,* p. 61; Cross, Privileged *Communications between Participants in Group Psychotherapy* (1970) Law and Social Order, 191, 199. . . .)

Given the importance of confidentiality to the practice of psychiatry, it becomes clear the duty to warn imposed by the majority will cripple the use and effectiveness of psychiatry. Many people, potentially violent—yet susceptible to treatment—will be deterred from seeking it; those seeking it will be inhibited from making revelations necessary to effective treatment; and, forcing the psychiatrist to violate the patient's trust will destroy the interpersonal relationship by which treatment is effected.[37]

Is Justice Clark correct? Should the court defer here to the legislature's fact-finding abilities? Or is he only using the time-worn argument, condemned by Chief Justice Vanderbilt's powerful dissent in *Fox v. Snow,* that legislatures, not courts, should make policy? Consider two possibilities. First, the court did in fact hear a wide variety of points of view on the policy

---

[37]Ibid., pp. 358–360. In 1984, Daniel Givelber, William Bowers, and Carolyn Blitch published the results of their survey of over 2,000 therapists nationwide. They conclude that most therapists found the *Tarasoff* ruling was consistent with their sense of professional ethics and that the ruling did not significantly impair their ability to treat their patients. See "*Tarasoff* Myth and Reality," 1984 *Wisconsin Law Review* 443 (1984). See also, Kathleen Quinn's "The Impact of Tarasoff on Clinical Practice," 2 *Behavioral Sciences and the Law* 319 (1984). Quinn, a doctor of medicine, goes so far as to say that the physician may encourage a potentially violent patient voluntarily to commit himself by reminding the patient that in the absence of voluntary commitment, the law may require the psychiatrist to warn potential victims. Compare "More Psychotherapists Held Liable for the Actions of Violent Patients," *Wall Street Journal* 2 March, 1987, p. 23.

questions. The American Psychiatric Association did file an amicus brief. Interest groups lobby courts much as they do legislatures. Is there any reason to believe that a legislature facing this issue would hear substantially more or different or better policy arguments? Does not Justice Clark's dissent tend to undercut his position? He appears to have digested and incorporated into his thinking a wide range of literature bearing on the subject. Second, if Clark's analysis is so compellingly correct, nothing in the common law prevents the California legislature from amending the statute Clark cites to include within its scope the type of situation that occurred in *Tarasoff.*

Any final analysis of this case must not lose sight of an important technical element in *Tarasoff.* The Supreme Court of California did not hold that the doctors and the board of regents were liable to the Tarasoffs. It held only that they might be if a full trial on the facts showed that the doctors had not used reasonable care in assessing the likelihood that Poddar would carry out his threat. In this case the trial judge did not allow a trial at all. The trial judge had ruled that the law did not permit the Tarasoffs to recover even if all their allegations were true. It is this interpretation of law that the California Supreme Court here reversed. Thus the case comes down to this: If a doctor has reason to believe the threat is a serious and real one, then he must warn the victim. It does not mean he must tell all.

How frequently do you think people who need psychiatric help will reason this way: "I need psychiatric help. I think I might kill someone. However, I've read about *Tarasoff* and I know that if I tell the psychiatrist the name of the person I might kill, the psychiatrist, if he or she thinks I really mean it, will warn the person whose killing I'm trying to avoid by seeking help. Therefore I won't seek help?" Do you believe the psychiatric profession will suffer a setback because people will reason that way?

There are two more interesting points in the *Tarasoff* case. One is the reliance of courts on law review articles for assistance in legal reasoning. I have not included the California court's footnotes in my quotations. A complete reading of this fascinating case will, however, reveal that the court relied very heavily on an analysis of this problem published in 1974 in the *California Law Review*.[38] The authors wrote the article precisely because they knew of the Tarasoff killing and recognized that it raised important legal questions. In doing so, they effectively wrote the majority's opinion.

Second, among the many amicus parties noted at the beginning of the *Tarasoff* opinion you will see the name Melanie Bellah. In October 1977, the Associated Press wire carried the following story:[39]

> SUICIDE WARNING NOT REQUIRED
>
> The [California] Court of Appeal has ruled that a psychiatrist cannot be sued for failing to warn parents of their 18-year-old daughter's potential for suicide.
>
> The court also ruled that the physician was not bound legally to restrain the young woman from killing herself.
>
> Melanie and Robert Bellah sought unspecified damages from Berkeley psychiatrist Dr. Daniel Greenson in the suicide death of their daughter, Tammy, on April 12, 1973.
>
> Tammy, a freshman at the University of California at Berkeley, had been under the care of the doctor, and the court said it appeared Greenson knew she was disposed to suicide.
>
> When Tammy died, her parents were temporarily living in New Jersey and claimed they had no personal contact with her and were unaware of her suicidal tendencies.
>
> The suit, filed two years later, alleged the doctor had failed to take measures to prevent Tammy's suicide and failed to warn others of her true condition.
>
> The appeal court noted the California Supreme Court's 1976 *Tarasoff* ruling that in certain circumstances a therapist had a duty to warn others when a patient was likely to harm another.
>
> "The [state Supreme] court did not hold that such disclosure was required where the danger presented was that

---

[38]John G. Fleming and Bruce Maximov, "The Patient or His Victim: The Therapist's Dilemma," 62 *California Law Review* 1025 (1974). One measure of freedom in the United States is surely that the law review of a state-run school can, without state interference, publish an article concluding that the very school ought to be found legally liable.

[39]*The Atlanta Constitution,* 7 October 1977, p. 14-B.

of self-inflicted harm or suicide or where the danger consisted of a likelihood of property damage," said the appeal
court.

Note that in the *Bellah* case the physician's own patient
died, but the court held that no law imposed potential liability
on the doctor. On the other hand, in *Tarasoff*, a third party
died and yet the court did impose a legal obligation on the
physician. Why this apparent anomaly? Could it be that
Tammy Bellah's condition might have worsened if her parents, when notified of her problem, had then intruded into
the therapeutic efforts of the doctor? Common law fact freedom marches on.

SUMMARY

- What is the historical origin of common law?
- Who was Henri de Bracton? How did his work over 700 years
  ago help produce the modern emphasis on reasoning by example in common law?
- Describe the recent transition from natural law to reasoning
  by example, and hence acknowledged and accepted judicial
  lawmaking today.
- Why don't general principles such as the rules of negligence
  and battery described in this chapter clearly resolve all legal
  problems of that type?
- How and why do the beliefs and values of individual judges
  influence the growth of law?
- How do legal principles move into common law and then out
  again? In analyzing reasoning in common law, why is it not
  sufficient to trace the rise and fall of such principles?
- How do the five justifications for stare decisis articulated in
  Chapter II apply to the cases described in this chapter?
- If judicial lawmaking is part of the common law tradition, are
  there any reasons why, in modern American political culture,
  judges should now discard that tradition and refuse to make
  new common law when the legislature has created no law of
  its own?

ILLUSTRATIVE CASE

Like *Tarasoff,* this case went to the court of appeals on a question of law before any trial occurred to test the actual facts.

Thus the court's holding here does not mean that defendant O'Daniels is liable to the plaintiff for damages. In a telephone conversation with Judge Andreen in July of 1983, I learned that the defendants had chosen not to appeal this ruling to the California Supreme Court.

Soldano v. O'Daniels
California Court of Appeals, Fifth District
190 *California Reporter* **310 (1983)**

ANDREEN, Associate Justice.

Does a business establishment incur liability for wrongful death if it denies use of its telephone to a good samaritan who explains an emergency situation occurring without and wishes to call the police?. . . .

Both briefs on appeal adopt the defense averments:

"This action arises out of a shooting death occurring on August 9, 1977. Plaintiff's father [Darrell Soldano] was shot and killed by one Rudolph Villanueva on that date at defendant's Happy Jack's Saloon. This defendant owns and operates the Circle Inn which is an eating establishment located across the street from Happy Jack's. Plaintiff's second cause of action against this defendant is one for negligence.

"Plaintiff alleges that on the date of the shooting, a patron of Happy Jack's Saloon came into the Circle Inn and informed a Circle Inn [bartender] that a man had been threatened at Happy Jack's. He requested the [bartender] either call the police or allow him to use the Circle Inn phone to call the police. That [bartender] allegedly refused to call the police and allegedly refused to allow the patron to use the phone to make his own call. Plaintiff alleges that the actions of the Circle Inn [bartender] were a breach of the legal duty that the Circle Inn owed to the decedent." . . .

There is a distinction, well rooted in the common law, between action and nonaction. (*Weirum v. RKO General, Inc.* (1975) 15 Cal.3d 40, 49). It has found its way into the prestigious Restatement Second of Torts (hereafter cited as "Restatement"), which provides in Section 314:

> The fact that the actor realizes or should realize that action on his part is necessary for another's aid or protection does not of itself impose upon him a duty to take such action.

The distinction between malfeasance and nonfeasance, between active misconduct working positive injury and failure to act to prevent mischief not brought on by the defendant, is founded on "that attitude of extreme individualism so typical of Anglo-Saxon legal thought." (Bohlen, *The Moral Duty to Aid Others as a Basis of Tort Liability,* part I, (1908) 56 U.Pa.L.Rev. 217, 219–220.). . . .

The refusal of the law to recognize the moral obligation of one to aid another when he is in peril and when such aid may be given without danger and at little cost in effort has been roundly criticized. Prosser describes the case law sanctioning such inaction as a "refus[al] to recognize the moral obligation of common decency and common humanity" and characterizes some of these decisions as "shocking in the extreme. . . . Such decisions are revolting to any moral sense. They have been denounced with vigor by legal writers." (Prosser, *Law of Torts* (4th ed. 1971) §56, pp. 340–341, fn. omitted.) A similar rule has been termed "morally questionable" by our Supreme Court. (*Tarasoff v. Regents of University of California* 551 P.2d 334 (1976).)

Francis H. Bohlen, in his article "The Moral Duty to Aid Others as a Basis of Tort Liability," commented:

> Nor does it follow that because the law has not as yet recognized the duty to repair harm innocently wrought, that it will continue indefinitely to refuse it recognition. While it is true that the common law does not attempt to enforce all moral, ethical, or humanitarian duties, it is, it is submitted, equally true that all ethical and moral conceptions, which are not the mere temporary manifestations of a passing wave of sentimentalism or puritanism, but on the contrary, find a real and permanent place in the settled convictions of a race and become part of the normal habit of thought thereof, of necessity do in time color the judicial conception of legal obligation. . . .

As noted in *Tarasoff v. Regents of University of California, supra,* the courts have increased the instances in which affirmative duties are imposed not by direct rejection of the common law rule, but by expanding the list of special relationships which will justify departure from that rule. . . .

Here there was no special relationship between the defendant and the deceased. It would be stretching the concept beyond recognition to assert there was a relationship between the defendant and the patron from Happy Jack's Saloon who wished to summon aid. But this does not end the matter.

It is time to re-examine the common law rule of nonliability for nonfeasance in the special circumstances of the instant case.

The Legislature has recognized the importance of the telephone system in reporting crime and in summoning emergency aid. Penal Code section 384 makes it a misdemeanor to refuse to relinquish a party line when informed that it is needed to call a police department or obtain other specified emergency services. This requirement, which the Legislature has mandated to be printed in virtually every telephone book in this state, may have wider printed distribution in this state than even the Ten Commandments. It creates an affirmative duty to do something—to clear the line for another user of the party line—in certain circumstances.

In 1972 the Legislature enacted the Warren-911-Emergency Assistance Act. This act expressly recognizes the importance of the telephone system in procuring emergency aid. . . .

The above statutes are cited without the suggestion that the defendant violated a statute which would result in a presumption of a failure to use due care under Evidence Code section 669. Instead, they, and the quotations from the prestigious national commissions, demonstrate that "that attitude of extreme individualism so typical of Anglo-Saxon legal thought" may need limited re-examination in the light of current societal conditions and the facts of this case to determine whether the defendant owed a duty to the deceased to permit the use of the telephone.

We turn now to the concept of duty in a tort case. The Supreme Court has identified certain factors to be considered in determining whether a duty is owed to third persons. These factors include:

> The foreseeability of harm to the plaintiff, the degree of cer-
> tainty that the plaintiff suffered injury, the closeness of the
> connection between the defendant's conduct and the injury
> suffered, the moral blame attached to the defendant's con-
> duct, the policy of preventing future harm, the extent of the
> burden to the defendant and consequences to the commu-
> nity of imposing a duty to exercise care with resulting liabil-
> ity for breach, and the availability, cost, and prevalence of
> insurance for the risk involved. (*Rowland v. Christian* (1968)
> 443 P.2d 561.)

We examine those factors in reference to this case. (1) The
harm to the decedent was abundantly foreseeable; it was immi-
nent. The employee was expressly told that a man had been
threatened. The employee was a bartender. As such he knew it
is foreseeable that some people who drink alcohol in the milieu
of a bar setting are prone to violence. (2) The certainty of decedent's injury is undisputed. (3) There is arguably a close connection
between the employee's conduct and the injury: the patron
wanted to use the phone to summon the police to intervene. The
employee's refusal to allow the use of the phone prevented this
anticipated intervention. If permitted to go to trial, the plaintiff
may be able to show that the probable response time of the police would have been shorter than the time between the prohibited telephone call and the fatal shot. (4) The employee's conduct displayed a disregard for human life that can be
characterized as morally wrong: he was callously indifferent to
the possibility that Darrell Soldano would die as the result of his
refusal to allow a person to use the telephone. Under the circumstances before us the bartender's burden was minimal and exposed him to no risk: all he had to do was allow the use of the
telephone. It would have cost him or his employer nothing. It
could have saved a life. (5) Finding a duty in these circumstances
would promote a policy of preventing future harm. A citizen
would not be required to summon the police but would be required, in circumstances such as those before us, not to impede
another who has chosen to summon aid. (6) We have no information on the question of the availability, cost, and prevalence of
insurance for the risk, but note that the liability which sought to be
imposed here is that of employee negligence, which is covered by
many insurance policies. (7) The extent of the burden on the
defendant was minimal, as noted.

The consequences to the community of imposing a duty, the remaining factor mentioned in *Rowland v. Christian, supra,* is termed "the administrative factor" by Professor Green in his analysis of determining whether a duty exists in a given case. (Green, *The Duty Problem in Negligence Cases,* I (1929) 28 Colum.L.Rev. 1014, 1035–1045. . . .) The administrative factor is simply the pragmatic concern of fashioning a workable rule and the impact of such a rule on the judicial machinery. It is the policy of major concern in this case.

As the Supreme Court has noted, the reluctance of the law to impose liability for nonfeasance, as distinguished from misfeasance, is in part due to the difficulties in setting standards and of making rules workable. (*Tarasoff v. Regents of University of California, supra.* . . .)

Many citizens simply "don't want to get involved." No rule should be adopted which would require a citizen to open up his or her house to a stranger so that the latter may use the telephone to call for emergency assistance. As Mrs. Alexander in Anthony Burgess' *A Clockwork Orange* learned to her horror, such an action may be fraught with danger. It does not follow, however, that use of a telephone in a public portion of a business should be refused for a legitimate emergency call. Imposing liability for such a refusal would not subject innocent citizens to possible attack by the "good samaritan," for it would be limited to an establishment open to the public during times when it is open to business, and to places within the establishment ordinarily accessible to the public. . . .

We conclude that the bartender owed a duty to the plaintiff's decedent to permit the patron from Happy Jack's to place a call to the police or to place the call himself. . . .

The creative and regenerative power of the law has been strong enough to break chains imposed by outmoded former decisions. What the courts have power to create, they also have power to modify, reject and re-create in response to the needs of a dynamic society. The exercise of this power is an imperative function of the courts and is the strength of the common law. It cannot be surrendered to legislative inaction.

Prosser puts it this way:

New and nameless torts are being recognized constantly, and the progress of the common law is marked by many cases of first impression, in which the court has struck out boldly to create a new cause of action, where none had been recognized before. . . . The law of torts is anything but static, and the limits of its development are never set. When it becomes clear that the plaintiff's interests are entitled to legal protection against the conduct of the defendant, the mere fact that the claim is novel will not of itself operate as a bar to the remedy." (Prosser, *op. cit. supra,* at pp. 3–4, fns. omitted.)

The possible imposition of liability on the defendant in this case is not a global change in the law. It is but a slight departure from the "morally questionable" rule of nonliability for inaction absent a special relationship. . . . It is a logical extension of Restatement section 327 which imposes liability for negligent interference with a third person who the defendant knows is attempting to render necessary aid. However small it may be, it is a step which should be taken.

We conclude there are sufficient justiciable issues to permit the case to go to trial and therefore reverse.

FRANSON, Acting P. J., and STANTON, J., concur.

QUESTIONS

1. Soldano overrules a long-standing common law rule. Do you agree that the old rule was "bad law"? (Remember that for the doctrine of stare decisis to come into play, you must believe that the old rule is unwise in the abstract.) If you so agree, do the principles of stare decisis permit overruling in this instance? Why or why not?
2. Note Judge Andreen's citation of *Tarasoff.* Is *Tarasoff* really a precedent for the *Soldano* holding? In what sense? In what sense is it no precedent at all?
3. Recall the cyclical model of common law principles. Of course it is too early to be sure, but might not *Tarasoff* mark the rise and *Soldano* the fall of the "special relationship" principle on such a cycle?
4. I edited out of the case many references to acts of the California legislature the purpose of which is to attempt to reduce the crime rate by increasing community responsibility. How might Judge Andreen have used such references to strengthen his argument?

5. Do you believe this case is only a "slight departure" from prior law? Why or why not?

6. Judge Andreen sent me copies of the parties' briefs in this case. The large majority of Judge Andreen's reasoning appears nowhere in either brief. That is, despite our adversary system, this judge felt no hesitation to go beyond the parties' arguments to decide on the basis that he and a unanimous court felt best. Are you comfortable with this practice?

7. Most modern common law opinions do not explicitly rest on a philosophy of innovation in common law as does the opinion in *Soldano.* What reasons might explain why such opinions are relatively rare? Is it necessarily helpful in every case for judges to follow the *Soldano* pattern? Why or why not?

8. On January 29, 1987, the *Wall Street Journal* quoted Dr. Jerome Groopman's claim that AIDS is "the public-health threat of the century. . . . We can't allow political sensitivities to prevent public health policy." The "political sensitivities" he referred to included proposals that would require AIDS victims to name past sex partners. Should a doctor who treats someone who tests positive for the AIDS virus be required to ask for the names of the patient's sex partners and notify them? Suppose (a) the patient is a married, bisexual male whose wife knows nothing about her husband's bisexuality, and (b) the physician treating the husband is a family physician who also treats the wife. Is this physician required to warn the wife who is also his patient? See "Asking AIDS Victims to Name Past Partners Stirs Debate on Privacy," *Wall Street Journal,* 29 January 1987, p. 1.

9. One of the most widely publicized common law rulings in this century occurred on March 31, 1987, when New Jersey Superior Court Judge Harvey R. Sorkow upheld the surrogate mother contract between William Stern, the biological father of "Baby M" and surrogate mother Mary Beth Whitehead.[40] Consider from among the many legal reasoning issues presented in this case these three issues:

   A. Are surrogate motherhood contracts desirable for society? Do they demean the value of marriage and family or enhance it?

   B. What result is in the best interest of Baby M? Is it not true that without the contract between Stern and Whitehead Baby M would not exist at all? In other words, is it not "pro life" to enforce such contracts?

[40]See *In the Matter of BABY "M,"* 525 A.2d 1128 (1987).

C. Judge Sorkow refused to treat the case as calling for the inter-pretation of New Jersey's adoption statutes. How convincing do you find the argument that, since adoption statutes were passed before surrogate motherhood by artificial insemina-tion was feasible, the New Jersey legislature did not intend adoption statutes to cover surrogate motherhood?

Chapter V

REASON AND THE CONSTITUTION

[Be it] regarded hereafter as the law of this Court, that its opinion upon the construction of the Constitution is always open to discussion when it is supposed to have been founded in error, and that its judicial authority should hereafter depend altogether on the force of the reasoning by which it is supported.

> —*Chief Justice Roger B. Taney, dissenting in* The Passenger Cases

We are under a Constitution—but the Constitution is what the Judges say it is.

> —*Charles Evans Hughes*

THE CONSTITUTIONAL PARADOX

This chapter explores an enduring paradox in legal reasoning: In no area of law is there more disagreement about legal reasoning principles, and more inconsistency in their practical application, than in constitutional law, yet the justifications the U. S. Supreme Court gives for its constitutional decisions have immensely more political significance than do the statutory and common law cases we have thus far covered.

Appellate judges make policy choices. These choices impose the power of government on individuals, and the reasons these judges give to justify their choices matter because our political culture values holding those who exercise power accountable. In statutory interpretation and common law reasoning, but not in constitutional law, the political process contains machinery for backstopping the justifications of appellate judges. A legislature, held accountable through the electoral process, can change an errant interpretation of a statute. Thus, in March, 1987, the U. S. Supreme Court interpreted federal legislation protecting the employment rights of the handicapped to cover persons with incurable and potentially communicable diseases. But Congress may abolish this ruling by altering the legislation if public concern, especially about the spread of AIDS, demands it.

Similarly, legislatures may modify or abolish any common law ruling. In the mid–1980s the majority of state legislatures considered "tort reform" legislation that would modify the common law of tort awards.

In constitutional law, on the other hand, no routine backstopping exists. The constitution is the law that defines and limits the powers of government, and the Supreme Court's applications of the Constitution limit by definition what the government can do. Short of holding a constitutional convention, those who dislike a constitutional ruling must either persuade the Court to change its mind or amend the Constitution. But a constitutional amendment requires approval of two thirds of both houses of Congress *and* three fourths of the states. Therefore, relatively small minorities can block a proposed amendment's passage. Only two of the eleven amendments ratified in the twentieth century (the Sixteenth Amendment, authorizing a federal income tax, and the Ninteenth, granting women's suffrage) can be said to have corrected controversial Supreme Court readings of the Constitution.

Thus, one side of the paradox takes shape. The Constitution claims in Article VI to be "the supreme law of the land,"

and the legal system—and usually the political system as well—have treated it that way from its beginnings. Yet judges without the backstop of electoral politics set aside, through the practice of "judicial review," legislative and administrative choices of the body politic.

Furthermore, the issues themselves are often fundamentally important. Courts strike down laws prohibiting abortions in the first trimester of pregnancy. Courts tell states what property they can and cannot tax. Courts order busing to integrate schools. Courts order legislatures to reapportion. Courts reverse the convictions of killers because of what some critics call "technicalities." The Court's call for ending racial discrimination or for permitting abortions in the first trimester of pregnancy have consequences far greater than the decision, in *Tarasoff,* to hold psychiatrists potentially liable for their failure to warn potential victims of their patients.

There are two more reasons why constitutional reasoning is politically so important. The document speaks frequently in general, ambiguous, and vague language. The Constitution's most frequently litigated clauses do little more than command the courts to *care* about basic political and governmental values without specifying with any precision the values or the problems to which the provisions apply.

- "Care," says the First Amendment to the courts, "that government not take sides on religious matters. Care that it not constrain religious freedom, or speech, or the press, unduly. But it's up to you to define religion, speech, and press and to decide when government action and those values simply cannot stand together.
- "Care," say the Fourth, Fifth, Sixth, and Eighth Amendments, "that government not become too zealous in fighting crime. Respect people's homes and property. Give them a fair chance to prove their innocence in court and do not punish the guilty too harshly. In short, be fair. But it's up to you to decide what's fair."
- "Men must be able to trade effectively," say the commerce clause and the contract clause. "Work it out so they can."

If we could assume that every governmental representative, the legislator before voting for a statute or the policeman before deciding to arrest, stopped and made a conscientious determination of the constitutionality of the decision, under our Constitution, we would still need a constitution-interpreting organization like the courts. The Constitution is so vague, general, and ambiguous that people with the best of intentions do not necessarily reach the same interpretation.

Finally, federalism compounds the problem. We have one national constitutional constitution but many state constitutions. If we take its legal status seriously, then the Constitution should mean the same everywhere, just as the Mann Act should not have one meaning in Utah and another in the District of Columbia. If we lived under a unitary government, then maybe (but only maybe) we could count on a conscientious Congress to determine uniform constitutional applications. Under our Constitution, however, Congress is neither structured nor empowered to review the constitutionality of the actions of state and local governments.

Hence, the finality of the Court, the importance of constitutional issues, the inconclusiveness of the Constitution's text, and the need for national uniformity would seem together to make mandatory the consistent use of stable and coherent patterns of legal justification. This is precisely what constitutional law over its 200-year history has never provided.

By the end of this chapter I hope to have persuaded you that, because "the Constitution is what the judges say it is," the "construction of the Constitution is always open to discussion." That is, the Court in interpreting the Constitution should play the role in political life not of an announcer of ultimate truth but of a facilitator of conversations about goodness in public life. This role is as delicate as any in our political system, and the Court has not always played it well. Dogmatic and inflexible constitutional rulings have gotten the Court into hot water more than once, yet the Court must preserve the idea that the Constitution, not what it or we may say about it, is the supreme law. As James Boyd White recently put it:

To say, as some do, that "we" ought to regard ourselves as "free" from the constraints of meaning and authority, free to make "our" Constitution what "we" want it to be, is in fact to propose the destruction of an existing community, established by our laws and Constitution, extending from "we" who are alive to those who have given us the materials of our cultural world, and to substitute it for another, the identity of which is most uncertain indeed. In place of the constituted "we" that it is the achievement of our past to have given us, we are offered an unconstituted "we," or a "we" constituted on the pages of law journals. One can properly ask of such a person, and mean it literally, "who are you to speak as you do? Who is the 'we' of whom you speak?" To answer that the new "we" is defined not by the Constitution we have, but by the Constitution we wish we had, is no answer at all; for who is the "we" doing the wishing? In the new world, who shall be king?[1]

THE FAILURE
OF CONVENTIONAL LEGAL REASONING

In 1985 Attorney General Edwin Meese called for a style of constitutional interpretation derived from the original understandings of the framers of the Constitution.[2] In this section I shall suggest that Meese's call was unrealistic. Neither the words of the Constitution nor the intent of the framers nor the purposes served by clauses separately or in combination provide uncontroversial methods of resolving cases

Words as Channels of Meaning

Article I, Section 10 of the Constitution prohibits the states from engaging in certain activities altogether. It prohibits them from making treaties, coining money, or keeping a state

---

[1]"Law as Language: Reading Law and Reading Literature," 60 *Texas Law Review* 415, at 443 (1982).

[2]Edwin Meese III, "Toward a Jurisprudence of Original Intention," 45 *Public Administration Review* 701 (1985).

militia during times of peace without Congressional permission. The section also includes these words: "No state shall . . . pass any . . . law impairing the obligation of contracts. . . . "

Debts provide the best example of the kind of contract the state may not impair under the contract clause. In the typical case of such a contract—"executory" contracts in legal language—Pauline borrows money, say from the bank, and promises to pay the money back some time in the future. Until she pays the money back (and at the stated time), she has a contractual obligation to do so. The contract clause prevents the state from impairing Pauline's "obligation" to repay. At minimum, these words seem clearly to mean the state can't pass a law saying people don't have to pay back what they owe, even if a popularly elected legislature voted to do so. Note also that the word "impairing" also presumably means something. An impairment is something different from a destruction. Someone with impaired vision is not necessarily totally blind. Thus the words would also seem to prevent the state from allowing Pauline to forget about paying the interest or to pay back years later than she promised.

During the Great Depression, a number of states passed laws allowing owners of homes and land to postpone paying their mortgage payments as the mortgage contracts required. These statutes forbade banks and other mortgage holders from foreclosing. The Depression, of course, destroyed the financial ability of hundreds of thousands of Paulines to repay mortgages on time, but these mortgage moratorium laws spared the Paulines from this peril. These laws spared the Paulines precisely and only because they impaired the bank's ability to recover the debt, yet the Supreme Court ruled, in *Home Building and Loan Association v. Blaisdell,* that these laws did not violate the contract clause.[3]

How can we defend such a result? Just as in nature, survival of economic and political values depends on adaptation, on changefulness, and on the ability to re-evaluate policies in

---

[3]*Home Building and Loan Association v. Blaisdell,* 290 U.S. 398 (1934). See also *East New York Savings Bank v. Hahn,* 326 U.S. 230 (1945) and *El Paso v. Simmons,* 379 U.S. 497 (1965).

light of new information. The Supreme Court rightly rejected the contract clause's words and upheld the Depression's mortgage moratorium laws because these laws were based on economic knowledge not fully available to the framers. In the forced panic sale of land following massive numbers of foreclosures of mortgages what would happen to the price of land? Supply and demand analysis predicted that the price would drastically decline, quite possibly to the point where creditors as well as debtors would lose because the land could be sold for only a fraction of what the banks had originally loaned on it. The Court upheld the law as a defensible method for attempting to prevent the further collapse of the economy.

A decision in the monumental school desegregation cases provides another example of prudent judicial flight from constitutional words. In its celebrated decision, *Brown v. Board of Education,* the Court held that the equal protection clause of the Fourteenth Amendment prohibited laws and policies designed to maintain segregation in public schools of the then 48 states.[4] The case concerned the problem of segregation of schools in the nation's capital. The Fourteenth Amendment's sentence containing the equal protection clause begins with the words "no state shall." It does not govern the District of Columbia. The original Bill of Rights does govern the national government and hence the district, but it contains no equal protection clause. The Court forbade segregation in the District's public schools by invoking the due process clause of the Fifth Amendment.[5] Unfortunately, the due process clause does not address the problem of equality. Its words—"No person shall . . . be deprived of life, liberty, or property, without due process of law. . . . "—seem to address the problem of the fairness of procedures, the "due process," in the courts. The Fourteenth Amendment contains *both* due process and equal protection clauses, which further suggests that they convey different messages.

Nevertheless, the Court rightly prohibited segregation in

<hr>

[4]*Brown v. Board of Education,* 347 U.S. 483 (1954).
[5]*Bolling v. Sharpe,* 347 U.S. 497 (1954). See also *Hirabayashi v. United States,* 320 U.S. 81 (1943).

the district. If the Constitution denies government the power to segregate schools by race, it is proper to avoid the absurdity of permitting segregation only in the national capital. It is proper to say in this instance that the due process clause of the Fifth Amendment *does* address this problem of equality despite its words.[6]

The Intent of the Framers and the Purpose of Constitutional Provisions

Searching for the actual intent of the framers of the original Constitution (or of its later amendments) proves just as frustrating as the search for legislative intent. The processes of constitution and statute making are equally political. People make arguments they don't fully intend in order to win support. Others do not express what they do intend in order to avoid offending. The painful process of negotiation and accommodation that produced the Constitution in 1787 left many questions unresolved. Most confounding of all, the au-

---

[6]Some of the Court's creative manipulations of words in constitutional law come disguised as statutory interpretations. For example Section 6(j) of the old draft law stated, "Nothing contained in this title shall be construed to require any person to be subject to combatant training and service . . . who, by reason of religious training and belief, is conscientiously opposed to participation in war in any form. Religious training and belief, in this connection, mean an individual's belief in a relation to a Supreme Being involving duties superior to those arising from any human relation, but do not include essentially political, sociological, or philosophical views or a merely personal moral code." In 1966, one Elliott A. Welsh, II, was convicted for refusing to submit to induction. He had applied for an exemption as a conscientious objector under Section 6(j), but he insisted that his feelings were not religious but moral, based upon "reading in the fields of history and sociology," he said. He believed that taking any life was "morally wrong" and "totally repugnant." The Court reversed Welsh's conviction. Hugo Black, speaking for himself and three other Justices (Blackmun did not sit; Harlan concurred on other grounds), said that Section 6(j) exempted all those who held moral and philosophical beliefs "with the strength of more traditional religious convictions." To avoid invalidating Section 6(j), Black made it say precisely what the words in Section 6(j) take pains to avoid. *Welsh v. United States,* 398 U.S. 333 (1970).

thors could have had no intent in relation to the new facts that have surfaced since their work concluded.[7]

Thus, the Court ignored the original purpose of the Sixth Amendment's command when it expanded the right to counsel. This amendment states in part that "In all criminal prosecutions, the accused shall enjoy the right ... to have the assistance of counsel for his defense." The framers who drafted it sought to alter the common law rule that prohibited accused felons from having any lawyer at all. They wanted to stop the government from preventing the accused from bringing his lawyer to court with him. It makes no reference to the problem that a man's *poverty* may stop him from hiring a lawyer. Yet in 1938 the Court held that these words required the federal government to provide lawyers for the poor and the court has since expanded the right to protect those accused of felonies and misdemeanors in state and local courts.[8]

And consider again the mortgage moratorium laws of the Depression. If we examine the purpose of the contract clause from the framers' viewpoint, we discover that they feared excessive democracy, feared that popularly elected legislators would enact the "selfish" interests of the masses. The masses contain more debtors than creditors, and it was precisely in economically difficult times that the framers most feared that debtors would put irresistible pressure on legislators to ease their debts. Hence the court in *Home Building and Loan* rejected more than constitutional words; it rejected the purpose of the provision. But it did so correctly because it understood, as presumably the framers did not, how postponing mortgage foreclosures could benefit creditors and debtors alike.

Finally, H. Jefferson Powell has recently shown two reasons why the leading figures of the founding period repeat-

[7]For further elaboration see my *Contemporary Constitutional Lawmaking: The Supreme Court and the Art of Politics* (Elmsford, N.Y.: Pergamon Press, 1985), pp. 52–55.

[8]*Johnson v. Zerbst,* 304 U.S. 458 (1938), *Gideon v. Wainwright,* 372 U.S. 335 (1963), *Argersinger v. Hamlin,* 407 U.S. 25 (1972). For a persuasive defense of this trend see Anthony Lewis's classic, *Gideon's Trumpet* (New York: Random House, 1964).

edly and expressly rejected the idea that their own actual hopes and expectations of the Constitution would dictate legal conclusions in the future. First, at common law, the reading of texts like wills and contracts rejected actual intent in favor of giving words their "reasonable," "grammatical," or "popular" meaning. Second, the framers, as members of the Protestant tradition, believed that texts ought to speak for themselves, unmediated by church or scholarly authority. They believed each person should be free to interpret biblical texts for himself and that complex scholarly interpretations— interpretations imposed by "experts"—had no presumptive authority.

Powell describes how George Washington required in his will the nonlegal arbitration of any ambiguity in administering its provisions precisely in order that the decision maker might consider Washington's actual intent in the matter. None of the debaters in Philadelphia acknowledged that their words might shape the future, and James Madison believed that usage ("usus") and the lessons learned from political practice should override any "abstract opinion of the text." Thus, as President he signed the Second Bank Bill. He thought the First U. S. Bank had been unconstitutional, but he approved the successor because the people had approved it and it had worked.[9]

Stare Decisis

In 1940 the Supreme Court held that a public school could require all children—including Jehovah's Witnesses, whose religious convictions forbade it—to salute the flag each day. In 1943 the Court overruled itself and held the opposite.[10] In 1942, four years after it required the federal government to provide counsel for the poor, the Court held that the states did not have to do so.[11] In the famous *Gideon* case cited above,

[9]H. Jefferson Powell, "The Original Understanding of Original Intent," 98 *Harvard Law Review* 885 (1985).

[10]*Minersville School District v. Gobitis,* 310 U.S. 586 (1940), and *West Virginia State Board of Education v. Barnette,* 319 U.S. 624 (1943).

[11]*Betts v. Brady,* 316 U.S. 455 (1942).

the Court changed its mind. In 1946 the Court refused to require state legislatures to make electoral districts roughly equal, but in 1962 the Court began to do just that.[12]

The Justices themselves have from time to time recognized the limited utility of stare decisis in constitutional law. After all, no legislature sits mainly to update constitutional policy in light of new conditions. It is not simply that the Court should correct its own mistakes—that, as indicated in Chapter III, is always wise policy. It is rather that wise policy at one time is not necessarily wise policy at another. If we take seriously the idea that the Constitution is law—ought to have teeth—then the courts must do the updating. As Justice William O. Douglas once said:

> The place of *stare decisis* in constitutional law is . . . tenuous. A judge looking at a constitutional decision may have compulsions to revere past history and accept what was once written. But he remembers above all else that it is the Constitution which he swore to support and defend, not the gloss which his predecessors may have put on it. So he comes to formulate his own views, rejecting some earlier ones as false and embracing others. He cannot do otherwise unless he lets men long dead and unaware of the problems of the age in which he lives do his thinking for him.[13]

Of course people rely on constitutional decisions. Teachers in 1943 believed they could require even Jehovah's Witnesses in the classroom to salute the flag. State judges in 1963 did not believe they had to appoint counsel in all felonies. Candidates for political office and their parties in the early 1960s may have created their election strategies assuming malapportionment in voting districts. The point is that constitutional values may be important enough to override reliance on past policy.

---

[12]*Colegrove v. Green,* 328 U.S. 549 (1946), and *Baker v. Carr,* 369 U.S. 186 (1962).

[13]William O. Douglas, "Stare Decisis," 4 *Record of the Association of the Bar of the City of New York* 152 (1949), pp. 153–154.

RESOLVING THE PARADOX

If *neither* the conventions of legal justification nor the back-stop of legislative correction of judicial decisions limits the Supreme Court's power and discretion, then what does? This question has preoccupied constitutional scholarship for nearly a century. The remainder of this chapter reviews two possible answers: Perhaps a theory of constitutional justification exists but the Justices have not yet learned to practice it. Or perhaps the political system imposes sufficient practical and informal checks on the court to compensate for the fact that judges aren't themselves elected. Although variations on these two themes encompass most modern constitutional jurisprudence, neither theme really resolves the paradox.

Theories About Constitutional Justification

The search for limits on the Supreme Court's power and discretion is not driven merely by the sometimes obsessive need of scholars to make the world neat and tidy. In the late nineteenth and early twentieth centuries the Supreme Court did try to proclaim itself the final arbiter of social and economic policy and of political morality. It actively thwarted economic and social reforms at all levels of government for the sake of then-popular beliefs in Social Darwinism, which seemed to many judges to equate unregulated private business activity with the improvement of the human race. So in *U.S. v. E.C. Knight* (1895) the Court aggressively reduced national power over commerce by defining the commerce power (contrary to precedents going back to John Marshall) to cover only the physical movement of goods among the states.[14] In 1905, in *Lochner v. New York,* the Court struck down statutory amelioration of harsh working conditions in bakeries by creating, under the Fourteenth Amendment's due process clause, a constitutional right to individuals' freedom to make any contracts they chose subject only to the "reasonable" exercise of the state's police power. The Court decided what was "reason-

[14]156 U.S. 1.

able."[15] In 1918, Congress forbade the shipment in interstate commerce of goods made with child labor. Although the statute seemed to honor restrictions on the commerce power set in *E.C. Knight,* the Court struck down this statute because there was nothing inherently harmful about the goods shipped.[16]

The Court's official version of Social Darwinism mistook the absence of regulation for free competition. Social Darwinism promised the improvement of the species through free competition, but such government regulations as the antitrust laws (which *E.C. Knight* curtailed) actually encouraged the sort of competition that Social Darwinism required; that is, the Court claimed the power to review and reverse social policy on the basis of a theory that contradicted itself. Thus, Justice David Brewer in 1893 told the New York Bar Association that strengthening the judiciary was necessary to protect the country "against the tumultuous ocean of democracy!" He believed that

> the permanence of government of and by the people . . . rests upon the independence and vigor of the judiciary, . . . to restrain the greedy hand of the many from filching from the few that which they have honestly acquired. . . . [17]

This claim to unlimited judicial power prompted a search for theories that would limit judicial power, a search that has continued to this day.

The first of these theories, authored by James B. Thayer of the Harvard Law School, tried to reaffirm the representative nature of American constitutional government. All acts of elected bodies carry a heavy presumption of constitutionality. The courts may properly overturn legislation only on a showing that the legislature has made a very clear mistake.[18]

Thayer's antithesis proved unsatisfactory for two reasons. First, like the "golden rule" of statutory interpretation,

[15]198 U.S. 45.

[16]*Hammer v. Dagenhart,* 247 U.S. 251.

[17]*Proceedings of the New York State Bar Association* (1893), p. 37.

[18]"The Origin and Scope of the American Doctrine of Constitutional Law," 7 *Harvard Law Review* 129 (1893).

it contained no standards for determining what counted as a clear mistake. From the perspective of David Brewer (and Justice Field, who thought the income tax marked the beginning of a war waged by the poor against the rich), economic regulation *was* a clear mistake. Thayer's position left to courts the responsibility for doing the extra-legal analysis necessary to decide what counts as a clear mistake: "The ultimate arbiter of what is rational and permissible is indeed always the courts, so far as litigated cases bring the question before them."

Second, if Thayer's theory did nudge the court into a posture of judicial self-restraint, the Court would then lack power to protect violations of civil liberties. Yet before the final collapse of the Court's economic activism in 1937, it had begun to move into the civil liberties area. In 1931 the Court struck down a Minnesota law permitting prior censorship of the press.[19] In 1932 it reversed the death sentences of six black defendants sentenced to death after a one-day trial in Scottsboro, Alabama, in which the six were denied adequate representation of counsel.[20]

The synthesis of the two extremes, the theory that justified judicial abstinence from evaluating the rationality of economic policy without curtailing its power to protect civil liberties, appeared quietly in the fourth footnote to a 1938 case in which the Court upheld congressional authority to regulate the ingredients in milk products processed for interstate commerce. The footnote read:

> There may be narrower scope for operation of the presumption of constitutionality when legislation appears on its face to be within a specific prohibition of the Constitution, such as those of the first ten amendments, which are deemed equally specific when held to be embraced within the Fourteenth. . . .
>
> It is unnecessary to consider now whether legislation which restricts those political processes which can ordinarily be expected to bring about a repeal of undesirable legislation, is to be subjected to more exacting judicial

[19]*Near v. Minnesota*, 283 U.S. 697.
[20]*Powell v. Alabama*, 287 U.S. 45.

scrutiny under the general prohibitions of the Fourteenth Amendment than are most other types of legislation. . . .

Nor need we inquire whether similar consideration enter into the review of statutes directed at particular religious . . . or national . . . or racial minorities . . . whether prejudice against discrete and insular minorities may be a special condition, which tends seriously to curtail the operation of those political processes ordinarily to be relied upon to protect minorities, and which may call for a correspondingly more searching judicial inquiry. . . . [21]

The first paragraph justified cases like *Near* because the First Amendment guarantees a free press, and *Powell* because the Fifth and Sixth Amendments guarantee a fair trial. In such cases the Court deemed that the Fourteenth Amendment's due process clause applied these federal restrictions to state and local governmental actions.

The note's second paragraph explained why the Court need not intervene in economic policy: Fights over allocation of economic resources—like the debate over the working conditions in bakeries in *Lochner*—are usually waged by well-organized groups on various sides of the issue. The political compromises among those interests may not equate with a professional economist's definition of rationality, but they are legally acceptable because all sides participate in the process. But if the electoral machinery itself breaks down so as to bias the messages policy makers receive, the Courts may intervene, e.g., as in the reapportionment cases.[22]

The footnote's third paragraph suggests that even when the machinery of electoral politics works properly, prejudice against racial, religious, or other minorities (including people accused of serious crimes like murder, rape, and robbery) may prevent them from being heard. The Court's leadership regarding racial segregation took place at a time when blacks in the deep South were systematically denied the chance to organize and vote.

---

[21]*United States v. Carolene Products Co.*, 304 U.S. 114, pp. 152–153.

[22]*Baker v. Carr*, 369 U.S. 186 (1962), and see *Reynolds v. Sims*, 377 U.S. 533 (1964).

John Hart Ely and Jesse Choper in two books published in 1980 developed the details of these theories.[23] To the three *Carolene Products* points Choper added a fourth: The Court should avoid upsetting political decisions about the balance of power between national and local government. The fact that state and local parties and elections select the members of Congress and that reelection depends on satisfying local demands ensures a rough balance of state and local power without help from the Supreme Court. (Indeed, a common modern complaint about Congress, particularly regarding its seeming inability to reduce the national budget deficit, holds that congressmen's outlooks are excessively parochial and local.)

Many more scholarly theories of the Court's role have emerged since 1937. Herbert Wechsler has advocated that the Court decide cases only on the basis of "neutral principles," on the basis of rules that future courts can apply in cases with very different partisan or political alignments. A principle protecting those who demonstrate for racial justice must be articulated in such a way as to protect demonstrating members of the American Nazi Party.[24] Alexander Bickel believed that, to preserve its capacity to announce such principles without endangering the Court's political support, the Court should exploit its many technical procedures by which it can avoid deciding at all.[25] This book's Appendix describes some of these techniques.

Despite the scholarly elegance of each of these theories, they do not answer our fundamental question. We seek legal and political dynamics that actually do limit the constitutional power of the Supreme Court, not merely a resolution of an academic debate about what might, in theory, limit the Court.

---

[23]John Hart Ely, *Democracy and Distrust: A Theory of Judicial Review* (Cambridge: Harvard University Press), and Jesse Choper, *Judicial Review and the National Political Process: A Functional Reconsideration of the Role of the Supreme Court* (Chicago: University of Chicago Press).

[24]Herbert Wechsler, "Toward Neutral Principles of Constitutional Law," 73 *Harvard Law Review* 1 (1959).

[25]Alexander Bickel, *The Least Dangerous Branch* (Indianapolis: Bobbs-Merrill, 1962).

We seek an understanding of the Court's actual practices that can assure us that its justifications are good, and the fact of the matter is that, in practice, the Court does not consistently follow these theories any better than it follows more conventional methods of legal reasoning.

Consider the Court's decision in *Griswold v. Connecticut,* in which the Court struck down state laws prohibiting the distribition of contraceptives. The "right of privacy" created by the Court to justify the result is hardly a "specific prohibition" in the Bill of Rights, and the people it protects—women and men both—are as far from an insular and discrete minority as we could imagine.[26] The Court's extension of the principle of privacy in the abortion case—including the right of a single female—might seem to practice Wechsler's neutral principles concept but for the fact that the Court also ruled that the Constitution permits government to deny funds for abortion to the indigent who are otherwise qualified to receive them.[27] Indeed Justice Stone, the coauthor of *Carolene Products'* footnote 4 voted (perhaps for Bickelian reasons) *against* allowing the Court to intervene in legislative reapportionment, in direct contradiction to his note's second paragraph.[28]

We have already seen that a precedent does not dictate how a judge applies it. (If it did, the case would usually not reach the appellate courts in the first place.) Just as "fact freedom" allows different judges to apply the same precedents in opposite ways, so each constitutional theory does not dictate or constrain. The history of judicial review, starting with *Marbury v. Madison,*[29] more resembles a tool bench where the judge decides how the case ought to come out and then chooses whatever tool seems handiest to get the job done. All academic theories about the Supreme Court's role fail to answer our question. Perhaps the political role of the Supreme Court

---

[26]*Griswold v. Connecticut,* 381 U.S. 479 (1965).

[27]*Roe v. Wade,* 410 U.S. 113 (1973), but *Harris v. McRae,* 448 U.S. 297 (1980).

[28]*Colegrove v. Green,* 328 U.S. 549 (1946).

[29]*Marbury v. Madison,* 5 U.S. 87 (1803). To reach the political result he wanted in this case, Chief Justice Marshall had to make five highly implausible readings of the laws relevant to the case.

makes theoretical consistency both impossible and unnecessary. We explore that possibility next.

Political Constraints on the Court

One school of thought, which political scientists have called "political jurisprudence," supplies constraints on the Supreme Court not through political theory or legal doctrine but from the practical operation of politics itself. This resolution of the constitutional paradox was expressed most pithily by Mr. Dooley's conclusion that "th' Supreme Court follows th' iliction returns." Martin Shapiro, a leading figure in political jurisprudence for a quarter of a century, put it this way:

> No regime is likely to allow significant political power to be wielded by an isolated judicial corps free of political restraints. To the extent that courts make law, judges will be incorporated into the governing coalition, the ruling elite, responsible representatives of the people, or however else the political regime may be expressed.[30]

Subject to a few historical exceptions, particularly the Court's advocacy of Social Darwinism and laissez faire economics, the theory holds that the Court rarely strays far enough from dominant popular opinion to worry about checking it through legal doctrine or theories of judicial review.[31] This approach combines historical observations of instances in which presidential selections of Justices have steered the Court onto more popular courses with analyses of the structural and procedural characteristics of the Court's work that make it politically responsive. Here are the major threads this perspective weaves together.

Many constitutional decisions do not invalidate the work of popularly elected legislators in the first place. They set aside, as in the decisions regarding search and seizure of criminal evidence and of interrogation of suspects, decisions of

[30]Martin Shapiro, *Courts: A Comparative Political Analysis* (Chicago: University of Chicago Press, 1981), p. 34.

[31]See Robert Dahl, "Decision-Making in a Democracy: The Supreme Court as National Policy Maker, 6 *Journal of Public Law* 294 (1958).

nonelected administrative personnel who are, like judges, only indirectly affected by electoral politics. In less than one-half of one percent of all statutes passed by Congress since World War II has the Court found a point to invalidate. In nearly all of these instances, the Court has invalidated not an entire statutory scheme or policy but only an offending clause or provision.[32] The most activist of courts touches only a tiny fraction of the democratic work of Congress.

Elected officials do not vote according to the "majority will" because on most policy issues before a legislature the public has no opinion whatsoever. The benefit of elections in the daily operation of politics comes from the fact that elected politicians listen to interest groups and individual citizens because they need as many votes from as many different sources as possible. Elections tend to overcome the natural inertia of all organized human effort. The legal process has a different but equally effective method for forcing judges to listen: Anyone can file a lawsuit about anything, and judges must listen to it at least long enough to determine that the lawsuit alleges no legal injury.

The President fills a vacancy on the Supreme Court on the average of slightly less often than once every two years. Even before Ronald Reagan's appointments of Sandra Day O'Connor and Antonin Scalia, the Nixon-Ford presidencies had named a majority of the Supreme Court bench, and this Burger Court very much slowed the expansion of the Warren Court's protection of the rights of the accused, just as President Nixon's "law and order" campaign had pledged.[33]

As we saw regarding the case of the sunken barges in Chapter IV, courts process information very much as other decision makers do. Various sides present positions. Lawyers file briefs containing abundant factual as well as legal assertions. They criticize the positions their opponents take. The capacity

[32]Through the year 1978, the Supreme Court had invalidated portions of about 100 Acts of Congress, 900 State Statutes, and 124 local ordinances. My thanks to Professor Sam Krislov for calling these tabulations to my attention.

[33]For a recent argument favoring independent Senate screening of the President's judicial appointments, see Laurence Tribe, *God Save This Honorable Court* (New York: Random House, 1985).

of judges to understand information depends on two things. First, does the issue really depend on the intelligent digestion and interpretation of a complex body of facts at all? Many of the most dramatic civil rights questions are so fundamentally normative and depend so extensively on moral rather than factual reasoning, that the technical competence of judges really does not seem relevant. The decision to forbid mandatory flag salutes does not depend on scientific analysis of data revealing the beneficial and harmful consequences of such practices. Second, when the issue does depend on an understanding of facts, then we should really expect judges to have the *capacity* to understand the facts before they proceed. Judges must understand the language through which the problem expresses itself. Most judges are well equipped to understand the dimensions of a right-to-counsel issue. Most judges are not equipped to understand the econometric analysis on which the Federal Reserve Board determines its national monetary policy. The problem must not be of the sort in which part of the information is necessarily hidden from judges, as it is in many foreign policy matters because the information is secret or because the only people who possess it do not live or work within the reach of the court's jurisdiction. Finally, if a given decision generates feedback information that will produce improved policy, the courts should have access to that information in the course of further litigation.[34]

Constitutional decisions possess all the characteristics of the common law tradition. No one decision permanently sets the course of law. The process is a thoroughly incremental one in which, case by case, new facts and new arguments pro and con repeatedly come before the courts. The law can change and adjust to new facts and conditions. A judicial commitment

---

[34]Lief H. Carter, "When Courts Should Make Policy: An Institutional Approach," in *Public Law and Public Policy,* John A. Gardiner, ed. (New York: Praeger, 1977), pp. 141–157; Donald L. Horowitz, *The Courts and Social Policy* (Washington, D.C.: The Brookings Institution, 1977); J. Woodford Howard, "Adjudication Considered as a Process of Conflict Resolution: A Variation on Separation of Powers," 18 *Journal of Public Law* 39 (1969); Stephen Wasby, "Horowitz: The Courts and Social Policy," 31 *Vanderbilt Law Review* 727 (1978).

to protecting liberties does not require the courts to articulate a complete theory of equal protection or due process.[35]

In the twentieth century the Court has avoided creating legal doctrine that appears to "take sides" along popular partisan lines. Decisions defending the freedom of civil rights activists to organize and demonstrate also protect neo-Nazis and Klansmen. The Burger Court voted without dissent against President Nixon's claim of executive privilege in the Watergate crisis. The Court steered a middle course regarding affirmative action when it ruled that race alone could not determine admissions policies.[36]

Although the Burger Court has sometimes forgotten the lesson, particularly in the legislative veto case, the structural core of American government is not and has never been the idea that power is separated. The main thrust of the Madisonian constitutional scheme was to prevent too much power from accumulating in one place. The dispersion of power takes place more through the sharing than the separating of power. Different institutions must compromise because none can act effectively without cooperating with the others. Perhaps therefore the indeterminacy of constitutional theory is a blessing in disguise, a measure of the success of Madison's vision.[37]

WHY THE PARADOX ENDURES

Do these indisputable characteristics of American politics resolve the paradox of constitutional law? Two lines of reasoning indicate that they do not. First, although these factors do

---

[35]Felix Cohen, "Transcendental Nonsense and the Functional Approach," 35 *Columbia Law Review* 809 (1935). See also Martin Shapiro, "Stability and Change in Judicial Decision Making: Incrementalism or Stare Decisis?" 2 *Law in Transition Quarterly* 134 (1964). And see Janet S. Lindgren, "Beyond Cases: Reconsidering Judicial Review," 1983 *Wisconsin Law Review* 583 (1983).

[36]*Regents of the University of California v. Bakke,* 438 U. S. 265 (1978).

[37]See Walter Murphy, James Fleming, and Will Harris, *American Constitutional Interpretation* (Mineola, N.Y.: Foundation Press, 1986), chap. 1–3, esp. pp. 48–55.

suggest no cause for immediate alarm about the Supreme Court's political role, they completely sidestep the original question. Legal reasoning ought to provide standards of satisfactory justification for specific case decisions. The political factors do not guide judges in the crafting of actual opinions. They provide some macroscopic reassurance, but it will hardly satisfy a losing litigant in a concrete case to learn merely that the President might appoint a new justice in a year or two.

Second, the reassuring argument may prove too much. The Constitution is in some respects an antimajoritarian document. The Constitution in part seeks to protect individuals from what Tocqueville called "the tyranny of the majority." It protects individuals, not demographically defined groups. The unpopular speaker and the deviant religious belief may thrive only if the courts are not politically too responsive. If James Boyd White, as quoted earlier in this chapter, is correct that we must sustain the belief that the Constitution is a central source of political structure and communal values— if we need to believe in *it*—then conventional political jurisprudence provides no satisfying solution to our problem.

The latest phase of political jurisprudence, the "Critical Legal Studies" movement, recognizes the two reservations I just described. Beginning in the mid–1970s, Duncan Kennedy, Roberto Unger, Mark Tushnet, Robert Gordon, Paul Brest, John Henry Schlagel, and other law professors who came of professional age during the antiwar movement of the 1960s began in their publications to assert that the political culture constrains court and legislature alike from protecting individual dignity adequately. But they also recognized that the solution lay in changing not legal doctrine but the political culture itself. The critical side of the movement has articulated a powerful case for abandoning the search for any doctrinal solution to the constitutional paradox.[38]

The positive contribution of Critical Legal Studies is less clear or convincing, in part because the very success of the movement's critique of doctrine makes a case that no doctri-

---

[38]I have treated the critical movement in my *Contemporary Constitutional Lawmaking,* especially pp. 98–101 and 127–133.

nal solution is possible. Nevertheless, Critical Legal Studies seems to move toward endorsing the idea that constitutional goodness depends on the Court's enhancing our capacity to converse about the moral or normative equality of our communal life. To accomplish this the Court must do more than protect First Amendment freedoms or individual privacy. It must protect individual integrity and dignity so that people feel empowered to participate in political life. To accomplish that the Court must in turn model good conversation. It must speak candidly about the world that law, politics, science, economics, and religion all inhabit.

The Critical Legal Studies movement has retained the radical or neo-Marxist orientation of its antiwar origins, but its substantive conclusions do not differ substantially from those reached by the more mainstream liberal philosophy of Ronald Dworkin, Walter Murphy, and Sotirios Barber.[39] Although mainstream liberalism persists in searching for a coherent constitutional philosophy, its approach emphasizes not legal solutions but the process by which we arrive at them. The Constitution reminds us that we aspire to achieve political goodness. We, being imperfect, will never achieve it, but it is essential that we not abandon our effort to combine the lessons of the past with our experience in the present to define what is politically good.

The final chapter, which presents my own theory of justification in all areas of law, will elaborate this approach. For now, the lesson is that a preoccupation with doctrine may do more harm than good. The judge or scholar who insists on a doctrinally elegant legal resolution of a case may shut himself off from the cares and aspirations of the litigants themselves. The people whose lives the courts shape will not likely have doctrinal elegance at the top of their list of priorities. Perhaps

---

[39]Dworkin, *Taking Rights Seriously* (Cambridge: Harvard University Press, 1978), and *A Matter of Principle* (Cambridge: Harvard University Press, 1985); Murphy, "The Art of Constitutional Interpretation: A Preliminary Showing," in M. Judd Harmon, ed., *Essays on the Constitution of the United States* (Port Washington, N.Y.: Kennikat Press, 1980); Barber, *On What the Constitution Means* (Baltimore: Johns Hopkins University Press, 1984).

this is what Justice Harry Blackmun meant in a recent interview:

> The notion of humility is central to an understanding of Justice Blackmun's place on the Court. He believes he is there to do justice, not merely to oblige its doctrinal demands, and his unprepossessing style serves to remind him of the constituency he has been sent there to serve. "Maybe I'm oversensitive," Justice Blackmun says, "But these are very personal cases. We're dealing with *people*—the life, liberty and property of *people*. And because I grew up in poor surroundings, I know there's another world out there we sometimes forget about."[40]

SUMMARY

- What is the "Constitutional paradox"?
- Which methods of legal reasoning approved in statutory interpretation and common law do not apply in constitutional law, and why?
- What political role did the Supreme Court assume in the period when it took Social Darwinism and laissez-faire doctrines seriously?
- What theories of judicial review substitute for the usual methods of legal reasoning?
- What forces lead the Supreme Court to respond to pressures from the political world?
- Why do neither theories of judicial review nor the structural and procedural characteristics that make the Supreme Court politically responsive resolve the constitutional paradox?
- How can the Constitution remain a viable source of political values if no doctrinal solution to the paradox exists?

ILLUSTRATIVE CASE

To understand the legal issues in the following case you need to know that the "equal protection clause" of the Fourteenth Amendment potentially invalidates any state law that classifies or differentiates people by sex. This body of law is complex and

---

[40]John Jenkins, "A Candid Talk with Justice Blackmun," *New York Times Magazine,* 20 February 1983, p. 20, at pp. 23–24.

unsettled, but please assume for the moment that *Craig v. Boren* 429 U. S. 190 (1976) states accepted law. In *Craig* the Court struck down a law that limited sale of 3.2 beer to men (but not women) in their late teens. The courts conventionally permit differentiations that bear a substantial relationship to legitimate public policies, but the Court in *Craig* required some evidence that young men more frequently caused social harm from drinking 3.2 beer than did young women. The state failed to produce such evidence, so the Court invalidated the sex-based classification. Consider by contrast the Supreme Court's conclusions about what the background facts do and do not prove in the following case. Assume that both male and female in this case were about 17 years old and that at least a half hour of fully consensual foreplay occurred before the act of statutory rape itself.

Michael M. v. Superior Court of Sonoma County
(California, Real Party in Interest)
460 U. S. 464 (1981)

Justice Rehnquist announced the judgment of the Court and delivered an opinion, in which The Chief Justice, Justice Stewart, and Justice Powell joined.

The question presented in this case is whether California's "statutory rape" law, Section 261.5 of the California Penal Code . . . violates the Equal Protection Clause of the Fourteenth Amendment. Section 261.5 defines unlawful sexual intercourse as "an act of sexual intercourse accomplished with a female not the wife of the perpetrator, where the female is under the age of 18 years." The statute thus makes men alone criminally liable for the act of sexual intercourse. . . .

We are satisfied not only that the prevention of illegitimate pregnancy is at least one of the "purposes" of the statute, but also that the State has a strong interest in preventing such pregnancy. At the risk of stating the obvious, teenage pregnancies, which have increased dramatically over the last two decades, have significant social, medical, and economic consequences for both the mother and her child, and the State.[a] Of particular concern

[a]The risk of maternal death is 60% higher for a teenager under the age of 15 than for a woman in her early twenties. The risk is 13% higher for 15-to-19-year-olds. The statistics further show that most teenage mothers drop out of school and face a bleak economic future. See, *e.g., 11 Million Teenagers,* supra,

to the State is that approximately half of all teenage pregnancies end in abortion. And of those children who are born, their illegitimacy makes them likely candidates to become wards of the State.

We need not be medical doctors to discern that young men and young women are not similarly situated with respect to the problems and the risks of sexual intercourse. Only women may become pregnant, and they suffer disproportionately the profound physical, emotional, and psychological consequences of sexual activity. The statute at issue here protects women from sexual intercourse at an age when those consequences are particularly severe.

The question thus boils down to whether a State may attack the problem of sexual intercourse and teenage pregnancy directly by prohibiting a male from having sexual intercourse with a minor female. We hold that such a statute is sufficiently related to the State's objectives to pass constitutional muster.

Because virtually all of the significant harmful and inescapably identifiable consequences of teenage pregnancy fall on the young female, a legislature acts well within its authority when it elects to punish only the participant who, by nature, suffers few of the consequences of his conduct. It is hardly unreasonable for a legislature acting to protect minor females to exclude them from punishment. Moreover, the risk of pregnancy itself constitutes a substantial deterrence to young females. No similar natural sanctions deter males. A criminal sanction imposed solely on males thus serves to roughly "equalize" the deterrents on the sexes. . . .

In any event, we cannot say that a gender-neutral statute would be as effective as the statute California has chosen to enact. The State persuasively contends that a gender-neutral statute would frustrate its interest in effective enforcement. Its view is that a female is surely less likely to report violations of the statute if she herself would be subject to criminal prosecution. In an area already fraught with prosecutorial difficulties, we decline to hold that the Equal Protection Clause requires a legislature to enact a statute so broad that it may well be incapable of enforcement. . . .

---

at 23, 25; Bennett & Bardon, "The Effects of a School Program On Teenager Mothers and Their Children," 47 *Am. J. Orthopsychiatry* 671 (1977); Phipps-Yonas, "Teenage Pregnancy and Motherhood," 50 *Am. J. Orthopsychiatry* 403, 414 (1980).

There remains only petitioner's contention that the statute is unconstitutional as it is applied to him because he, like Sharon, was under 18 at the time of sexual intercourse. Petitioner argues that the statute is flawed because it presumes that as between two persons under 18, the male is the culpable aggressor. We find petitioner's contentions unpersuasive. Contrary to his assertions, the statute does not rest on the assumption that males are generally the aggressors. It is instead an attempt by a legislature to prevent illegitimate teenage pregnancy by providing an additional deterrent for men. The age of the man is irrelevant since young men are as capable as older men of inflicting the harm sought to be prevented. . . .

Accordingly, the judgment of the California Supreme Court is affirmed.

JUSTICE STEWART concurring. . . . Young women and men are not similarly situated with respect to the problems and risks associated with intercourse and pregnancy, and the statute is realistically related to the legitimate state purpose of reducing those problems and risks.

As the California Supreme Court's catalog shows, the pregnant unmarried female confronts problems more numerous and more severe than any faced by her male partner.[b] She alone endures the medical risks of pregnancy or abortion. She suffers disproportionately the social, educational, and emotional consequences of pregnancy. Recognizing this disproportion, California has attempted to protect teenage females by prohibiting males from participating in the act necessary for conception.

The fact that males and females are not similarly situated with respect to the risks of sexual intercourse applies with the same force to males under 18 as it does to older males. The risk of pregnancy is a significant deterrent for unwed young females that is not shared by unmarried males, regardless of their age. Experienced observation confirms the commonsense notion. that adolescent males disregard the possibility of pregnancy far more than do adolescent females. And to the extent that Section 261.5 may punish males for intercourse with prepubescent fe-

[b]The court noted that from 1971 through 1976, 83.6% of the 4,860 children born to girls under 15 in California were illegitimate, as were 51% of those born to girls 15 to 17. The court also observed that while accounting for only 21% of California pregnancies in 1976, teenagers accounted for 34.7% of legal abortions.

males, that punishment is justifiable because of the substantial physical risks for prepubescent females that are not shared by their male counterparts. . . .

[Concurring opinion of Justice BLACKMUN omitted.]

Justice BRENNAN, with whom Justices WHITE and MARSHALL join, dissenting. . . .

The plurality assumes that a gender-neutral statute would be less effective than Section 261.5 in deterring sexual activity because a gender-neutral statute would create significant enforcement problems. The plurality thus accepts the State's assertion that

> a female is surely less likely to report violations of the statute if she herself would be subject to criminal prosecution. In an area already fraught with prosecutorial difficulties, we decline to hold that the Equal Protection Clause requires a legislature to enact a statute so broad that it may well be incapable of enforcement. Ante, at 473–474. . . .

However, a State's bare assertion that its gender-based statutory classification substantially furthers an important governmental interest is not enough to meet its burden of proof under *Craig v. Boren*. Rather, the State must produce evidence that will persuade the court that its assertion is true. See *Craig v. Boren*, 429 U. S., at 200–204.

The State has not produced such evidence in this case. Moreover, there are at least two serious flaws in the State's assertion that law enforcement problems created by a gender-neutral statutory rape law would make such a statute less effective than a gender-based statute in deterring sexual activity.

First, the experience of other jurisdictions, and California itself, belies the plurality's conclusion that a gender-neutral statutory rape law "may well be incapable of enforcement." There are now at least 37 States that have enacted gender-neutral statutory rape laws. Although most of these laws protect young persons (of either sex) from the sexual exploitation of older individuals, the laws of Arizona, Florida, and Illinois permit prosecution of both minor females and minor males for engaging in mutual sexual conduct. California has introduced no evidence that those States have been handicapped by the enforcement problems the plurality finds so persuasive. Surely, if those States could provide such evidence, we might expect that California would have introduced it.

In addition, the California Legislature in recent years has revised other sections of the Penal Code to make them gender-neutral. For example, Cal. Penal Code Ann. Sections 286(b)(1) and 288a(b)(1), prohibiting sodomy and oral copulation with a "person who is under 18 years of age," could cause two minor homosexuals to be subjected to criminal sanctions for engaging in mutually consensual conduct. Again, the State has introduced no evidence to explain why a gender-neutral statutory rape law would be any more difficult to enforce than those statutes.

The second flaw in the State's assertion is that even assuming that a gender-neutral statute would be more difficult to enforce, the State has still not shown that those enforcement problems would make such a statute less effective than a gender-based statute in deterring minor females from engaging in sexual intercourse. Common sense, however, suggests that a gender-neutral statutory rape law is potentially a *greater* deterrent of sexual activity than a gender-based law, for the simple reason that a gender-neutral law subjects both men and women to criminal sanctions and thus arguably has a deterrent effect on twice as many potential violators. Even if fewer persons were prosecuted under the gender-neutral law, as the State suggests, it would still be true that twice as many persons would be *subject* to arrest. The State's failure to prove that a gender-neutral law would be a less effective deterrent than a gender-based law, like the State's failure to prove that a gender-neutral law would be difficult to enforce, should have led this Court to invalidate Section 261.5....

Justice STEVENS, dissenting.

Local custom and belief rather than statutory laws of venerable but doubtful ancestry will determine the volume of sexual activity among unmarried teenagers. The empirical evidence cited by the plurality demonstrates the futility of the notion that a statutory prohibition will significantly affect the volume of that activity or provide a meaningful solution to the problems created by it . . . [T]he plurality surely cannot believe that the risk of pregnancy confronted by the female—any more than the risk of venereal disease confronted by males as well as females—has provided an effective deterrent to voluntary female participation in the risk-creating conduct. Yet the plurality's decision seems to rest on the assumption that the California Legislature acted on the basis of that rather fanciful notion.

In my judgment, the fact that a class of persons is especially vulnerable to a risk that a statute is designed to avoid is a reason for making the statute applicable to that class. The argument that a special need for protection provides a rational explanation for an exemption is one I simply do not comprehend.[c]

In this case, the fact that a female confronts a greater risk of harm than a male is a reason for applying the prohibition to her—not a reason for granting her a license to use her own judgment on whether or not to assume the risk. Surely, if we examine the problem from the point of view of society's interest in preventing the risk-creating conduct from occurring at all, it is irrational to exempt 50% of the potential violators.... And, if we view the government's interest as that of a *parens patriae* seeking to protect its subjects from harming themselves, the discrimination is actually perverse. Would a rational parent making rules for the conduct of twin children of opposite sex simultaneously forbid the son and authorize the daughter to engage in conduct that is especially harmful to the daughter? That is the effect of this statutory classification.

If pregnancy or some other special harm is suffered by one of the two participants in the prohibited act, that special harm no doubt would constitute a legitimate mitigating factor in deciding what, if any, punishment might be appropriate in a given case. But from the standpoint of fashioning a general preventive rule—or, indeed, in determining appropriate punishment when neither party in fact has suffered any special harm—I regard a total exemption for the members of the more endangered class as utterly irrational.

In my opinion, the only acceptable justification for a general rule requiring disparate treatment of the two participants

[c]A hypothetical racial classification will illustrate my point. Assume that skin pigmentation provides some measure of protection against cancer caused by exposure to certain chemicals in the atmosphere and, therefore, that white employees confront a greater risk than black employees in certain industrial settings. Would it be rational to require black employees to wear protective clothing but to exempt whites from that requirement? It seems to me that the greater risk of harm to white workers would be a reason for including them in the requirement—not for granting them an exemption.

in a joint act must be a legislative judgment that one is more guilty than the other. The risk-creating conduct that this statute is designed to prevent requires the participation of two persons—one male and one female.[d] In many situations it is probably true that one is the aggressor and the other is either an unwilling, or at least a less willing, participant in the joint act. If a statute authorized punishment of only one participant and required the prosecutor to prove that that participant had been the aggressor, I assume that the discrimination would be valid. Although the question is less clear, I also assume, for the purpose of deciding this case, that it would be permissible to punish only the male participant, if one element of the offense were proof that he had been the aggressor, or at least in some respects the more responsible participant in the joint act. The statute at issue in this case, however, requires no such proof. The question raised by this statute is whether the State, consistently with the Federal Constitution, may always punish the male and never the female when they are equally responsible or when the female is the more responsible of the two.

It would seem to me that an impartial lawmaker could give only one answer to that question. The fact that the California Legislature has decided to apply its prohibition only to the male may reflect a legislative judgment that in the typical case the male is actually the more guilty party. Any such judgment must, in turn, assume that the decision to engage in the risk-creating conduct is always—or at least typically—a male decision. If that assumption is valid, the statutory classification should also be valid. But what is the support for the assumption? It is not contained in the record of this case or in any legislative history or scholarly study that has been called to our attention. I think it is supported to some extent by traditional attitudes toward male-female relationships. But the possibility that such a habitual attitude may re-

---

[d]In light of this indisputable biological fact, I find somewhat puzzling the California Supreme Court's conclusion, quoted by the plurality, *ante,* at 467, that males "are the *only* persons who may physiologically cause the result which the law properly seeks to avoid." 25 Cal. 3d 608, 612, 601 p. 2d 572, 575 (1979) (emphasis in original). Presumably, the California Supreme Court was referring to the equally indisputable biological fact that only females may become pregnant. However, if pregnancy results from sexual intercourse between two willing participants and the California statute is directed at such conduct I would find it difficult to conclude that the pregnancy was "caused" solely by the male participant.

flect nothing more than an irrational prejudice makes it an insufficient justification for discriminatory treatment that is otherwise blatantly unfair. For, as I read this statute, it requires that one, and only one, of two equally guilty wrongdoers be stigmatized by a criminal conviction. . . .

Nor do I find at all persuasive the suggestion that this discrimination is adequately justified by the desire to encourage females to inform against their male partners. Even if the concept of a wholesale informant's exemption were an acceptable enforcement device, what is the justification for defining the exempt class entirely by reference to sex rather than by reference to a more neutral criterion such as relative innocence? Indeed, if the exempt class is to be composed entirely of members of one sex, what is there to support the view that the statutory purpose will be better served by granting the informing license to females rather than to males? If a discarded male partner informs on a promiscuous female, a timely threat of prosecution might well prevent the precise harm the statute is intended to minimize.

Finally, even if my logic is faulty and there actually is some speculative basis for treating equally guilty males and females differently, I still believe that any such speculative justification would be outweighed by the paramount interest in evenhanded enforcement of the law. A rule that authorizes punishment of only one of two equally guilty wrongdoers violates the essence of the constitutional requirement that the soverign must govern impartially.

I respectfully dissent.

QUESTIONS

1. From the perspective of the average layman, does California's statutory rape statute treat men and women unequally? Why or why not? By what legal route does the Court conclude that there is no unconstitutional inequality here? On what assumptions about differences between male and female psychology and sexual behavior does the decision rest?
2. Is this decision consistent with the precedent of *Craig v. Boren?* If not, how much does the inconsistency bother you? Why should it, particularly if disregard for precedent is acceptable in constitutional law?
3. Males under the age of 18 are a group that lacks direct ac-

cess to the normal electoral and legislative political processes. Why? How significant should that fact be in this
case?

4. Do you think the authors of the Fourteenth Amendment intended the equal protection clause to cover sale of 3.2 beer
   to male versus female customers? to cover "statutory" rape
   statutes? to cover sex issues at all, given that women did not
   have the vote when the amendment was passed? How much
   attention do the opinions in this case pay to these questions?
5. Are you satisfied that the majority opinion rests logically on
   a "neutral principle"? What might that principle be?
6. This case is a rich blend of case facts, background facts, and
   values. I find the dissenters' treatment of the background
   factual assumptions much more realistic than those in the
   majority opinions. However, I have deliberately omitted one
   important fact in this case itself, namely, that the girl testified that just before the intercourse she resisted and that Michael M. punched her two or three times on the chin, which
   punches eventually raised bruises. Construct a theory explaining how the presence of that fact in the case itself could
   subconsciously determine the Court's answer to the question of constitutional law.
7. Professor Bradley C. Canon has recently analyzed the various forms judicial activism can take.[41] His analysis is particularly useful because it shows how a decision that appears
   highly active on one dimension may be inactive on another.
   His six dimensions are:

   A. Majoritarianism—Does the decision nullify an act of an
   elected legislature?

   B. Interpretive stability—Does the decision overrule prior court
   precedent?

   C. Interpretive fidelity—Does the decision contradict the man-
   ifest intent of the framers?

   D. Substance—Does the decision make new basic policy for the
   society, e.g., public school desegregation?

   E. Specificity—Does the decision require people to follow specific, court-created rules?

   F. Availability of political alternatives—Are other political insti-

---

[41]"A Framework for the Analysis of Judicial Activism," in Halpern and
Lamb, eds., *Supreme Court Activism and Restraint* (Lexington, Mass.: Lexington
Books, 1982), chap. 15.

tutions equally able and willing to formulate effective policy in the area the decision touches?

Is the majority opinion in *Michael M.* active in some respects and restrained in others?

8. Comment, with reference specifically to the opinions in *Michael M.*, on the following complaint of Thomas Geoghegan, an attorney in Chicago who refers to himself as "an aging activist."

> No one fully knows why it happened. But for some reason, the law went from fast-forward in the Warren Court era to very fast-forward in the Burger era. The appellate volumes (F.2d's) and the district court volumes (F.Supp's) stopped being the story of liberty. Instead, they became like raw microfiche, conceptual reasoning with no offswitch, a bunch of law clerks citing each other in a madder and madder blizzard of words.
>
> Supreme Court opinions are the most bloated of all. Even the academics are complaining. In the 1960s Black, Douglas, and other great judges were readable, and short. But in the Burger era there has been a shocking decline into babble. One reason, I believe, is that judges are now afraid. They do not know how far to the right they are supposed to go, so they throw up verbal smoke screens. If you know what is right, like Black or Douglas or even a conservative like Harlan, it is easy to be brief.[42]

9. Chief Justice Rehnquist's majority opinion in *U.S. v. Salerno* upheld against due process and Eighth Amendment attack a federal statute allowing pretrial detention without bail of legally innocent persons who are found to present a threat to the safety of other persons or to the community if released. Does the following excerpt from the majority opinion strike you as an example of a verbal smoke screen?

> As an initial matter, the mere fact that a person is detained does not inexorably lead to the conclusion that the Government has imposed punishment.... Unless Congress expressly intended to impose punitive restrictions, the punitive/regulatory distinction turns on "'whether an alternative purpose to which [the restriction] may rationally be connected is assignable for it, and whether it appears excessive in relation to the alternative purpose assigned [to it].'"

[42]"Warren Court Children," *New Republic,* 19 May 1986, p. 17, at p. 18.

We conclude that the detention imposed by the Act falls on the regulatory side of the dichotomy. The legislative history of the Bail Reform Act clearly indicates that Congress did not formulate the pretrial detention provisions as punishment for dangerous individuals. Congress instead perceived pretrial detention as a potential solution to a pressing societal problem. There is no doubt that preventing danger to the community is a legitimate regulatory goal.[43]

---

[43]107 S. Ct. 2095 (1987), excerpt from the opinion printed in the *New York Times*, Wednesday, 27 May, 1987, p. 8.

Chapter VI

LAW AND REASON

The ultimate goal is to break down the sense that legal argument is autonomous from moral, economic and political discourse.
   —Duncan Kennedy

When judges make law and scholars propose rules of law, they necessarily rely on their vision of society as it is and as it ought to be. If law is to be made well, those visions must be accurate and attractive.
   —Mark Tushnet

I can offer you no final truths, complete and unchallengeable. But it is possible that this one effort will provoke other efforts, both in support and contradiction of my position, that will help us understand our differences and perhaps even discover some basic agreement.
   —New York Governor Mario Cuomo, addressing the Catholic Bishops

In the three branches of law we have now covered, appellate judges do not discover the law's right answer. They choose how the case before them will come out from at least two, and sometimes many, plausible but opposing arguments. We do not understand the psychological process by which judges actually choose results. We do, however, expect them to justify their choices because they exercise power over the litigants and because, given the common law tradition, each opinion carries the potential to shape decisions and doctrines in the future. Of course many opinions will not in fact influence the future, but at the time a judge authors an opinion he cannot predict whether or how a future judge will use it. Justices should write all opinions as if they will matter in the future.

We are now confronted with one final puzzle in legal reasoning. If indeterminacy in law makes judicial justifications so important, it won't do for a judge to pretend that his solution follows from law that was clear all along. On the other hand, the appellate opinion telling us what the law *ought* to mean should not rest on the judge's own political agenda or self-interest either. The judicial opinion must, in other words, reassure us of its impartiality. Hence the puzzle: If neither legal rules on one hand nor the judge's personal beliefs and desires on the other, provide working material for a good legal justification, what does?

At the beginning of this book I sketched my solution. The well-reasoned opinion, i.e., the good judicial justification, "harmonizes" these four elements present in all cases: the rules of law on the books, the facts of the conflict proved at trial, social background facts, and norms and moral values articulated in the community. A good opinion thus seeks to reassure both the litigants and all potential readers that we can make the world we inhabit orderly, coherent, and morally satisfying.

This chapter fills in the details of that sketch, defends it, and applies it to appellate cases. To do so I shall refine the definition of law and develop a theory of impartiality. As you cover this material keep in mind that law ought overall to encourage social cooperation. We seek a model of legal justifying that maximizes our ability to settle disputes peacefully and that encourages us to talk constructively to others about our differences. If you reject these propositions, you will probably reject the model I propose here, though I hope we could talk about even this difference.

LAW AND THE STATE

Law is the process by which people try to conduct their affairs in terms of rules created by government, by the "State." Rules on the books do not by themselves make law. The legal process operates only to the degree that people agree on ways of deciding what the rules mean in the context of their situation and abiding by the results that the legal process declares.

The legal process resolves disputes, sometimes between two individuals and sometimes among a variety of contending interests and groups. Sometimes the legal process induces social change, while at other times it lags well behind such changes. But law is not the only method—probably not even the primary one—that individuals, groups, and societies use to handle disputes. Loving, going home to mother, shaking hands on the gentleman's agreement, exercising power, unconsciously conforming to informal social rules we call customs, and many other activities in private and public life reduce conflict and cope with social change. As Malcolm Feeley writes:

> Law does not perform a unique social function, nor is it a singular form of social control. . . . Legal rules are only one of a number of systems of rules, often overlapping and entwined, which shape people's aspirations and actions, and by which they are judged and resolve their troubles.[1]

Thus, one way to narrow the judge's field of vision—and

[1]Malcolm M. Feeley, "The Concept of Laws in Social Science," 10 *Law and Society Review* 497 (1976), p. 501. For a particularly promising altenative to traditional litigation in problem solving, see Roger Fisher and William Ury, *Getting to Yes: Negotiating Agreement Without Giving In* (New York: Penguin Books, 1981).

hence his responsibilities—is to remind him that he need not attain perfection in every case. By perfection I mean the discovery of, or the creation of, a legal rule that produces one right solution in every case. Previous chapters have explained why judges cannot attain this kind of perfection, but I am arguing here as well that they do not need to do this. Law is ultimately one of many ways of meeting needs that people feel and try to satisfy. Other activities and relationships can compensate if and when the legal system fails to address these interests.

But what kinds of needs do law and other social processes jointly try to satisfy? *Social processes including law seek to satisfy, above all, the psychological need for structure in people's lives, the need to believe that physical forces and moral norms can answer questions and relieve people from questioning some concepts altogether. When society fails to meet its members' need for structure, law cannot achieve its immediate goal of promoting social cooperation.* Note carefully that this statement emphasizes the importance of the belief in structure, not the structure itself. We do not lead our daily lives by constantly testing every decision against the rules of physics or of religion or of law, but we need to believe they are there if we need them.

Having precepts and resolving cases in terms of them help maintain that confidence in structure. For the legal system, success arises primarily from settling cases "well enough" that people will abide by the final decision. Success does not require settling them "to perfection."

Social groups of all sorts—sororities, street gangs, symphony orchestras, and political science departments—develop formal and informal conventions that provide a sense of structure so that work and play can proceed. The regularization of dispute settling in labor-management relations, by creating rules for collective-bargaining agreements and resolving industrial disputes in terms of the rules, has in this century substantially changed the workplace.

And yet we do not call these lawlike uses of rules "law." *Law* governs through rules made and enforced by the government, the state. What should it mean to a judge to define law this way? Why does it matter whether a unit of government on one hand or General Motors on the other creates and enforces a rule?

We can examine why it matters in two ways. The first method examines law as a practical aspect of politics; the second scrutinizes law in ethical and philosophical terms. Both try to see the world as it really is; both attempt to view law through the eyes of both the governors and the governed.

The political view of the importance of government in law is essentially one of degree. Law is the process that fosters and legitimates the interests of the powerful. Government matters simply because it creates and limits the arena in which the most important battles for power in society occur. One cannot gain position to make law in government without being powerful. Of course, elections try to equalize the unequal power that flows from differential distributions of wealth, but that is one small part of politics. Law results from the unending struggle for power in society because government and the power struggle are only different labels for a single phenomenon. When judges decide, they simply reinforce the interests of the powerful. From this standpoint, the content and quality of legal reasoning become no more than rationalizations for the exercise of judicial power.[2]

There is certainly some truth in the political approach, at least if its proponents avoid the circular error of defining the powerful in terms of the interests that law promotes. I do, however, think this view seriously misleads us. The political aspect encourages us to think about law exclusively in power terms so that we do not recognize that ethics, beliefs about right and wrong, have a meaning and power of their own. It encourages us, for example, to think of the proceedings in the House of Representatives in 1974 concerning Richard Nixon's impeachment solely (as Nixon himself did!) in terms of relative party strength, the resources of the pro- and anti-Nixon forces, their strategies and tactics, and so on.

But is not the essence of Watergate very different? Did

[2]See Lawrence M. Friedman, *The Legal System* (New York: Russell Sage Foundation, 1975), and see also Arthur F. Bentley, *The Process of Government* (Chicago: University of Chicago Press, 1908).

not Watergate uncover a feeling shared throughout the community that *if* the President violated a set of values, he should no longer hold office? The values were not absolute. No doubt many people who possessed the feeling could not articulate the values precisely, nor did everyone even agree on the standards by which to judge Mr. Nixon. Nevertheless, the community did share the belief that *some* structure limits presidential power, that the President may have exceeded it, and that the situation absolutely had to be *judged*.[3] This second ethical point of view makes the existence and quality of judgment absolutely central in the legal process.

Viewed ethically, when government—rather than General Motors or the management of the Seattle Symphony—creates the rules, legal reasoning becomes more important because:

- The government's rules speak to the public, to the community, to everyone, in a way that General Motors' rules (or for that matter, the Pope's rules) do not.
- The community is the greatest source of disruption and uncertainty in our lives because it exposes us to the work of strangers that we individually cannot control: crimes, nuclear wars, and changes in moral standards. The community is the place where people's psychological need for confidence in structure is greatest, for it is the one place that binds everyone and beyond which we will find no social structure at all. The rules that the *government* makes and enforces must maintain confidence in structure, confidence that even strangers can share values.
- People need to maintain this confidence even when they cannot express precisely the"right" limit or value by which to judge a concrete situation. They take most seriously the idea that the community has value in it.

The judicial process and legal reasoning therefore play

---

[3]See Joseph R. Gusfield's review of Friedman's "The Legal System," 29 *Stanford Law Review* 371 (1977), p. 381.

a major part in preserving the confidence that the community can reconcile rules, facts of disputes, social conditions, and ethics. Our confidence does not rest entirely or immediately on the quality of legal reasoning, but the language of legal justification is one important means by which those who govern can reassure us that our communal life is "accurate and attractive." Unlike other social processes in and out of government, courts must make *some* decision, must reach some closure on the problems litigants bring to them. Regardless of the wisdom of the solution, we need to believe that our community contains points where decisions and action replace indecision and drift. This book has criticized so many conventional practices, habits, and assumptions in legal reasoning precisely because legal reasoning is so important. Reason must "break down the sense that legal argument is autonomous from moral, economic, and political discourse" or it will ultimately destroy our confidence in community.

In sum, the political view of law presumes that the state consists of people vying to have their specific wants, the policies they espouse, written into law. The ethical view, on the other hand, asserts that everyone, including the most apolitical of citizens, simply by virtue of living in a community, needs to believe that values hold the community together. In the political view, whatever decision occurs must be right. In the ethical view, the quality of judgment, the ability of judges to convince us they take the task of harmonizing seriously, is both problematic and very important.

Thus, the ethical view of the legal process holds that, despite its potentially infinite complexity and uncertainty, law must contain a method of applying the abstractions of law to human affairs. This does *not* require finding the perfect solution. It is much more important that the process *attempt* to reach acceptable reconciliations of facts, social conditions, laws, and ethical values. Viewing law as a process of resolving disputes in terms of rules made and enforced by the state helps us to identify the special reconciling and harmonizing role of legal reasoning.

We must now shift our attention to the precise definitions of impartiality and judgment. Before we do so, however, you should understand the complexity of the problem that legal reasoning addresses.

The modern view of man teaches that neither judges nor anyone else ever will actually identify a structure that holds society together. Rules are ambiguous. People constantly disagree about the nature of social conditions and about ethical values. Virtually every problem, the more we think about it, reduces to an unsolvable riddle, a tension between opposing goods, an antinomy. Paul Freund eloquently identifies three such antinomies: triumph and fraternity, knowledge and privacy, and personal security and moral responsibility.[4] Duncan Kennedy reduces these to just one, the tension between individualism and altruism.[5] In this section, I have suggested that law need not resolve the unresolvable. I have urged that ongoing attempts to reach defensible but imperfect reconciliations of competing forces will suffice to maintain the necessary confidence in community structure.

IMPARTIALITY

Imagine yourself in each of these three situations:

1. A midsummer afternoon in Wrigley Field. The Cubs versus the Cardinals. You are calling balls and strikes behind home plate.

2. A late Saturday night in Atlantic City in early September. You are judging the finals of the Miss America Pageant.

3. Eight-thirty in the evening, the home of your young family. The children are squabbling. They appeal to you for judgment.
   Laurie: "Mommie, Robbie bit me!"
   Robbie: "I did not!"
   Laurie: "You did too! Look! Tooth marks!"

---

[4]Paul Freund, "Social Justice and the Law," in Richard B. Brandt, ed., *Social Justice* (Englewood Cliffs, N.J.: Prentice-Hall, 1962), p. 94.

[5]Duncan Kennedy, "Form and Substance in Private Law Adjudication," 89 *Harvard Law Review* 1685 (1976), p. 1713.

Robbie: "But Mom! Laurie took my dime!"
Laurie: "I took your dime cuz you stepped on my doll and broke it."
Robbie: "But it was an accident, dum-dum."
Laurie: "I am not a dum-dum, you fathead!"

Each of these situations calls for judgment. Each judge makes decisions that affect the claims of others, and he decides before an audience that has some expectations about *how* the judge should decide. Without necessarily determining *what* the judge should conclude, the audience knows what the judge should look at and will test the judgment against these expectations. Even the children seeking justice from their mother do so.

To judge is to decide the claims of others with reference to the expectations of an audience that define the process of decision. We shall see shortly where this definition leads in law. For the moment, consider what these three nonlegal judging situations do and do not have in common.

First and most important, notice that the three are not equally reasoned. Reasoning, defined as a choice that depends on calculations about future consequences, influences the umpire calling balls and strikes only indirectly. Occasionally, he may reflect on the fact that if he calls a pitch wrong he may be beaned by flying beer bottles. Basically, however, he simply tries to fit physical—visual—evidence to a category, ball or strike, predetermined by the rule. He judges because the audience, baseball fans, has specific expectations of how umpires should behave. In most households the mother, at the other extreme, cannot escape from making some calculation about the effects of her decision on the children, or at least on her own sanity.

The second difference is that rules do not equally affect all three situations. The umpire works with an elaborate set of written rules about baseball, most of which he commits to memory. He decides most questions literally in a second or less by applying the rules to the facts. In baseball, time is of the essence, which is why its rules are so elaborate. Additionally, baseball allows for precise rules because, as in most sports, we can pinpoint what matters to us in time and space.

On the other hand, we cannot define male or female beauty so precisely in time and space. Beauty contest judges exercise more discretion because their rules do not so precisely tell them what to seek.[6] Finally, the squabbling children may invoke no family rule at all. The family may have no regulation forbidding or punishing Robbie's toothy assault on his sister and his lie, and no conventions governing Laurie's theft or their gratuitous exchange of insults. Expectations, not precepts, create the need for judgment.

Third, these three kinds of judges have different opportunities to make rules for the future. The parent can explicitly respond to the squabble by announcing what is right and wrong and declaring its official policy for the future. Such a setting of limits may be precisely what the children hope the judge will do. But beauty contest judges may do so only informally and the umpires hardly at all, given audience expectations of their roles.

The definition and discussion of the nature of reason made clear, I trust, that not all reasoning is legal reasoning. Legal reasoning involves judgment, deciding the claims of others in front of some audience, before a "public." We have also seen, from the example of the baseball umpire, that not all judgment involves reason. Law therefore employs reasoned judgment, and I shall develop that concept momentarily. First, however, we must pin down that quality inherent in all judging, whether reasoned or not: "impartiality."

Impartiality is not a mysterious concept. The *American Heritage Dictionary* defines "partial" as "pertaining to only part;

---

[6]There is another interesting difference: With rare exceptions, when he calls the game on account of rain or ejects an ornery manager or player, the umpire has minimal control over who wins. But the beauty contest judges *declare* the winner. This differential effect on the outcome explains why we have only one home plate umpire but several judges in contests of beauty and on our appellate courts. (Notice that when the umpire does make discretionary calls he is also more likely to consult other umpires than when he calls balls and strikes.) For a fascinating description of how a new sport, competitive female body building, failed to grow precisely because the relevant audience could not agree on how such contests should be judged, see Charles Gaines and George Butler, "Iron Sisters," *Psychology Today*, November 1983, pp. 64–69.

not total; incomplete." To decide impartially is to leave the final decision open until all the relevant information is received. It means that the information — the placement of the pitch, the beauty contestant's stage performance, and the children's actual behavior—rather than a personal affection or preference for one "party" determines the result.

While impartiality is not itself a difficult concept—we have all judged and been judged in our lives—it is often difficult for audiences to satisfy themselves that judges actually decide impartially. How can judges satisfy audiences that they decide impartially? Initially, a judge may succeed if his mistakes cancel out, if his errors favor both sides equally. But the loser, being the loser, will probably not take a balanced count of errors. The judge's only long-range security, therefore, is to care about and try as best he can to fulfill the expectations of judgment that the audience imposes.[7]

To judge is to be judged. The argument assumes, of course, that audiences can, in fact, distinguish their expectations of the process of decision from their hopes that one side—their side!—will win. I am convinced that people can do so, though I rely more on my experience as a sports fan, employee, teacher, and parent than I do on psychological experimentation. Teams can lose championships, employees can receive poor assignments, students can receive disappointing grades, and children can be ordered to wash the dishes, all without doubting that the judges, by caring about standards of decision, have acted fairly.

Professor Robert Cover has written:

> The judicial whim argument entails a common error or oversimplification. The critical dimension of the rule of law is not the degree of specificity with which an actor is con-

[7]Robert G. Dixon, Jr., also identified judicial neutrality with judges' "style of operation," not the substance or impact of the outcome. See "The 'New Substantive Due Process' and the Democratic Ethic: A Prologomenon," 1 *Brigham Young University Law Review* 43 (1976), p. 76. Harold Berman and William Greiner describe this judicial style of decision as operating deliberately and publicly. Judicial decisions should reflect "an explicit community judgment and not merely an explicitly personal judgment." *The Nature and Functions of Law,* 3rd ed. (Mineola, N.Y.: Foundation Press, 1972).

strained, but the very fact that the actor must look outside his own will for criteria of judgment. There is a difference—intelligible to most pre-adolescents—between the directions "Do what you want" and "Do what you think is right or just."[8]

To "look outside his own will for criteria of judgment": If we have any single key to legal judgment, it is here.

IMPARTIALITY AND JUDGMENT IN LAW

To judge is to decide the claims of others before an audience. The judgmental decision need not be reasoned, as the umpire's calling of pitches reveals. But judgmental decisions must be impartial, which means in the end they must, to appear impartial, conform to audience expectations of the process of decision.

Since appellate legal decisions are judgmental, we must determine the audience's expectations of that decision process. But the discussion of law's relationship to the state has already determined that. I believe that the audience of law, the community, expects the process to reassure it that society can reconcile and harmonize facts, rules, social conditions, and moral values. This is the test of judicial impartiality and hence of reason in law. When judges explain their results in judicial opinions, they must attempt to convince us that the result does *not* depend on a fact at issue between the parties that we know is false, does *not* depend on false assumptions about social conditions, does *not* depend upon a tortured reading of a rule, and does *not* depend on an ethical judgment that the community would reject. The result need not please everyone, but that is not the point. Judges cannot and need not discover one right solution that everyone somehow believes best. They con-

[8]Robert Cover, book review of R. Berger, *Government by Judiciary, New Republic,* 14 January 1978, p. 27. Two recent essays in which judges vigorously defended the impartiality of the appellate courts are Harry T. Edwards' "Public Misperceptions Concerning the Politics of Judging," 56 *Colorado Law Review* 619 (1985), and Patricia Wald's "Thoughts on Decisionmaking," 87 *West Virginia Law Review* 1 (1984). Compare the Australian film *Breaker Morant.*

vince us of their impartiality as long as they convince us that they have *attempted* to describe these four elements accurately and to reconcile them as best as they can in the circumstances.

And now something like a complete picture of the legal process begins to take shape: Law is not a "natural science." We cannot experimentally tests its propositions to demonstrate their truth or error. Nor is law a purely logical process that, like mathematics, is subject mainly to the test of internal consistency. Instead, the common law tradition gives us a process of asserting and persuading through language. Facts, rules, and values are processed through the judge's use of words to express his thoughts about them. Some thoughts may persuade more effectively than others, but we cannot prove them absolutely true or false in either the logical or empirical sense. Thus, when facts, rules, and values in a case are genuinely controversial, different judges can reach conflicting results in that case yet still reason impartially in law.

Let me summarize. Citizens living in communities need the reassurance that the community has the capacity to reconcile the concrete facts of a dispute with the conditions and events of life, the formal rules of the community, and the citizens' beliefs, often themselves in conflict, about right and wrong. I have asserted that this need is real in our political lives just as we need nourishment, sleep, and sex in varying degrees in the biological part of our existence. People do not care in this regard exclusively that public policy impose any specifically favored value of their own on society, though, of course, they often do care about policies. People, at a deeper level, are frightened by the prospect that their community may lose its structure, its embodiment of place and of limits, altogether. People expect the kind of reasoning I have described from courts because other institutions only rarely face the task of dealing with the facts of specific human conflicts, rules, social conditions, and fundamental values all at the same time.

I do not mean that citizens daily review legal opinions to satisfy themselves as to the quality of legal reasoning, for, of course, they do not. But parties to lawsuits, and their friends, and the legal profession—the immediate audience—do care about the fairness of decisions. When legal parties, lawyers, and news commentators increasingly report dissatisfaction with judges; when, over thousands of people and thousands of cases the message emerges that judges somehow are "out of touch," then the community begins to lose confidence in its own capacity to reconcile the four factors. If judges assume that no one decision matters, cumulative damage will occur.

Legal reasoning as I have defined it matters primarily because communities need to retain confidence in limits, and reasoning can reinforce that confidence. Even for purely normative questions, questions of personal taste that cannot be resolved factually or scientifically, reasoning can improve judgment. For example, suppose that, offended by the rock music coming from my daughter's room, I tell her to turn off the music. She asks me why. I can, of course, say, "Because I say so." But I could, as an alternative, reason with her. If I say it's too loud, and mean it, I then give her the option to turn it down but not off, to satisfy us both. Or, I may say I don't like rock music. "Why not?" she then asks. "It's all beat. The tunes are monotonous." "But Dad, you play 'Bolero' on the hi-fi over and over." And suddenly, by reasoning with her honestly, I must confront what matters to me in music. Perhaps I will fail in that conversation to explain to my self or her a complete philosophy of aesthetics in music. However, I will begin to care about deeper structures and values in my life. By caring, my values may even change, but it is more important that I reassure my daughter of my capacity to care about structure and values. Do not characters in movies and literature become heroic when we believe they are in touch with values, although perhaps not ours, and live by them?

APPLYING THE THEORY

To bring this abstract theory down to earth, let us apply it to some of the cases this book has applauded and some this book has criticized.

Consider first the *Prochnow* blood test case at the end of Chapter I. We are tempted to condemn the case for flying in the face of science: the court reached a result that we all know couldn't be true. If so, we would be criticizing the case for its failure to harmonize the social background facts in the case. But the difficulties with the *Prochnow* opinion go deeper. If the opinion means to tell us that juries should be free to speculate on whether God or nature or some hidden force temporarily suspended the laws of science, the opinion should have addressed that claim head-on. Such a principle would revolutionize our entire notion of how law works, for if a jury verdict based on speculations about God's will can stand, a jury can find anything it wants, and no appellate court would ever overturn a jury verdict for being inconsistent with the weight of the evidence. The opinion should have mentioned this because the point needs extended discussion to say the least.

We have seen another less supernatural and more plausible explanation for the *Prochnow* result. Perhaps the legislature favors fatherhood so strongly that it authorizes juries to disregard science for the sake of allowing children to grow up with fathers. But that point deserves airing too, partly to give the legislature a chance to react if the court has misread the statute, and partly because the position makes so little intuitive sense. If the legislature in fact felt that way, why would it have authorized introducing blood test evidence at all? The majority opinion read the statute legalistically, that is, without attention to the other three elements in legal reasoning. It said the words of the statute make the tests admissible but not conclusive, therefore the law allows juries to disregard the tests. But an entirely plausible alternate reason exists for not making the tests conclusive: the laboratory might have gotten Robert's blood sample confused with another sample. If the plaintiff offers evidence that the blood tests were in error, or worse, corruptly falsified, then of course the test shouldn't be conclusive. But here the plaintiff introduced no such evidence.

In short, the Wisconsin Court majority might have reached the same result, in favor of Robert's paternity, if it had argued the value of fatherhood. It could have harmonized all four elements by saying, "We know all about science, and we know the blood tests in this case are incompatible. We admit that no evidence in the trial contradicted the blood tests, but we read the purpose of this law to favor paternity and we

believe this value is a value widely shared in the community."
That reasoning would give us a coherent vision of the community that we can discuss and seek to sustain or change. Instead
the majority implies that we live in a confusing and unknowable world in which anything can happen, one in which we
can't trust either science or God or the conventional trial
court methods of fact finding.

Repouille v. U.S. and *Michael M.* also fail for the same reason. In both of these cases a clear and recent precedent stated
law that seemed to apply directly to the case. The *Francioso*
opinion said that the naturalization decision should rest on
judgments about the person seeking naturalization, not on the
nature of incest in the abstract. Yet in *Repouille* Learned Hand
did quite the opposite. *Craig v. Boren* held that the state bears
the burden of proving a rational relationship between a law
that classifies people by their gender and the achievement of
a valid public policy goal. Show us, said the *Craig* majority,
that discriminating against young men will actually reduce
traffic accidents, and the Oklahoma beer policy can stand.
But you can't just guess. Justice Rehnquist in *Michael M.*
does the opposite. He's satisfied with California's guess that
law enforcement will benefit from punishing only men for underage voluntary sex in the absence of any proof. Both *Repouille* and *Michael M.* lead us to believe that law doesn't matter.
Both increase our confusion.

I do not argue that *Repouille* and *Michael M.* "came out
wrong." I argue that the results were not well reasoned or justified. A different opinion could have persuasively justified the
result each case reached by giving reasons to overrule the
precedent or distinguish the precedent through fact freedom,
but the opinions we read fail to do so. They are incoherent.
They only confuse lawyers who must advise future clients with
similar cases—confuse and thereby perhaps encourage litigation when law should instead encourage cooperation.

You should, I hope, be able to see in each of the cases
this book has criticized one or more of the four elements that
were not harmonized. The evidence introduced in trial about
baseball in *Toolson* made a strong case that baseball was a business in interstate commerce that monopolized. Why does the

Court ignore that evidence? In *Lochner,* the bakers' hours case, the Court ignored the social background evidence that baking was unhealthy. *Repouille* and *Michael M.* ignore the law itself. The majority in *Fox v. Snow* ignored the ethical value of carrying out the hopes of those who write wills, and so on.

We should, of course, turn this analysis on the cases these pages have applauded. *Hynes,* the diving board case, harmonizes (a) the fact in Harvey's case that the wire might have killed him had he been a swimmer lawfully using the river, and the fact that the railroad had not maintained the wires and poles; (b) the social background fact that property boundaries become increasingly hard to know and learn as life becomes more complex, urban, and interconnected; (c) a plausible reading of the thrust of the *Hoffman* and *Beck* precedents; (d) the deeply ethical value that law should promote cooperation, that the law of tort ought to encourage the railroad to prevent the dangerous wires it owns and controls from injuring others.

FOR FURTHER STUDY

These pages have developed a model of judicial justification that challenges some conventional ideas about law. Legal rules do not resolve disputes automatically or by themselves. Law is not the province of highly trained experts whose decisions flow from their professional expertise.[9] Law is profoundly political and ought to remain so in the sense that it encourages discourse among different social groups and interests. The "harmony test" of goodness in judicial opinions seems in the last analysis more like aesthetics than law.

But how well does this approach itself harmonize with developments in the much larger world of modern philosophy itself? This book cannot answer that question at length. However, recent Western social thought, especially since the Viet-

---

[9]See William Barrett's rejection of the belief that technical expertise can resolve conflicts effectively in *The Illusion of Technique,* (Garden City, N.Y.: Anchor Press, 1978).

nam War, has produced a virtual explosion of theories in a variety of fields that closely parallel my own. This section briefly reviews the more prominent of these in the hope that some readers will care to pursue these issues further.

Law and Language

A substantial literature, much of it influenced by the later Wittgenstein, rejects the belief that people use language to describe an objective reality. Verbal and nonverbal languages create the world that we experience. Professor Murray Edelman's essay "Political Language and Political Reality" is the most accessible description of this trend for the general reader.[10] Edelman writes:

> In short, it is not "reality" in any testable or observable sense that matters in shaping political consciousness and behavior, but rather the beliefs that language helps evolve about the causes of discontents and satisfactions, about policies that will bring about a future closer to the heart's desire, and other unobservables . . .
>
> While language, consciousness, and social conditions are replete with contradictions, they shape each other so as to make it possible for people to live with themselves, with their moral dilemmas, and with chronic failure to resolve the dilemmas and contradictions.

The capacity of language to make life livable despite its contradictions depends on the bonds that good communication itself creates. Thus the late Lon Fuller, a professor of jurisprudence whose work exposed many of the contradictions in law, wrote:

> If I were asked . . . to discern one central indisputable principle of what may be called substantive natural law . . . I would find it in the injunction: Open up, maintain and preserve the integrity of the channels of communication.[11]

[10]"The 1984 Lasswell Symposium," reprinted in *PS*, Winter 1985, pp. 10–19.

[11]*The Morality of Law* (New Haven: Yale University Press, 1964), p. 186. See more recently Peter Teachout's superb analysis of Fuller's jurisprudence in "The Soul of the Fugue: An Essay on Reading Fuller," 70 *Minnesota Law Review* 1073 (1986).

Joseph Singer reminds us that people can develop and maintain close friendships with each other even though they disagree about almost everything. The talk itself, despite endless
disagreement, cements the friendship.[12]

Law and Literature

The modern role of language I just described blurs the conventional distinction between fiction and nonfiction. Political
and legal languages inevitably edit, simplify, and thereby
change what they represent. We might therefore call them
works of fiction, and many recent essays elaborate the similarities between law and literature, poetry and theater. Indeed,
Justice John Paul Stevens has stated that the study of poetry is
the best undergraduate preparation for the study of law.[13]

Ronald Dworkin has defended his position that political
and moral principles can in theory generate right answers to
legal cases by the use of literary analogies, but the literary
theorist Stanley Fish casts substantial doubts on Dworkin's aesthetics.[14] More helpful analyses of how literary and theatrical
understanding can increase our appreciation of law's constructive social character come from James Boyd White and
Milner Ball.[15]

---

[12]*The Player and the Cards: Nihilism and Legal Theory,* 94 *Yale Law Journal* 1
(1984). See John Stick's extended disagreement with Singer in "Can Nihilism
Be Pragmatic?" 100 *Harvard Law Review* 332 (1986).

[13]See George Gopen, "Rhyme and Reason: Why the Study of Poetry Is the
Best Preparation for the Study of Law," 46 *College English* 333 (1984). Cf. Mary
Jo Salter's remark concerning the poetry of Emily Dickinson, "So much has
been made of Dickinson's liberties with rhyme and meter that it is easy to
forget just how deliberately and even mathematically she often got things
'wrong' in order to get them right." "Occupational Therapy," The New Republic, 2 March 1987, p. 40, at p. 41.

[14]The exchange is described in my *Contemporary Constitutional Lawmaking,*
supra pp. 117–123. And see Stanley Fish, "Fish v. Fiss," 36 *Stanford Law Review*
1325 (1984), in which Fish argues that all forms of interpretation, including
legal and literary interpretation, are constrained primarily by politics, not by
rules. See also my "Die Meistersinger von Nurnberg and the United States
Supreme Court," 18 *Polity* 272 (1985).

[15]See White's recent collections of essays in *When Words Lose Their Meaning*
(Chicago: University of Chicago Press, 1984), especially the essay "The Judicial
Opinion and the Poem: Ways of Reading, Ways of Life," and *Heracles's Bow*

Modern Social Philosophy

Two recent books by Richard Bernstein provide useful summaries of the "new pragmatism" in Western philosophy. Following the Civil War, in which, as in so many wars, people justified killing each other for the sake of a doctrine or ideology they believed to be absolutely true, the philosophy of pragmatism began to take shape. Pragmatism, especially in the hands of John Dewey, emphasizes that experience, not doctrine, shapes our beliefs and actions and that human cooperation depends on not taking doctrine too seriously.[16] The articles collected in a recent *Southern California Law Review* symposium applied many of the elements of modern pragmatism to law and legal interpretation.[17]

Miscellaneous Sources

Some fascinating recent articles are less easily classified. Richard Danzig's evaluation of the psychology of Felix Frankfurter's jurisprudence in the flag salute cases nicely uncovers the processes by which judges inevitably transform (or fictional-

---

(Madison: University of Wisconsin Press, 1985). See Ball's "The Play's the Thing: An Unscientific Reflection on Courts Under the Rubric of Theater," 28 *Stanford Law Review* 81 (1975) and *The Promise of American Law* (Athens: University of Georgia Press, 1981). See also James E. Murray, "Understanding Law as Metaphor," 34 *Legal Education* 714 (1984), and Robin West, "Jurisprudence as Narrative: An Aesthetic Analysis of Modern Legal Theory," 60 *N.Y.U. Law Review* 145 (1985).

[16]See Richard Bernstein, *Beyond Objectivism and Relativism* (Philadelphia: University of Pennsylvania Press, 1983), and *Philosophical Profiles* (Cambridge-shire: Polity Press, 1986). Bruce Kuklick traces the origins of modern pragmatism as far back as the New England puritanism of Jonathan Edwards, which reinforces the case for pragmatism as the core of mainstream American political thought. See *Churchmen and Philosophers* (New Haven: Yale University Press, 1985).

[17]"Symposium on Interpretation," 58 *Southern California Law Review* 1 (1985, 2 vols.), especially Christopher Stone, "Introduction: Interpreting the Symposium," p. 1. Stone writes that "one necessary element of interpretation is the potential for legitimate ambiguity.... [W]here we see interpretation, we should expect, in the nature of the activity, to find more than one satisfactory answer" (p. 3).

ize) the material they work with.[18] Much recent philosophy of science develops political and aesthetic explanations for how scientific knowledge changes. Thomas Kuhn's *The Structure of Scientific Revolutions* is now a classic.[19] Philip Kitcher's rebuttal of such religious arguments against evolutionary theory as "creation science" develops aesthetic principles like "unification" and "fecundity" to define the scientific enterprise.[20]

Finally, a case can be made that the "new pragmatism's" emphasis on experience, and on the central place of art in making raw experience meaningful, is in fact ancient and universal. Eugene Webb recently summarized the thought of Eric Voegelin this way:

> An excessive concentration on the (conscious) expression of truth can obscure what to a thinker like Voegelin (or, for that matter, to such thinkers as Socrates, Plato, or Aristotle) is the central aim of philosophical inquiry: the pursuit of wisdom, which is to say, the attempt to dwell consciously in reality. Propositional truth may point in the direction of philosophical wisdom or sketch its outline, but existential truth is its very core.[21]

If existential or experiential truth is the core of wisdom, it may follow that seeking and claiming to have found "the right answer" may undercut what it most needed in democratic government, the capacity to adapt. Even more important, a democracy presumes its citizens competent to assess and speak on political matters, and therefore legal matters, without acquiring expert training first. The very claim to have achieved the right answer undermines the nature of democratic discourse, a point expressed by Mario Cuomo's epigraph at this chapter's beginning.

---

[18]"Justice Frankfurter's Opinions in the Flag Salute Cases: Blending Logic and Psychologic in Constitutional Decisionmaking," 36 *Stanford Law Review* 675 (1984). See also Robin West's "Law, Rights, and Other Totemic Illusions: Legal Liberalism and Freud's Theory of the Rule of Law," 134 *Pennsylvania Law Review* 817 (1986).

[19](Chicago: University of Chicago Press, 1970).

[20]*Abusing Science: The Case Against Creationism* (Cambridge: MIT Press, 1982).

[21]"Politics and the Problem of a Philosophical Rhetoric in the Thought of Eric Voegelin," 48 *Journal of Politics* 260 (1986).

CONCLUSION

The modern expectation of judgment in communities accepts openness and imperfections in reasoning, and recognizes that law should change with changes in the life with which law deals. Courts as well as other institutions must act to preserve the sense that the modern community has value in it, even though caring about the striving for values may itself be the only value the process preserves. It is perfectly possible to reason about values and thus to sharpen a mutual understanding of what matters in law just as my daughter and I can sharpen our mutual understanding by discussing values in music, even though we never agree about which pieces of music are good.

If modernity robs us of the security of religious, political, legal, or ethical absolutes, it does not rob us of the value of the attempt to articulate standards that make sense of what we know and believe. Judges should and can make the attempt.

And judges often do. Let me conclude by letting a judge speak for himself:

> I have never had the misfortune to be closely associated with a truly conservative judge. I do not mean "conservative" in its ordinary sense. A more apt word is, perhaps, "sterile." I have in mind sterile intellectualism that is not in the least offended but, instead, is delighted that there may be no reason for decision other than that the rule "was laid down in the time of Henry IV." I have known very few such judges, and them only at a distance, but I have read others. This is the kind of judge who, if he is a trial judge, likes to say from the bench, "This is not a court of justice; it is a court of law." When I was a young judge (under age forty) I said it once or twice myself and am sorry for it. This is cold intellectualism that finds no room at the inn for people. This type of legal mind is concerned with "legal problems" —entirely unaware that the term is a misnomer, that there are only peoples' problems for which the law sometimes may afford answers. The life principle of such a judge is stare decisis. He fervently believes that it is far, far better that the rule be certain and unjust than that he tinker with it. It is a delight to him to construct painstakingly, with adequate display of erudition, an edifice of logic and prece-

dent upon which justice may be sacrificed. . . . When one reads such an opinion, complete with pious disavowal of judicial power to usurp the legislative prerogative, the feeling comes though that the author is not sorry that he cannot and may even be glad that the legislature will not. Such a judge categorically rejects Holmes' aphorism that the life of the law is not logic but experience, and such a judge, of course, has never entertained the following thought of Yeats: "God guard me from those thoughts men think In the mind alone; He that sings a lasting song thinks in (the) marrowbone."[22]

SUMMARY

- How has this chapter defined law, judging, and impartiality?
- How does the fact that law involves rules made and enforced by the government help define the character and desired qualities of legal reasoning?
- What benefits flow from reasoning about problems, even when the problems involve values, like taste in music, about which no one can prove that one position is objectively right or wrong?
- How can reason produce several inconsistent but equally justified resolutions of a legal conflict?

ILLUSTRATIVE CASE

Professor Sanford Levinson of the University of Texas School of Law has presented his students with the following problem at the beginning of their study of constitutional law. It is the concluding piece in the long symposium on interpretation cited in this chapter.[23] How would you answer the questions he poses?

In 1970 a number of concerned citizens, worried about what they regarded as the corruption of American life, met to consider what could be done. During the course of the discussion, one of the speakers electrified the audience with the following comments:

[22]J. Braxton Craven, Jr., "Paean to Pragmatism," 50 *North Carolina Law Review* 977 (1972), pp. 979–980.

[23]"On Interpretation: The Adultery Clause of the Ten Commandments," 58 *Southern California Law Review* 719 (1985).

The cure for our ills is a return to old-time religion, and the best single guide remains the Ten Commandments. Whenever I am perplexed as to what I ought to do, I turn to the Commandments for the answer, and I am never disappointed. Sometimes I don't immediately like what I discover, but then I think more about the problem and realize how limited my perspective is compared to that of the framer of those great words. Indeed, all that is necessary is for everyone to obey the Ten Commandments, and our problems will all be solved.*

Within several hours the following plan was devised: As part of the effort to encourage a return to the "old-time religion" of the Ten Commandments, a number of young people would be asked to take an oath on their eighteenth birthday to "obey, protect, support, and defend the Ten Commandments" in all of their actions. if the person complied with the oath for seventeen years, he or she would receive an award of $10,000 on his or her thirty-fifth birthday.

The Foundation for the Ten Commandments was funded by the members of the 1970 convention, plus the proceeds of a national campaign for contributions. The speaker quoted above contributed $20 million, and an additional $30 million was collected, $15 million from the convention and $15 million from the national campaign. The interest generated by the $50 million is approximately $6 million per year. Each year since 1970, 500 persons have taken the oath. *You* are appointed sole trustee of the Foundation, and your most important duty is to determine whether the oath–takers have complied with their vows and are thus entitled to the $10,000.

It is now 1987, and the first set of claimants comes before you:

(1) Claimant *A* is a married male. Although freely admitting that he has had sexual intercourse with a number of women other than his wife during their marriage, he brings to your atten-

---

Cf. Statement of President Ronald Reagan, Press Conference, Feb. 21, 1985, *reprinted in* N.Y. Times, Feb. 22, 1985 § 1, at 10, col. 3: "I've found that the Bible contains an answer to just about everything and every problem that confronts us, and I wonder sometimes why we won't recognize that one Book could solve a lot of problems for us." [note in original]

tion the fact that "adultery," at the time of Biblical Israel, referred only to the voluntary intercourse of a married woman with a man other than her husband. He specifically notes the following passage from the article *Adultery,* I JEWISH ENCYCLOPEDIA 314:

> The extramarital intercourse of a married man is not *per se* a crime in biblical or later Jewish law. This distinction stems from the economic aspect of Israelite marriage: The wife as the husband's possession . . . , and adultery constituted a violation of the husband's exclusive right to her; the wife, as the husband's possession, had no such right to him.

A has taken great care to make sure that all his sexual partners were unmarried, and thus he claims to have been faithful to the original understanding of the Ten Commandments. However we might define "adultery" today, he argues, is irrelevant. His oath was to comply with the Ten Commandments; he claims to have done so. (It is stipulated that *A,* like all the other claimants, has complied with all the other commandments; the only question involves compliance with the commandment against adultery.)

Upon further questioning, you discover that no line-by-line explication of the Ten Commandments was proffered in 1970 at the time that *A* took the oath. But, says *A,* whenever a question arose in his mind as to what the Ten Commandments required of him, he made conscientious attempts to research the particular issue. He initially shared your (presumed) surprise at the results of his research, but further study indicated that all authorities agreed with the scholars who wrote the *Jewish Encyclopedia* regarding the original understanding of the Commandment.

(2) Claimant *B* is *A's* wife, who admits that she has had extramarital relationships with other men. She notes, though, that these affairs were entered into with the consent of her husband. In response to the fact that she undoubtedly violated the ancient understanding of "adultery," she states that that understanding is fatally outdated:

 (a) It is unfair to distinguish between the sexual rights of males and females. That the Israelites were outrageously sexist is no warrant for your maintaining the discrimination.

 (b) Moreover, the reason for the differentiation, as already noted, was the perception of the wife as property. That notion is a repugnant one that has been properly repudiated by all rational thinkers, including all major branches of the Judeo–Christian religious tradition historically linked to the Ten Commandments.

(c) She further argues that, insofar as the modern prohibition of adultery is defensible, it rests on the ideal of discouraging deceit and the betrayal of promises of sexual fidelity. But these admittedly negative factors are not present in her case because she had scrupulously informed her husband and received his consent, as required by their marriage contract outlining the terms of their "open marriage."

(It turns out, incidentally, that A had failed to inform his wife of at least one of his sexual encounters. Though he freely admits that this constitutes a breach of the contract he had made with B, he nevertheless returns to his basic argument about original understanding, which makes consent irrelevant.)

(3) C, a male (is this relevant?), is the participant in a bigamous marriage. C has had no sexual encounters beyond his two wives. (He also points out that bigamy was clearly tolerated in both pre- and post-Sinai Israel and indeed was accepted within the Yemenite community of Jews well into the twentieth century. It is also accepted in a variety of world cultures.)

(4) D, a practicing Christian, admits that he has often lusted after women other than his wife. (Indeed, he confesses as well that it was only after much contemplation that he decided not to sexually consummate a relationship with a coworker whom he thinks he "may love" and with whom he has held hands.) You are familiar with Christ's words, *Matthew* 5:28: "Whosoever looketh on a woman to lust after, he hath committed adultery with her already in his heart." (Would it matter to you if D were the wife, who had lusted after other men?)

(5) Finally, claimant E has never even lusted after another woman since his marriage on the same day he took his oath. He does admit, however, to occasional lustful fantasies about his wife. G, a Catholic, is shocked when informed of Pope John Paul II's statement that "adultery in your heart is committed not only when you look with concupiscence at a woman who is not your wife, but also if you look in the same manner

at your wife." The Pope's rationale apparently is that all lust, even that directed toward a spouse, dehumanizes and reduces the other person "to an erotic object."

Which, if any, of the claimants should get the $10,000? (Remember, *all* can receive the money if you determine that they have fulfilled their oaths.) What is your duty as Trustee in determining your answer to this question?

More particularly, is it your duty to decide what the best *single* understanding of "adultery" is, regarding the Ten Commandments, and then match the behavior against that understanding? If that is your duty, how would you go about arriving at such an understanding? You may object to the emphasis that is being placed on *your* deciding. Instead, you might wish to argue that someone else, whether a discrete person or an authoritative institution, has the capacity to decide, and your role is simply to enforce that understanding. This argument is certainly possible. To whom, though, would you look to for such authoritative resolution?

Is it possible that your duty, rather than seeking the best single definition of adultery, is instead to assess the plausibility of the various claims placed before you? That is, are there several acceptable answers to the question of what constitutes adultery? Is it enough that you find an argument plausible even though you personally reject it as ultimately mistaken? That is, *you* might not have behaved as did a given claimant, considering *your* understanding of "adultery," but does this automatically translate into the legitimate rejection of someone else's claim to have remained faithful to the Commandment?

Is the "sincerity" or "good faith" with which an argument is made relevant? Would it make a difference to you, in *A's* case, whether he had researched the original understanding of the Commandment *after* he had engaged in his liaisons? What if he had learned about ancient Israel only a week before, after consulting the best lawyer in town who will receive one fourth of the $10,000 as a contingency fee should you award the money to *A?*

Let us stipulate that you deny the $10,000 award to *A, B,* and *D,* who promptly race to the nearest courthouse and sue you in your capacity as Trustee. They claim that you have violated your duty to enforce in good faith the terms of the Foundation's contract with the oath–takers. You may further assume that there are no special contract problems involved: the court determines that an enforceable contract was created by taking the oath and by the oath-takers' detrimental reliance on the Foundation's promise to award the money in return for the expected behavior. *D* testified, for example, that one reason for his painful decision not to consummate the affair was his family's need for the $10,000. The only question before the court, therefore, is who breached the contract, the claimants or you.

What questions should the court ask in reaching its decision? How, if at all, do they differ from the questions you have asked as Trustee? Is it the task of the court to determine whether you "got it right" as to what "adultery" means, or is it sufficient that you attempted to fulfill your duties conscientiously and that your views are plausible, even if the court might disagree with you? If you choose the latter alternative, consider the following (possible) paradox: If *your* position should be upheld because of your good-faith belief in a plausible view, independently of the court's agreement with you, how can you justify not applying a similar test in regard to the claimants?. . .

QUESTIONS

1. Consider the differences between the role of baseball umpire and appellate judge. Are the rules of baseball less ambiguous than legal rules? If so, by what standard are they less ambiguous? What discretionary calls do umpires make? Does the home plate umpire make a discretionary call when he adjusts the strike zone to fit the varying size of the batter? Umpires do not all agree that they should admit it when they know they have made a mistaken call. Most feel they will lose their credibility if they admit error. Do you agree with this position?[24] Rulings on the field are rarely appealed and even more rarely overturned. One recent exception, the 1983 "pine tar" controversy, made the law reviews. See Donald Rapson, "A 'Home Run' Application of Established Principles of Statutory Construction," 5 *Cardozo Law Review* 440 (1984).

[24]See Ron Luciano, *The Umpire Strikes Back* (Toronto, N.Y.: Bantam Books, 1982); Jay Baum, *Umpiring Baseball* (Chicago: Contemporary Books, 1979); Joe Brinkman and Charlie Euchner, *The Umpire's Handbook* (Lexington, Mass.: Stephen Greene Press, Inc., 1985); Tom Gorman and Jerome Holtzman, *Three and Two* (New York: Charles Scribner's Sons, 1979).

2. The death penalty continues to raise difficult legal questions that vividly illustrate the interconnectedness of law, politics, ethics, and science. Consider these two examples:

   A. In an attempt to meet the spirit of the constitutional prohibition on cruel and unusual punishment, many states have authorized executions by lethal injection. But medical ethics prohibit physicians and nurses from assisting in the taking of lives. J. D. Autry, who was executed in 1984, took over 10 minutes to die because the needle delivering the chemicals was improperly inserted in his vein by inadequately trained people. Autry was conscious, moved about, and complained of pain for most of the 10 minutes. Does such a problem call for judicial intervention?[25]

   B. The Supreme Court's current position on the constitutionality of the death penalty requires that the death penalty be imposed in a uniform manner according to explicit statutory guidelines, but the *Wall Street Journal* reported widespread agreement among practitioners that the death penalty is not so imposed. Killers of whites are much more likely to receive a death sentence than killers of blacks. Michael Bowers, Attorney General of Georgia, said "we cannot have perfection in our judicial system." He added that we rather need "a greater decisiveness by the judiciary." Do you agree?[26]

3. It is often said that people go to court to vindicate their rights, but does defining the issues in lawsuits in strong human rights terms only exacerbate the losing litigant's disappointment and frustration? The difficulty with defining legal issues in rights terms is particularly vivid in the literature treating the "Baby Doe" issue: Should a newborn infant with severe and permanent mental impairment and life-threatening physical impairments as well simply be allowed to die? Carl Schneider points out that strong right-to-life claims compete directly with a strong parental claim of right to decide what is best for their children. He questions whether defining the problem as a rights problem can lead to a politically acceptable solution.

---

[25]See "A 'Civilized' Way to Die?" *Newsweek*, 9 April 1984, p. 106.

[26]"Death–Penalty Edicts Compound Confusion, Say Critics of the Court," 10 May 1984, p. 1. The article reports recent statistics indicating that "a person in Georgia is 10 times more likely to receive a death sentence for killing a white man than for killing a black." In April 1987 the U.S. Supreme Court, 5–4, upheld Georgia's practice. *McCleskey v. Kemp*, 107 S Ct. 1756 (1987).

I wish to raise, cautiously, the possibility that, as a matter of practical psychology, to frame the question of neonatal euthanasia in terms of parents' rights is to encourage parents to be "self-regarding." In one sense, of course, rights are "other-regarding": rights are an acknowledgment by society that its members have claims against it. But by the same token, and I think more commonly in ordinary thinking, rights are claims by individuals against society, and are "self–regarding." Thinking in terms of rights encourages us to ask what we may do to free ourselves, not to bind ourselves. It encourages us to think about what constrains us from doing what we want, not what obligates us to do what we ought. Legal rights are significantly different from moral rights in this respect: When philosophers talk about rights, they talk of a complex web of relationships and duties between individuals. When lawyers talk about rights, they tend to talk about an area of liberty to act without interference. This difference is inevitable, since law's scope must be less than morality's, but this inevitability probably does not greatly affect the psychological consequences of the system of legal rights.

It is of course true that the system of legal rights is not entirely self-regarding, for most rights find some kind of limit in a conflicting right. But in the context of our discussion, that limit is precisely the problem, for it is not restrictive enough. Rights not only conflict with rights, "they conflict in the demands they make upon us with moral considerations to which the concept of a right does not seem to apply at all: the requirement that we help someone in need, the generosity or kindness we ought to extend to persons simply out of love and affection for them. . . ." Rights discourse in the law encourages us to think of the claims of others on us in terms of their legal rights; the danger is that it may thereby encourage us to feel those rights fully describe the limits of what we should do for them. . . .

As a logical matter, of course, one may have a right without exercising it or feeling encouraged to use it. But I have been speculating about what we might call the socio-psychological consequences of the mode of rights discourse in the United States today. My sense, which is strong but not susceptible to ready proof, is that that mode has encouraged us to feel that "to demand our rights, to assert ourselves as the moral agents we are, is to be able to demand that we be dealt with as members of the community of human beings." The civil rights movement taught us the reasons for that attitude. But attitudes appropriate to civil rights may be inappropriate to privacy rights. Civil rights are rights to participate in self-government and society. Such participation is at least a virtue and may be a duty. But privacy rights are in a sense the opposite of civil rights—they are rights *not* to be affected by government and society—and to forego their use can be a virtue and even a duty. A person may, for example, have a privacy right to father more children than he can support, but he presumably has a moral duty to refrain from exercising that right. . . .

Because of the difficulties I have described with the rights approach to neonatal euthanasia, and because I share the skepticism of other commentators about "legalizing" these decisions by adopting the committee solution, I share their reluctance to change the law on the books, despite its disjunction with law in action. I would, at least temporarily, retain the law on the books while society, in the numerous ways available to it, debates the social and moral problems neonatal euthanasia presents. I am drawn to this hesitant conclusion because I see human life as an ultimate value; because I believe the helpless and deformed deserve compassion, not calculation; and because I believe it would be degrading to live in a society which permitted children to die because they are burdensome. I concede that there will be cases in which euthanasia is proper, though I believe such cases are extraordinary and few. But like other commentators, I do not see how standards can be written which limit euthanasia to those few cases, which do not depersonalize questions of life and death, which do not dangerously diffuse responsibility for people's lives, which do not ask the state to endorse the principle that some lives are not worth living. Perhaps these are very personal reasons, but they seem to me directed toward a question of legitimate public concern.

I see this, then, as a matter involving important moral principles. Others see it as a matter involving important human rights. The danger of either view is that both moral principles and human rights are commonly felt to be, and to some extent ought to be, uncompromisable. But in a complex democracy, some compromise of both principles and rights, some decent respect for the opinions of others, some realization that time has upset many fighting faiths, are necessary. It seems to me a fault of the rights approach that it impedes compromise. Defining something as a right masks the nature and complexity of the interests actually at stake. Defining the

interests at stake as rights makes accommodation more difficult, since we lack a hierarchy of rights that would help us
choose between them. Defining the interests as rights turns the
accommodation of interests into the breaching or defining
away of a right and thus a political and moral wrong. On the
other hand, a virtue of the present state of the law is that it
may ease compromise. First, the dichotomy between the law
on the books and the law in action represents a compromise, a
compromise all the more attractive because unacknowledged.
Second, at least until recently, each state was able to regulate
the problem in its own way. Since there are still important differences in social attitudes between many states, this federalist
flexibility seems to me to permit a useful, though neglected,
form of compromise . . . .[27]

**Do you agree with Schneider's argument? To what extent
does Schneider's position illustrate a pragmatic model of the
legal process?**

4. Many of the problems this book has described occur in the
   legal systems of other developed countries. In 1986 the European Court of Justice in Luxembourg heard arguments in a
   lawsuit challenging West Germany's ban on most imported
   beers. Germany has limited foreign competition against German beer in Germany by invoking the Bavarian law of 1516
   requiring that beer be made only with malted cereals, hops,
   water, and yeast. Germany contended in court that the law
   protects the health of German beer drinkers.[28] What further
   information would persuade you to rule for or against Germany? Consider also the intriguing story reported by Reuters
   in late 1986.

MOSCOW—The Soviet Communist Party called Saturday for a
reorganization of the legal system to balance the fight against
crime with the protection of citizens' rights.

---

[27]"Rights Discourse and Neonatal Euthansia," 30 *Law Quadrangle Notes* (University of Michigan Law School), Winter 1986, pp. 33–40. Compare Charles
Krauthammer, "What To Do About 'Baby Doe,' " *The New Republic,* 2 September 1985, pp. 16–21.

[28]"Ruling Is Expected Today on German Beer Imports," *Wall Street Journal,*
12 March 1987, p. 29.

A resolution from the party's Central Committee said that despite the development of democracy in the country, the people's interests still were not fully protected.

The work of the courts, prosecutors and police also should be reorganized to "ensure the defense of state interests and the rights of citizens," the resolution said, but it did not make clear precisely what reform was contemplated.

The resolution, carried by the official Tass news agency, coincided with a report that the justice minister and 23 other officials in the republic of Byelorussia had been fired over a miscarriage of justice in the town of Vitebsk.

The republic's newspaper, Sovietskaya Belorussiya, said criminal charges would be brought against those found responsible for punishing innocent people in the town to make crime detection statistics seem healthier than they were.

Earlier Saturday, the Communist Party newspaper Pravda reported.that the public prosecutor of a Ukrainian region and his assistant also had been fired over the arrest of a local reporter who exposed police abuses.[29]

5. What characterizes a good lawyer? Stewart Macaulay has reviewed some empirical studies showing how lawyers define and differentiate their status and prestige within the profession. See "Law Schools and the World Outside Their Doors."[30] But my question concerns skill, not status. What is the essence of this skill? In addition to the several answers this chapter has already provided, consider the following passage. It is from an essay titled "Thomas More's Skill."

Skill, character and knowledge. This lawyer skill is not a matter of principles. Lawyers use legal principles, but they use them more to garnish their work than to carry it out. Lawyers, when being candid, admit scant regard for legal principles. Nonlawyers may think that lawyers disdain principles, or that we disdain the idea of government under law. But the lawyer thinks of legal principles as something to be taken apart and made to fit the client's needs. The lawyer thinks this work *is* government under law. Principles and facts are the lawyer's raw materials. What is sacred in the law is not legal principles. The sacred thing in the law, to a lawyer, is the fact that those who

[29]"Officials Urge Reform of Soviet Legal System," *Atlanta Journal and Constitution,* 30 November 1986, p. 43A.
[30]*Legal Education* 506 (1982).

have power are bound to respect skill and knowledge in the wielding of power—skill and knowledge even among those who merely wield power, who do not have it. This is, at last, we think, the political side of a respect for *character*. With regard to what is *legal*, principles come last. Thomas More understood that. He lived it. It was important to him. Bolt understands that; it is part of the reason he thinks that More's life might stand up as an illustration of the courage to preserve one's soul—one's unbudgeable self—in the modern world.[31]

Is the good lawyer necessarily a virtuous person, defined as one who knows he lives and works in a moral system and who seeks to better both himself and his world?[32]

I can think of no more suitable way to close this book than to urge readers to explore further the nature of legal skill by reading two of this century's finest plays, Robert Bolt's *A Man for All Seasons* and Herman Wouk's *The Caine Mutiny Court-Martial.* In each drama a heroic lawyer's skill is very much an extension of his character. In both dramas circumstances force the heros, Thomas More and Barney Greenwald, into adversarial positions. Each hero agonizes profoundly because each sees clearly the great costs that rejection of the value of cooperation brings.

[31]Thomas Shaffer, *On Being a Christian and a Lawyer, supra,* chap. 18 (written in collaboration with Stanley Hauerwas), p. 195.

[32]See David Luban, ed. *The Good Lawyer* (Totowa, N.J.: Rowman & Allanheld, 1983). See also Geoffrey Hazard, "Arguing the Law: The Advocate's Duty and Opportunity," 16 *Georgia Law Review* 821 (1982), and *Ethics in the Practice of Law* (New Haven: Yale University Press, 1978). Compare "Damage Control: After 137 People Died in Its Texas Jet Crash, Delta Helped Families," *Wall Street Journal,* 7 November 1986, p. 1, which includes these two paragraphs:

After the victims of any such disaster have been buried, lawyers quickly begin negotiations intended to reduce the value of the lost lives to a financial equation. "I find it distasteful," says San Francisco attorney Richard Brown, "but the courts place a relative value on human lives. You're worth more if you are a parent with minor children than if you are a (single) adult."

And in court, the victims' lives are examined closely. The strength of a marriage, relationships with children and parents, drinking, work habits, even sexual conduct all can become part of determining what a life was worth in dollars. The husband of a Delta flight attendant killed in the accident says investigators combed his neighborhood several weeks after the funeral asking neighbors whether he and his wife fought or had drinking problems.

Appendix

Introduction to Legal Procedure and Terminology

A litigant disappointed with the outcome of a trial may file an appeal alleging that the trial court judge erroneously interpreted the law. Trial judges may err in their rulings on evidence and motions during the trial or in their instructions to the jury, or their findings of law at the end of the trial if they sit without a jury.

This **appellant** (the party making the appeal) need not technically have lost the trial. The United States Football League in 1986 won a $3 judgment in its antitrust suit against the National Football League, but it appealed, claiming that since it won at all, antitrust law required a much larger judgment in the USFL's favor. The NFL, the **appellee** on appeal, technically lost the trial, but its officials expressed satisfaction with the trial outcome.

Appeals challenge interpretations of law in lower courts. Chapter I introduced you to the case of the stolen airplane, *McBoyle v. United States.* Federal law prohibited the transportation across state lines of vehicles known to be stolen, but the specific words of the statute seem to refer only to vehicles that operate on the ground. The lower courts held that Mr. McBoyle did nevertheless violate the statute. He appealed on the ground that this interpretation of the scope of the statute was too broad.

This appendix introduces you to the basic terms and concepts of legal procedure that define how cases—here the *McBoyle* case—move through the legal system. Key terms appear here in boldface. In due course you will read Justice Holmes's opinion for the U. S. Supreme Court in this case. Many of the concepts developed in Chapters I and III will help you evaluate the soundness of Justice Holmes's argument.

Lawsuits grow out of the complex of our daily relationships with each other. People constantly act in ways that affect others. Often our acts, consciously or not, help. Sometimes they hurt. The laws made by the government specify a set of obligations to and expectations of other people. More precisely, rules of law define a set of injuries that the policy has deemed serious enough to warrant using the power of the government, through the courts, police, and so on, to recify.

Legal rules do not provide remedies for many of life's injuries. My teenage daughter, for example, claims to be genuinely embarrassed if I wear the same pants, jacket, and tie to work two days in a row. But if she, or one of my students, filed a lawsuit to recover money **damages** from me to compensate her for her embarrassment or to obtain a court **injunction** against my wearing the same clothes two days running, the trial court would dismiss the suit on the ground that the **plaintiff** (the person filing the lawsuit) had **no cause of action** against the **defendant.** That is, no branch of the government has made a legal rule specifying that embarrassment caused by another's clothing is **actionable** in court. A cause of action existed in *McBoyle* because the plaintiff, in this case the United States government, could claim that the defendant, Mr. McBoyle, violated a legal rule enacted by Congress: the National Motor Vehicle Theft Act. No statutes, common law cases, or bureaucratic regulations protect against the hurt we call embarrassment, so embarrassment does not constitute a legal cause of action. There are, however, common law rules of negligence. If I wear a combination of pants, jacket, and necktie that causes a student of mine to have a severe seizure, if that student then explains to me the problem and asks me not to wear that combination again, and if I then forget and cause a second seizure requiring medical attention, the rules of negligence would give my student a cause of action against me.

The legal system normally classifies legal actions as either **civil** or **criminal**. As long as we don't think about it too much, we think we know the difference: In a criminal case a governmental official—a **prosecutor**—has the responsibility for filing complaints for violations of laws that authorize the judge to impose a punishment—usually fine, imprisonment, or both—on behalf of the polity. *McBoyle* is a criminal case, prosecuted by a U.S. Attorney working for the U.S. Department of Justice, because the National Motor Vehicle Theft Act prescribes a punishment for those convicted under it.

In a civil case, on the other hand, the plaintiff seeks a judicial decision that will satisfy him personally. Civil remedies usually consist of a court award of money damages to compensate for harm already done or of a court order commanding the defendant to stop doing (or threatening to do) something injurious.

In practice these distinctions between civil and criminal actions tend to break down. Units of government, acting as civil plaintiffs, may file lawsuits to enforce policies that benefit the entire country. The United States government does so when it files civil antitrust actions. A private citizen may file and win a civil rights complaint in which the judge imposes "punitive damages" on defendants. Then damages awarded can far exceed the harm the plaintiff actually experienced. The kind of rule on which a lawsuit is based very much shapes the **evidence** that the parties introduce in trial. We can, for example, imagine that when the owner of the airplane Mc-Boyle transported got it back, he found that it needed $1,000 of repairs. The owner of the plane might file a civil suit against McBoyle seeking to recover damages from McBoyle to pay for the repairs plus the damage the owner suffered by not having use of his vehicle. At this imaginary trial, McBoyle's lawyers might try to introduce evidence that the airplane needed the repairs before McBoyle transported it. In the actual criminal case, however, the facts at issue and the evidence presented are completely different. The evidentiary questions at this trial might wrestle with whether McBoyle knew the plane was stolen. In the actual criminal trial, McBoyle denied any involvement, but the trial court found that he had hired a Mr. Lacey to steal the airplane directly from the manufacturer and fly it to Oklahoma. The jury found that McBoyle paid Lacey over $300 to so so. See *McBoyle v. U.S.,* 43 F. (2d) 273 (1930).

The four elements of legal reasoning introduced in Chapter I include two kinds of facts about which lawyers and judges may reason. One set of facts we may call the facts of the dispute at issue between the parties. These are events and observations that the people in the lawsuit must either prove or disprove through their evidence to prevail at trial. Thus the United States government had to prove that McBoyle knew the plane he transported was indeed stolen. These facts are settled one way or the other by the **trier of fact:** a jury or a judge sitting without a jury. (Jury trials are longer and more costly than "bench trials." The large majority of lawsuits filed are in fact settled by negotiation without any trial, and most trial court proceedings take place without juries.)

A second kind of fact, which I have labeled "social background facts," also influences legal reasoning. In *McBoyle,* the court, including the trial judge, must interpret the word "vehicle" in this statute so as to decide whether it covers airplanes. Social background facts help decide that question: How common were airplanes when Congress passed the statute in 1919? Did Congressional debates discuss and reject the idea of including the word "airplanes" in the statute? What social problem prompted busy Congressmen to pass the National Motor Vehicle Theft Act? Every state had laws prohibiting theft. Why, historically, was a national law about stealing and transporting motor vehicles necessary in 1919?

Notice that, unlike the facts at issue between the parties, these social background issues have no direct connection with the parties at all. They do not have to be proved at trial. Sometimes lawyers at trial will address them, but just as often these factual issues will arise only on appeal, where the lawyers will argue them orally or in their written briefs. Furthermore, judges are free to research such issues on their own or through their clerks with no help from the parties before them, and base their legal conclusions on them. Often the social background facts appear only implicitly in the opinion. They are the judge's hunches about the way the world works that we can only infer from what the judge does say. Every appellate opinion reviewed in these pages rests on such explicit or implicit hunch assertions.

In addition to the requirement of a cause of action, litigants must meet a number of other procedural requirements before courts will decide their case "on the merits." For our purposes we may divide these procedures into requirements for **jurisdiction** and **justiciability.**

"Jurisdiction" prescribes the legal authority of a court to decide the case at all. More specifically, a court must have (a) **jurisdiction over the subject matter** and (b) **jurisdiction over the person** before it can decide. Neither of these requirements is terribly mysterious. Subject matter jurisdiction refers to the fact that all courts are set up by statutes that authorize the court to decide some kinds of legal issues but not others. A local "traffic court" has jurisdiction to hear only a small subset of cases: criminal traffic violations. State probate courts hear issues about the wills and estates of the deceased. The federal court system has a variety of specialized courts, such as the United States Customs Court and the United States Court of International Trade. In both federal and state judicial systems, some courts have statutory authority to hear a broad scope of cases. These are called courts of "general jurisdiction." The U.S. District Court and (in most states) state "superior courts" serve as the trial courts in which most serious lawsuits begin. The U.S. District Court for the Western District of Oklahoma is such a court, and it therefore had subject matter jurisdiction to try the criminal case against McBoyle.

Jurisdiction over the person refers to the fact that agents of a court must catch the defendant and serve him with the papers notifying him that a suit has been filed against him before the court can enter a judgment against him. The agents who "serve process" on defendants—sheriffs in the states and U.S. marshalls in the federal system—only have authority to find people and serve notice on them within the geographic territory the court governs. A sheriff working for a Superior Court in Georgia cannot serve someone who lives in Alabama unless the sheriff can catch the person (or attach land of his) in Georgia. This jurisdiction over the person is sometimes called "territorial jurisdiction."

McBoyle's case raised an interesting problem of jurisdiction over the person. Federal law requires that defendants be tried in the district where the crime was committed. McBoyle claimed that because he never flew the airplane, or left Illinois for that matter, he could not have committed a crime in the Western District of Oklahoma, Mr. Lacey's destination. The U.S. Court of Appeals for the Tenth Circuit rejected that argument, saying that the crime ran with the airplane, and that the crime was committed in Oklahoma, even if McBoyle wasn't in Oklahoma at the time. See 43 F. (2d) 273 at 275 (1930).

Most courts in the United States possess authority to decide what the U.S. Constitution (in Article III) calls "cases" and "controversies." Over the years this phrase has become synonymous with a genuinely adversarial contest in which plaintiff and defendant desire truly different outcomes. Judges cannot initiate lawsuits. They respond to the initiatives taken by the litigants.

Rules of **justiciability** ensure that judges decide true adversary contests. These rules serve three functions: (a) To avoid wasting judicial time and resources on minor matters; (b) to improve the quality of information that reaches them by

hearing different points of view; (c) to justify refusing to decide politically delicate cases that might damage the courts'
political popularity.

Thus courts generally refuse to hear **moot** cases, cases in
which the harm the plaintiff tried to prevent never happened
and, for whatever reasons, cannot happen in the future. Plaintiffs must have **standing,** which means that the plaintiff must
be among those directly injured (or directly threatened) by the
defendant's actions. Thus, to have standing to challenge the
constitutionality of statutes prohibiting abortions in the first
trimester of pregnancy, the plaintiff might have to be a woman
either pregnant or capable of becoming pregnant. **Exhaustion**
requires that plaintiffs exploit their primary opportunities for
settling a case, especially through bureaucratic channels, before going to court, and **ripeness** requies that the defendant
actually threaten what the plaintiff fears. Thus, partly to avoid
getting itself in hot political water, the U.S. Supreme Court at
first refused to consider the constitutionality of Connecticut's
laws against distribution and use of birth control devices. It
insisted that Connecticut wasn't bothering to enforce these
laws and that therefore the case wasn't ripe. No justiciability
problems arose in *McBoyle.*

McBoyle's case reached the U.S. Supreme Court in this
fashion: The trial court found McBoyle guilty. (In criminal
cases the trial court expresses its **disposition** in terms of guilt
and innocence. Civil dispositions find defendant "liable" or
"not liable.") McBoyle appealed, and the Court of Appeals,
ruling on both the jurisdictional claim and the statutory interpretation claim, **affirmed** (upheld) the trial court's decisions
on these two matters of law. McBoyle appealed again, and the
U.S. Supreme Court **reversed.** Here is Justice Holmes's opinion for the court:

McBoyle v. United States
Supreme Court of the United States
283 U.S. 25 (1931)

Mr. Justice HOLMES delivered the opinion of the Court.

The petitioner was convicted of transporting from Ottawa,

Illinois, to Guymon, Oklahoma, an airplane that he knew to have been stolen, and was sentenced to serve three years' imprisonment and to pay a fine of $2,000. The judgment was affirmed by the Circuit Court of Appeals for the Tenth Circuit. 43 F.(2d) 273. A writ of *certiorari* was granted by this Court on the question whether the National Motor Vehicle Theft Act applies to aircraft. Act of October 29, 1919, c. 89, 41 Stat. 324, U.S. Code, title 18, § 408. That Act provides: "Sec. 2. That when used in this Act: (a) The term 'motor vehicle' shall include an automobile, automobile truck, automobile wagon, motor cycle, or any other self-propelled vehicle not designed for running on rails. . . . Sec. 3. That whoever shall transport or cause to be transported in interstate or foreign commerce a motor vehicle, knowing the same to have been stolen, shall be punished by a fine of not more than $5,000, or by imprisonment of not more than five years, or both."

Section 2 defines the motor vehicles of which the transportation in interstate commerce is punished in Section 3. The question is the meaning of the word "vehicle" in the phrase "any other self-propelled vehicle not designed for running on rails." No doubt etymologically it is possible to use the word to signify a conveyance working on land, water, or air, and sometimes legislation extends the use in that direction, e.g., land and air, water being separately provided for, in the Tariff Act, September 21, 1922, c. 356, § 401 (b), 42 Stat. 858, 948. But in everyday speech "vehicle" calls up the picture of a thing moving on land. Thus in Rev. St. § 4, intended, the Government suggests, rather to enlarge than to restrict the definition, vehicle includes every contrivance capable of being used "as a means of transportation on land." And this is repeated, expressly excluding aircraft, in the Tariff Act, June 17, 1930, c. 497, § 401 (b), 46 Stat. 590, 708. So here, the phrase under discussion calls up the popular picture. For after including automobile truck, automobile wagon, and motor cycle, the words "any other self-propelled vehicle not designed for running on rails" still indicate that a vehicle in the popular sense, that is a vehicle running on land, is the theme. It is a vehicle that runs, not something, not commonly called a vehicle, that flies. Airplanes were well known in 1919 when this statute was passed, but it is admitted that they were not mentioned in the reports or in the debates in Congress. It is impossible to read words that so carefully enumerate the different forms of motor vehicles and have no reference of any kind to aircraft, as including airplanes under a term that usage more and more precisely confines to a different class. The counsel for the petitioner have shown that the phraseology of the statute as to motor vehicles follows that of earlier statutes of Connecticut, Delaware, Ohio, Michigan, and Missouri, not to mention the late Regulations of Traffic for the District of Columbia, title 6, c. 9, § 242, none of which can be supposed to leave the earth.

Although it is not likely that a criminal will carefully consider the text of the law before he murders or steals, it is reasonable that a fair warning should be given to the world in language that the common world will understand, of what the law intends to do if a certain line is passed. To make the warning fair, so far as possible the line should be clear. When a rule of conduct is laid down in words that evoke in the common mind only the picture of vehicles moving on land, the statute should not be extended to aircraft simply because it may seem to us that a similar policy applies, or upon the speculation that if the legislature had thought of it, very likely broader words would have been used. United States v. Bhagat Singh Thind, 261 U.S. 204, 209, 43 S.Ct. 338.

Judgment reversed.

Chapter III returns to the issues *McBoyle* raises and suggests that Holmes's opinion is not very persuasive. If you have not read Chapter III, consider the relevance to this case of the concept of territorial jurisdiction covered above. Assume that Congress passed the National Motor Vehicle Theft Act in response to the growing problem of car theft. The territorial principle complicates state law enforcement. Georgia police can't prowl around in Alabama looking for people who steal the cars of Georgians, but it is easy to drive a Georgian's car to Alabama. Doesn't this same purpose cover airplanes? And do you think the law was as unclear as Holmes says about the morality of what McBoyle did?

Index

Index of Cases

BOLDFACED page numbers indicate pages on which a significant excerpt from an opinion in the case begins. All other page numbers denote in-text case references. This index excludes cases of minor significance, for example, cases cited within other quoted cases and materials. Case citations are provided in the text.